GORDON MILNE

Shankly, My Dad and Me

GORDON MILNE

Shankly, My Dad and Me

with Steve Younger

pitch

First published by Pitch Publishing, 2023

Pitch Publishing
9 Donnington Park,
85 Birdham Road,
Chichester,
West Sussex,
PO20 7AJ
www.pitchpublishing.co.uk
info@pitchpublishing.co.uk

A CIP catalogue record is available for this book
from the British Library.

ISBN 978 1 80150 654 0

Typesetting and origination by Pitch Publishing

Printed and bound in Great Britain by TJ Books, Padstow

Contents

Dedication

For Andrew, Graham, and Ian

Foreword by Mark Lawrenson

WE ALL know how these forewords work: waxing lyrical about the subject and their achievements. This one is easy, though, as I'm writing about one of the nicest people in the game, and the fittest octogenarian I know.

Gordon was a gifted footballer who became a much sought-after manager and coach across Europe and Japan. Like myself, he is a Prestonian who played for the Lilywhites, but he truly made his name at Liverpool. Signed by the late, great Bill Shankly (himself a former Preston North End player), Gordon made nearly 300 appearances for the Reds. A right-half – sorry, midfield player – he also played 14 times for England and was desperately unlucky to miss out on a place in Sir Alf Ramsey's World Cup-winning squad of 1966.

Plenty of silverware was accrued at Anfield though, and after leaving Liverpool a spell at Blackpool was followed by his appointment as player-manager of non-league Wigan Athletic, where his love affair with management began. He went on to spend the best part of 30 years in the managerial hot seat(s); a remarkable achievement, and one almost unheard of in the Russian roulette of today's game.

Always insightful, always considered, Gordon is still regularly called upon by many in the game for his thoughts and opinions, which are always astute – and always balanced, of course! To this day he remains the voice of reason, and compassion too.

He always was – and still remains – a class act.

Mark Lawrenson

Foreword by Gary Lineker

I CAN see him now, trotting on to the Leicester training ground in his shorts – always in his shorts. Whether it be 25 degrees or minus 5, you would never see him wearing tracksuit bottoms. He'd jog out, touch his knees a dozen or so times, fire out a couple of quips – often towards me about my perceived lack of enthusiasm for training – then the session would begin.

I'm too young to remember Gordon as a player but from training alongside him you could see he was technically gifted: a neat and tidy midfield player, one who went on to enjoy a distinguished career. Having spotted his talent at Preston North End, Bill Shankly made Gordon one of his first signings for Liverpool. He forced his way into the England side, but just missed out on England's greatest-ever footballing triumph, the 1966 World Cup win. I wonder why? I also wonder why I never asked him about it. Was it injury, or form? A huge blow, or expected? Hopefully the answers lie in this tome.

It was as a manager I knew Gordon. He joined Leicester City in 1982, replacing Jock Wallace. The two characters couldn't have been more different. Jock was intimidating, a giant of a man with a fierce Scottish accent who played direct, up-and-at-'em football. Gordon was a softly spoken (mostly), diminutive chap who liked to play an attacking, more possession-based game. This suited me down to the ground, and under his stewardship we scored goals – lots of goals.

I learned an enormous amount from Gordon and will forever be grateful he joined the club. From an entirely selfish perspective, he was the right man at the right time for a striker who relied on being in the right place at the right time. Not only was he tactically adept, but he also had a way of getting the best out of players without hurling abuse at them (which, ridiculously, was the way in those days). He was a calming influence with a waspish sense of humour, albeit not always deliberately so. I recall an incident at St Andrew's when, as we entered the tunnel after full time, we were spat at by Birmingham City fans. One of our players returned fire. Gordon was not impressed, pointing his finger at the offender, saying, 'That is totally unacceptable. If ever someone spits at you, you just have to swallow it.' A couple of us tried to suppress our giggles, with little success. To this day I'm not sure Gordon realises what he said.

Despite a great appreciation of what the gaffer had done for me, in 1985 I felt it was time to move on. It was an incredibly difficult decision, but Gordon couldn't have been more supportive. I moved to Everton, but our paths would cross again in Japan with Grampus Eight. We weren't a great side. The club struggled and when the Japanese coach moved upstairs, such was my respect for Gordon, as a man and as a manager, I persuaded the club to appoint him as the new coach. He had been enormously successful in Turkey with Beşiktaş, but unfortunately Japan didn't work out too well. Therefore, I would like to take this once-in-a-lifetime opportunity to apologise to Gordon for encouraging him to take the Grampus job in the first place! Turkey beckoned again, followed by a spell as director of football at Newcastle United when Sir Bobby Robson was at the helm.

This promises to be a fascinating and entertaining book about the life of a genuine football man. I haven't seen Gordon personally in too many years, but in a few weeks' time, we're getting the Leicester band back together to celebrate his 86th birthday. I wonder – will he turn up in shorts?

Gary Lineker

Preface

PROFESSIONAL FOOTBALL has dominated my life for as long as I can remember. As the only son of a player and manager, the game was immediately and forever in my blood. Now, I find myself in a position to place on record stories from my footballing life, drawn from and inspired by my father's handwritten journals. To this day, they still fascinate; reminders of a bygone era shared with his close friend and team-mate Bill Shankly, along with the likes of Stan Mortensen, Billy Wright, Sir Stanley Matthews and, of course, Sir Tom Finney; all top players with careers compromised by the Second World War.

Now, long past the end of my own career, another challenge has arisen. For the last couple of years my sons Andrew, Graham and Ian have continually pestered me to follow my father's example: 'Put it down on paper.' As I sit in my office on a rainy day, cup of tea in hand, nothing gives me greater pleasure than picking one of dad's journals from the shelf and thumbing through it for the umpteenth time. With that in mind, I recognised my sons were right: it was up to me to continue the story my father began so many years ago. And, in conclusion, if my three sons feel the same – or even half – the comfort and pleasure I feel when looking back through my father's eyes, I'll be happy, contented and will consider the mission accomplished.

Introduction

I'VE READ numerous books written by footballers, some extremely good, others less so. I'm no literary critic, much less an author, but to my mind many such publications ultimately turn out to be little more than lists and statistics: games played, goals scored, medals won and lost. There's nothing wrong with that, of course – numbers are the currency of a footballer, after all – but nowadays, facts and figures are a mere mouse click away and, to be honest, don't really interest me.

I imagine most walks of life are the same; the minutiae of any job can become tiresome, and the world's favourite game is no different. As a footballer, you don't do much more than train and play, then do it all again. (And you actually spend far more time training than playing.) It's not complicated, or shouldn't be, but to me there's only so much of that you can write about. It's what surrounds the minutiae that keeps the interest alive: the who, the what, the how and the why; the goodies, the baddies, the heroes and the villains. I've had innumerable encounters with all the above, many of which are retold here.

In that sense – and I mean this sincerely – this book isn't really about me. It's about those I've met along the way; the interest is in them and the journey I've been on, beginning in Preston, ending in Turkey, with plenty of mileage in between. Thanks to the route

I picked, I was fortunate enough to be in the right place at the right time on more than one occasion: choosing Liverpool over Arsenal meant I was at the heart of the creation of a footballing dynasty; success at Wigan led to international management, in turn leading to a wonderful decade at Coventry City; when that came to an end, five great years at Leicester City followed; my old pal Jim Smith's resignation presented an incredible opportunity for me at the League Managers' Association; and without an off-the-cuff meeting with Bobby Robson, would I have ever gone to Turkey? Would Japan have been in my thoughts were it not for my connection with Gary Lineker?

Every day I give thanks that football found me. I'm grateful for all I've experienced and truly appreciate everything the game has given me. To have had the career – the life – I've had in football, to have undertaken such a journey, remains humbling to this day. It's a journey that has taken me from Lancashire to the Land of the Rising Sun. There have been bursts of speed and sudden breakdowns; short hops, long treks, pit-stops and layovers, all alongside an ever-changing cast of fellow travellers, some heading in the same direction, others on a direct collision course. It's these figures who define my story; this is, in a way, as much their story as it's mine, so writing about them rather than just myself ... well, I hope you don't feel short-changed.

I hope this offers you a different kind of read. More than anything else, I hope you enjoy.

Prologue

MY EARLIEST memory is of kicking a tired old football against the garage door in the driveway of my parents' home in Preston. I must have been three or four years old at the time, and it was something I did as often as I could, again and again and again. The garage wasn't the sturdiest of structures, the double doors a bit rickety. The driveway sloped down towards the road, so assuming I didn't miss the target, the ball would always return to me. The gates at the bottom of the drive meant I couldn't get out into the road; not that I wanted to, although if the ball somehow found its way over those gates, I'm sure I'd have thought differently.

One day, there I was, doing what I did, when a friend of my dad appeared. He lived across the road and had popped round for a cup of tea with my parents. On seeing me, he decided the tea could wait and joined my game instead. He played with the same enthusiasm as I did, if not more. The two of us took turns and the garage door rattled, albeit somewhat louder when he found the target.

He clearly enjoyed his football as much as I did, and we played together for a good half-hour. He did this sort of thing a lot, and if it wasn't with me, it would have been with someone else. This man loved football so much, if he saw anyone playing, anywhere, he'd join in. He was a regular visitor to our house, a friendly face, but I had no idea who he was or what he did. I'd soon find out though. His name was Bill Shankly.

Chapter 1

FOOTBALL FOR me began on the streets, and I loved the winter fixtures the most. As the nights drew in and the streetlights flickered into life, excitement began to build. I was lucky, my house was directly opposite a lamppost, so I was always playing home games. From somewhere long forgotten we'd acquired the match ball – actually, a battered old tennis ball – the safeguarding of which was my responsibility. So precious and highly treasured, under no circumstances could we allow it to go astray; between games it remained locked away safely in the garden shed. It also fell to me to provide the goalposts – four tin cans, filled with sand for stability (enabling us to play 'rebounds' – we were no mugs), and painted white to stand out in the seemingly ever-present gloom. These I stored under the hedge in my parents' front garden, instantly available whenever they were required. They were safe there; what would anyone else want with four tins full of sand?

All the houses had coal fires, which in winter were rampant. Coupled with the poor streetlighting, the smoke these fires produced created an eerie, almost unreal atmosphere. This was a time when Wolves entertained the likes of Honvéd in early European fixtures, some of the first night matches to be televised. Floodlights were rare, but such occasions – smoke and smog from the house fires mixing with the steam and smoke from the terraces, all drifting through the floodlights and the shadows – were incredibly atmospheric; there was a magic to the murkiness. And to us, under our streetlights, it felt the same, as if somehow, something special had been added, something very different to playing in daylight.

As soon as enough reprobates had gathered, a game would start, although kick-off couldn't take place until I supplied the goalposts and the ball. The pitch itself – commonly known as the road – was around ten yards wide and bordered by a kerb on each side, ready-made touchlines off which the ball would constantly rebound (the 'ball-in-play' statistics were unusually high). We'd begin with a relatively well-proportioned pitch, which, over the course of the game, would be extended several times; as the numbers grew, so would the pitch. When it became too crowded – and it always did – we'd simply move the goalposts further back. During peak participation, all sense of pitch proportion would be lost and could lead to a playing area ten yards wide but a hundred yards long.

Three against three was enough to commence, but that would quickly become four vs four, five vs five, and so on. There was no limit, and you'd often go a long time without getting a kick. Players would drift in and out – 'You're playing this way; you're playing that way.' But so long as the teams were equal ('Hang on, they've got two more bloody players than us!') the game would roll on. Lads would pop up from nowhere, appearing out of the shadows, then you'd look around and couldn't see someone who was there five minutes ago.

What fascinated me, and still does, is that no matter how many players made up a team, and despite chasing a small ball around in the gloom, you could always identify who was a team-mate and who wasn't, even though players were clad in all sorts of garments and came in all shapes and sizes: the one with the big mouth (who couldn't play); the one with the torn trousers who never said a word (but who could play – the quiet ones could always play, it seemed); the one who ran around all night, never got near the ball, but never stopped smiling, loving every minute.

There were few cars around then so, despite the odd interruption, we weren't stopping and starting all the time. And if someone came along on a bike, they'd simply ride along the footpath next to the touchline. None of this was of any real consequence though; this was a time of innocence and freedom. Parents didn't worry because they knew where their kids were (in my case, invariably outside my own house). And in those magical moments, we were all playing at Wembley, for sure. We'd play two or three times a week, at least. Some games were bigger than others, but Friday night was always the biggest, a key component of the build-up to the weekend and the real business of First Division football.

As the evening ran its course, players would slowly disappear with a myriad of excuses: homework, tea's ready, tired, fed up, had enough, I shouldn't be here anyway. See you tomorrow. The numbers would dwindle back down to three-a-side, frequently the same six who had started the game all those hours ago (we'd have played all night if we could). The game would gently peter out, the goalposts stashed back under the hedge and the tennis ball returned safely to the shed. Until next time.

* * *

My dad Jimmy joined Preston North End in 1932, transferring from his first professional club, Dundee United. He and my mother, also from Dundee, married in June 1934. Preston owned several houses near Deepdale, the club's home ground, all within walking distance of each other, and they encouraged players to rent them for a nominal monthly fee as an incentive when signing. It was a fair deal for both parties and my parents duly moved into their first real home. Soon to join them in the neighbourhood – directly across the road, to be precise – were a new team-mate of my dad, and his wife, a Mr and Mrs Shankly, fellow Scots from similar stock.

After training it was quite common for Mr Shankly to call round for a cup of his favourite herbal tea (he was always extremely dedicated, looking after himself, trying to eat and drink well). I remember Mum's good-natured exasperation at having to buy it in specially – herbal tea wasn't easy to find in Lancashire! Shanks was always friendly and very family oriented, never failing to ask, 'How's the wee man coming along?' as I slept in my pram outside the front door. In later years my dad wrote in his journal: 'Bill was always playing football in the street with my son Gordon … Bill was a lad; if Gordon went out with the ball, Bill would be there. I think he must have been looking for him coming out.'

How could one ever imagine, more than 20 years later he'd call at that very same house to offer that very same 'wee man' the opportunity to join him at Liverpool Football Club? You wouldn't throw your toys out of the pram at that offer.

* * *

It was every boy's dream. On Lowthorpe Road I lived practically next door to the football ground my favourite team called 'home'. Preston North End have played at Deepdale since 1875 and were founder members of the Football League in 1888. Now, in the mid-to-late 1940s, PNE was my world. What's more, my dad, who played for the club for almost a decade prior to the Second World War, was now an integral member of the staff. He even held keys to the ground!

Late on Friday afternoons before home matches, one of my dad's many responsibilities was to provide plenty of hot water available for baths and showers the following day. This was produced by a coke-burning boiler the size of a small bus, which also provided heating for the rest of the main building. The boiler could never sleep, and every Friday had to be full to the brim, guaranteeing Tom Finney and the boys a hot shower after the match. I'd stoke the boiler with my dad before Saturday's big match, although every match was a big one to me. On entering the boiler room, close to the treatment room at the far end of the building, my dad and I would be faced with a mountain of coke piled to the ceiling as the hungry boiler roared away.

My dad also had to ensure the home dressing room was in pristine condition. Preston North End was a club with a great tradition and took pride in doing things well and in the right way. I'd help lay out the kit, a truly special task. I felt important; I was a crucial member of the backroom staff and loved every minute. It was paradise. Shirts were placed on hangers and hung on the pegs above the benches, with the numbers facing outwards, 1–11 in numerical order. The shorts (anything but short) were neatly folded and placed on a lilywhite towel (PNE's nickname was the Lilywhites, after all) alongside the thick, woollen, hairy socks. These were well matched with the shinpads, which were truly something else: leather facing, with cane strips woven in and filled out with an unidentified material that resembled modern sofa stuffing; far from attractive but, when 'take no prisoners' was a primary tactic of all teams, absolutely essential.

Boots were placed neatly on the floor beneath the benches, facing outwards. Made of leather with built-in toecap, their leather studs were hammered in with nails then filed down to the players' preferred lengths, a practice that on matchday habitually led to chaos: with kick-off looming, players would be filing away frantically to achieve the most suitable stud length for the condition of the pitch.

I vividly remember taking much longer over Tom Finney's boots. Picking them up, putting them down, even smelling the dubbin (a type of wax used to preserve and soften the leather, which supposedly made the boots more comfortable). This had a unique and potent aroma, one long associated with dressing rooms up and down the country. It was the smell of football, the memory of which remains with me to this day. My hero's boots were in perfect condition, correctly placed, just waiting for the great man himself to step into them. What magic would they produce tomorrow? I'd go to bed dreaming of what was to come.

Also neatly presented and ready to go were the 'kicking-in' balls – 'T-Balls' as they were known, due to their stitching resembling the letter T. (I'd been well trained by my dad in the art of lacing footballs, first by watching and then by practising. Armed with a lacer and a tightener I soon became quite competent and eventually earned the honour of preparing the 'T-Balls' for matchday kick-ins.) These balls had an inflatable bladder that was carefully inserted before being inflated by a hand pump. Once inflated the balls were carefully laced up: parallel lacing with no kinks; any kink meant 'start again'. The lacing was the most important step, not only for appearance but because players' foreheads would meet that part of the ball on a regular basis; any knots or kinks would only add to the discomfort of what was already a painful practice. And if there were any knots – whoever prepared that ball, watch out! Placed in a corner of the dressing room, tomorrow these balls (by now gleaming with dubbin too) would be carried out by the players just before kick-off.

After a final check to ensure the boiler was full, we'd exit past the treatment room where an hour earlier I'd witnessed my dad massaging (another of his responsibilities) my idol Sir Tom Finney in preparation for tomorrow's match. In the long empty corridor, the silence was only broken by the echo of our footsteps, creating a sense of mystique. We'd check the home team's dressing room door was locked before taking a sharp left turn towards the players' entrance at the end of the corridor beyond the match officials' room. The remaining lights were switched off, the double doors securely locked behind us, and we'd step into the night. I was always reluctant to leave what was to me a privileged and magical world. I'd laid out the kit, the boots, the balls, had ensured there would be plenty of hot water for the bath at full time, and had witnessed my idol receiving treatment from my father. In my young mind the coliseum was ready, the main gladiator was ready – let battle commence. I'd sleep well that night.

Public transport, bicycles and of course shanks's pony were the main means of transport to the matches (this even included the players), and living so close to the ground I decided to start my first-ever business enterprise: looking after supporters' push bikes and motorcycles. A reasonably sized front garden sat alongside our concrete drive leading to a wooden gate built by my dad that sat on top of an old air-raid shelter he'd also constructed, one with just enough space for all the family. (Had any enemy aircraft dropped a stray one on Dad's masterpiece we'd have known about it; I'm no expert but with just a corrugated iron roof covered in turf, I'm not too sure the shelter was bomb-proof!) The gate accessed the back garden, also a decent size. I'd fashioned a wooden sign that I fastened to the gate post, white letters on a black background: 'Road cycles 3d, Motorbikes 6d, Cars 1/'. There was only space for one car, though, and as this would take up most of the drive, I realised it wouldn't be good for business. I quickly removed the car option from the sign. The venture proved popular, and on matchdays both front and back gardens were packed, mainly with bicycles.

Supporters travelled from far and wide, in all weathers too. One chap cycled from Longridge, half a dozen miles away, but confessed he'd gladly walk both ways just to watch Tom Finney play. He used to bring half a dozen eggs for my mum and as a result always parked his bike, at no charge, in pole position for a quick getaway. And we always had boiled eggs for breakfast on Sundays.

Because of my dad's job I received a pass, giving me access to the main stand. Ten minutes after kick-off I'd sprint down the road, leaving my mum and my Aunty Grace (Mum's sister who lived with us) in charge of the 'parking'. They'd keep watch and deal with any latecomers (there were always plenty). I'd tear down the road as fast as I possibly could, desperately hoping I hadn't missed a goal, although being so close to begin with I'd already know from the roar of the crowd.

Fifteen minutes before full time I'd have to leave, again hoping not to miss anything important, to manage the inevitable post-match chaos and to ensure my clients all got away safely – and on the same bikes they arrived upon! While disentangling three or four machines, tempers could and would flare as everyone wanted to leave at the same time; the prevention of civil war in the back garden of a semi-detached Lancashire home was my chief priority. Fraught situations would often be defused, however, when someone mentioned Tom's second goal, or was it three or four players he went past before squaring for Tommy Thompson to tap home? Men in flat caps and raincoats reliving these moments by telling anyone who would listen, many with bicycle clips already around their ankles. In these five-minute shows of genuine emotion, they'd be pirouetting and gesticulating, waving their arms and raising their voices, attempting to explain the magic they'd just witnessed. Eventually, with the last few bicycles disentangled, handlebars and saddles thankfully facing in the right direction, my customers would head off into the evening, by now – and again, thankfully – contented. Like them, I also had so much to thank Sir Tom for.

* * *

There was another big Tom at Preston at that time: Tommy Docherty. Another strong Scot, much like Shanks in character, build and background. Both were hungry, aggressive, took no prisoners and would play all day. Football was their lives. And, of course, they both adored Tom Finney too. If you were making a movie about Shanks, the Doc would have been ideal for the role, and he wouldn't have needed to rehearse either!

His route to Deepdale would take him past our house and he'd often call in to say hello to my mum or Aunty Grace. Grace was an integral part of the family who had worked in a munitions factory during the war, so when it came to chit-chat and banter, she could mix it with the best of them. She loved the Doc and could give him a run for his money any time. He'd only stay for ten minutes or so, long enough to have them in stitches and to take on board a couple of wee sherries: 'Good for instant energy,' according to him. He was a one-man whirlwind, always fully motivated, ready and able to light up the dressing room, which, with his sherries inside him (not that he needed them), he did time and again. Even the senior players let him get on with it; he was never pulled up because he brought the passion and atmosphere at vital times – and no time was more vital than pre-match. The Doc would get everybody on their toes.

To this day, even having passed away in 2020, Tommy remains one of the funniest men in football. My memories of that Preston team in which he played are of a dressing room and training ground full of good humour, mickey-taking and great camaraderie. Certain boundaries could and would be crossed on occasion, in ways that wouldn't be tolerated today, but as was befitting of the times, it was always done in good faith, never with any spite. Some things the Doc used to say to Willie Cunningham, it's unbelievable how Willie never strangled him! And those two were team-mates for Scotland too! Willie accepted it for what it was, though, as we all did. Alongside the enjoyment, this behaviour also brought togetherness, both vital to any dressing room. It became contagious, even more so when mixed with the desire for victory. Tommy Docherty, and that team, only knew one way to play: they played to win.

Chapter 2

THROUGHOUT MY school days my only ambition was to be a professional footballer. Day and night this consumed me, but as those days and nights were coming to a close, it dawned on me: it was decision time – what was I going to do? I remember conversations with school pals, all facing the same dilemma. Would I be working in a bank or garage? In engineering, or insurance? None of these appealed; in fact, the very thought of such employment frightened me to death.

There were plenty of jobs available to school leavers, an abundance of choice. My father insisted I have a profession upon which I could rely in later life. He knew the owner of a local building firm who also ran a cabinet-making business, as well as looking after PNE's maintenance work, and was (along with his business partner brother) an avid supporter and season ticket holder. He offered me a five-year apprenticeship as a carpenter/joiner (I'd turn out to be no good at either) and, with the workshop only a ten-minute bicycle ride from home, this was an offer too good to refuse. My introduction to the real world began.

Menial work was the introduction for the new boy: keeping the workshop clean, bagging shavings and sawdust to be sold on later and, of course, making the tea. This involved a nightmare trek across the road to a small knitwear factory (we had an agreement to use their facilities for the tea run) housing around 75 women and girls, all beavering away on various machines. At the far end of the factory floor was a boiler generating all the hot water required. Much later in life I'd face numerous hostile, intimidating and sometimes embarrassing situations, but none came close to the tea run. Nothing was ever as stressful as balancing eight tin mugs on a piece of plywood, walking gingerly on a polished factory floor in big heavy boots, desperately trying not to spill the precious beverages on board: tea, coffee, Bovril – if any went down it would be nothing short of disaster. Tentatively picking my way through a jungle of female voices, all taking the mickey and with frequent lewd comments and suggestions that would have made the Kop blush, was sheer hell. Those ten minutes felt like ten years. There was no happier 16-year-old in the world when Barons Ltd eventually purchased their own boiler. We could finally brew up in-house.

During my apprenticeship I was training two nights a week, 6.30–8.30. Adjacent to Deepdale was a floodlit area, a rarity in those days. I'd jump on my bike immediately after work and be at the ground by 6pm. We'd change in the visitors' dressing room where clothes pegs were at a premium. The rule was one peg per person, so with 30-odd players involved, competition was fierce; arrive late and your clothes would end up wherever you could find a space for them. After one particularly long day in the machine shop, I was in a hurry to change. Removing my work boots produced a flurry of sawdust on to the polished floor. Worse was to follow when removing my overalls (really a boiler suit), as wood shavings and lots more sawdust descended around my feet. Sweating and embarrassed, I felt my skin flush. It was hilarious to the others, many of whom had office jobs or worked in shops and arrived in nice clean shoes and clothes. Somehow, though, after training, the sawdust and shavings had disappeared. I never discovered who swept them away but was eternally grateful, and ensured it never happened again.

As I gained more experience I'd occasionally join up with senior tradesmen on the outside; much more interesting and liberating, as confinement to the workshop wasn't where I wanted to be. With bicycles the main mode of transport for the working man, I soon learned the finer arts of shipping timber from the workshop to wherever it was required, balancing as much as I could handle on my shoulder, one hand supporting the load, the other trying its best to steer in the right direction without losing control of the bike. Should the load be too big to carry manually, my precious bicycle was turned into a two-wheel mobile timber yard, rope or string used to (hopefully) secure the cargo to the handlebars and saddle, somewhat restricting in terms of control and influence over the intended distance and direction of travel.

In many cases control, influence and dignity were thrown out of the window. The disasters are too many to catalogue, although one or two stand out: bringing traffic to a standstill on the main street in Preston; causing total chaos as the saddle fell off my bike and timber scattered left, right and centre; and freewheeling down a posh driveway before abandoning ship and crashing into the customer's prized plant pots and smashing them to pieces. In that instance, to say the lady of the house wasn't pleased would be quite the understatement. Her husband (fortunately, for me, a PNE supporter) politely suggested my future may lie elsewhere. My senior workmate, who had watched through his hands, horrified, agreed. They weren't wrong.

* * *

Past our workshop at the end of the road was a large chemist's shop that I regularly cycled past. The shop was owned by a Mr John Brooks, a wonderful man who became a close friend right up until his recent passing at the ripe old age of 97. John was old school, always wearing the white coat, a terrific storyteller and a lovely man. One day, while freewheeling by, absent-mindedly staring through the shop window, a very attractive dark-haired girl in the obligatory white coat caught my attention. There were others, too, all in white coats (the boss ran a tight ship) but this one stood out. Love at first sight, in a young man's eye? Perhaps. What I knew for sure, though, was that cycling past that shop would never be the same again. From now on, as I passed, I'd always slow down, trying to steal a long, lingering glance – more a stare, really – desperately hoping to glimpse that lovely dark-haired assistant. I was mostly unsuccessful, however, and several times nearly finished up under a bus.

We eventually met, purely by chance, at the local park's tennis courts. My pal Dave Kerry (a young pro at Preston) and I were knocking a few tennis balls to each other one summer's evening – posing, really, if I'm being honest. Two attractive young girls were playing on an adjacent court. Edith and Barbara were their names. Unknown to us all, that day was the beginning of two relationships that would stand the test of time. Edith and I have been married for more than 60 years, Dave and Barbara for more than 57 until he sadly passed away. Two close pals marrying two best friends. Not a bad doubles pairing, that.

* * *

By April 1958 my apprenticeship was drawing to a close. As the weeks swiftly evaporated, looming large and edging ever closer was the compulsory National Service (for younger readers this meant I had no choice but to join the military), a two-year venture into the unknown. What would happen to my fledgling football career? Would it be forgotten? Would *I* be forgotten? Would I remain in Britain or be posted overseas? Would I, to all intents and purposes, simply disappear for two vital years (I was 21 years old when conscripted)? It was scary, not least because the East Lancashire Regiment to which I was assigned was an infantry outfit trained for combat. The most likely destination for such a regiment was Malaya (now Malaysia), where communist forces sought independence from the British Empire, a very real conflict.

With that in mind, the thought of playing football against the likes of Tommy Banks and co. (more on them later), as fearsome as they were, suddenly seemed more attractive a prospect than ever before. At the very least I knew after a game against them I'd go home. Now there were no guarantees, wherever I was heading, that I'd make the return journey. Nothing could be taken for granted. It was truly daunting, and no other period of my life had a more profound effect upon me.

The day arrived and I reported to my new residence. Fulwood Barracks was just two miles from home but on arrival it could have been two *thousand*. It seemed as if a wall of steel – a real one, rather than the fabled Bolton Wanderers defence – encased the entire camp. I've never felt as alone or lost as I did at that moment. My intake consisted of 80 young men – boys, really – split into four groups of 20, lads from all walks of life, mostly from Lancashire, Liverpool and Manchester. Many were only 18, an age that if you had no trade saw you immediately summoned to the 'cause'. Unsurprisingly, my unit was a motley crew, although we weren't alone in that regard.

We lined up to receive our equipment. The only question I remember being asked was, 'Boot size?' The vast amount of equipment was thrown at me by unsmiling veterans who glanced me up and down before deciding what size would fit me. We were issued with our heavy-duty uniform: overcoat, beret, belt, gaiters, trousers, shirts, rucksack … I remember it was piled so high and wide in my arms I could barely see over or around it, and anyone looking in my direction couldn't see me either as I desperately tried to balance the load.

We were shepherded to our digs, a large, single, stone building running the length of the parade ground – home for the next ten weeks. Like a granite tenement, although not nearly as grand, the building housed all the new recruits and was split into multiple sections, each unit of 20 men in its own quarters. It couldn't have been mistaken for anything but a military building – certainly no holiday home. Inside, on the cold stone floor, were two parallel rows of single steel-frame beds, facing each other in the traditional barrack-room way. A steel locker, 6ft tall and 3ft wide, stood next to each bed. At each end of the room was a large window, one looking out upon the parade ground, where we'd spend hours after, breaking in new boots (hopefully the right size), the other offering a view of the bathroom facilities. Nice.

Dave Kerry, conscripted six months before me (with a good job in the catering department), was a valuable source of guidance for what lay ahead. One early tip he threw my way was to not grab a bed by the door, as when the duty sergeant arrived for his daily inspection it would be the first bed he'd see. Humiliation of new recruits sat high on the agenda of the duty sergeant and was to be avoided whenever possible. I made sure I was through the door early and dumped my equipment on a bed in the far corner next to the back wall with that view of the toilets. I'd made my first military decision, a good one, as any inspection would come as far as my bed but no further. The space between my bed and the wall was a 'dead' area that no one cared about. More importantly, I was at the end of the row so there would be no one snoring to my right. To this day I remain grateful to Dave as the situation was daunting enough already: 20 beds for 20 different characters who had just been thrown together, having only met a few short minutes ago. That first night together, not knowing what tomorrow might bring, I believe many of us didn't sleep well. I know I didn't. Opposite me was a lovely, young, chubby lad from east Lancashire, very innocent, who worked for the family business and, dare I say it, was even more naive than the rest of us. The situation was foreign to us all, but seemingly more so to him.

The rude awakening was literally that, as the duty sergeant burst through the door at 6am. Of course, with hindsight comes clarity, but that morning, at that time of the day, I could never have known I was about to embark upon a period in my life where every day I'd experience first hand, up close and in person what could be achieved through repetition, discipline and organisation. It was full-on, an almost overwhelming introduction to rules and the values of maturity, responsibility, discipline and loyalty. The ability – and necessity – to work as a group and support your mates would be steamrollered into us day after day, constantly, without a break, for two months.

Getting to know each other was a long process. Among our ranks were three real hard cases (or so they thought) – two Mancunians and a Scouser – a potent enough combination in itself, never mind the rest of us. They were clearly intent on playing by their own rules, steadfastly adamant that conformity wasn't for them (or so they thought again), and even less keen on obeying orders. A couple of days in, the guard house soon saw them change their ways. The guard house (essentially a solitary confinement unit where 'rebel' recruits were housed until lessons were learned) wasn't a pleasant place to be. Punishment also came via early wake-ups, extreme physical challenges and trials of endurance.

Initially we were a ramshackle bunch. Some struggled to identify their left foot from their right; others, when marching, would turn in the opposite direction to the blue-faced sergeant major's instruction, causing a head-on collision with those who had turned correctly, ensuring complete chaos and inevitable punishment. Gradually, however, the extra drill work began to pay off and the message started to get through: we'd only succeed by working together. Many of the young lads had problems with coordination and concentration, and were naturally uncomfortable and embarrassed during the drills, but little by little, day by day, a genuine understanding developed between us. For some, this was borne of a sense of self-preservation: 'The sooner we sort this out, the better for all of us.' Slowly but surely, we began to get the hang of things, although mistakes and punishments weren't eradicated entirely. There were rhetorical questions such as: why do we have to iron our overcoats and uniforms, wash our shirts and bedding for a daily 6.30 inspection? Most of us didn't know how to switch an iron on! And there were only two irons between us, neither in the best condition to begin with.

During those early, endless, full-on days the pressure began to tell. Lights out at 10pm brought time for reflection; thoughts and fears remained ever-present. The sound of sobbing frequently soundtracked the darkness, accompanied by shouts of, 'F***ing shut up!' The response, often in a wonderfully aggressive Scouse accent, of, 'F***ing leave him alone!' confirmed acceptance and understanding, from some at least, of what we were all close to at times. Consequently, the togetherness that had begun to develop on the parade ground began to grow stronger, and the midnight melody would eventually fade away.

As an infantry battalion our training was extremely physical and aggressive, and it wasn't long before we were issued our first rifles, with one heavily emphasised instruction: they were *never* to leave our sides. These vital pieces of equipment would soon be required on our parade ground drills too. An hour before one such drill my chubby young pal opposite me innocently asked, 'Do we 'av to tek us guns, Corporal?' sounding as if he was off on a Sunday morning pigeon shoot.

The corporal wasn't best pleased. 'GUNS?!?! F***ING GUNS?!?! THAT'S A WEAPON, SOLDIER, A LETHAL F***ING WEAPON! A LETHAL F***ING WEAPON THAT ONE DAY COULD SAVE YOUR F***ING LIFE! IT IS NOT A F***ING GUN!' The corporal marched out of the room, slamming the door behind him. It was the cue for an outburst of laughter from the entire unit; totally spontaneous but, most importantly, completely collective. To this day I remain utterly convinced that the corporal knew exactly what he was doing; he knew his response would, in a strange sort of way, strengthen the bond between us. And he was right. I've often thought he knew it would work because he'd seen it all before; he'd probably been on the receiving end himself. Either way, it worked, we were laughing together as a group, and especially with our friend who had been offered those few words of wisdom.

Days were now flying by. The group that initially couldn't put two steps together, sounding like an old supermarket trolley being dragged over cobblestones, was soon transformed into a single slick unit, everyone in unison. Backs were straight, heads were high and confidence was bursting from our bulging chests. Something special had happened.

The drill sergeant now screamed, 'LISTEN TO IT! LISTEN TO IT! LEFT, RIGHT, LEFT, RIGHT! LISTEN TO IT!' He could barely contain his pride; 20 individuals now drilling together as one, 40 boots hitting the ground simultaneously, a battalion in perfect harmony. On the range, bullets were hitting bullseyes, sandbags were stabbed cleanly and ropes were climbed quickly (with no one falling off). There was a true sense of togetherness and achievement.

Passing out parade was only days away, the culmination of ten weeks of intensive, rigorous, exhausting work, a period that influenced the lives of so many of us for the better. Even the hard cases had softened, becoming integral to the unit and like the rest of us would emerge from this adventure as better people, doing everything in their power not to let their mates down; reunited with the rest of us, they too had flourished. We now had a week to prepare as a single unit of 80 men, having been four separate entities for nine weeks. In a way, it felt like a 'job well done'.

Family members were invited to witness their loved ones' big day, not knowing what to expect. They were in for an unexpectedly pleasant, heart-warming surprise. The boys who had left home ten weeks earlier were now men, unrecognisable in military uniform and immaculately turned out: boots so polished they resembled mirrors; trousers with creases like razor blades (soap applied on the inside of the trouser leg, then being pressed, did the trick); shiny buttons glinting in the lunchtime sunshine; weapons professionally, confidently and steadily held against the shoulder. As we paraded in front of the commanding officer and his senior staff, every element combined to present a sense of enormous pride shared among ourselves and our families. It was quite a feeling.

For me, that feeling intensified even further when I was presented with the award of best recruit from my intake. I accepted with equal measures of pride and humility, having travelled into the unknown with a group of perfect strangers before arriving at my destination a much wiser and all-round better person. And all because of those strangers; it was all thanks to them. To this day, I remain in their debt.

* * *

Throughout basic training I, along with senior military personnel, had remained in touch with Preston North End regarding my standing with the club once I'd passed out. It looked likely I'd be posted locally, meaning I could further my Preston career and also be available (if selected) for the representative army team, at that time full of distinguished names such as Jimmy Armfield (a future great friend and team-mate with Blackpool and England), Gerry Hitchens of Aston Villa and England, and Sheffield Wednesday's Tony Kay (in later years he and I were considered by many to be in direct competition for an England spot). Cliff Britton, the Preston manager, informed my father that the club and the military were 'working on it'. I was looking forward to a ten-day break before my posting was announced, and was confident of the outcome.

On posting day we gathered at the barracks to learn our fates. After addressing us with a few short words, the commanding officer unveiled a huge poster listing our names alphabetically. There was the inevitable, immediate stampede (many were hoping for the 'exotic' posting in Malaya) but I waited, confidently biding my time. Eventually I strolled casually towards the poster before finding my name. Then I saw what was written next to it and felt all the wind in my body – and I mean all of it – rush out of me. It was as if I'd been punched – very hard – in the stomach. I must have read it 20 times, stood stock still, in total disbelief. The confidence I'd possessed only 30 seconds earlier had vanished instantly, already a distant memory. I was completely numb. I stood there so long that I eventually found myself alone, my comrades having long since departed.

I can't remember anything of the walk to my parents' house, sat in the shadow of the Deepdale Kop, a shadow that now seemed to have taken on a whole new meaning, because in two weeks' time I'd have to return to the barracks to be issued with my jungle greens, receive the necessary injections and prepare for immediate departure – to Malaya. My world had come crashing down around me and left me in a state of shock, surrounded by the debris. 'What can I do?' I had no answers. My father subsequently held more meetings with Cliff Britton, but all calls and requests to the military fell on deaf ears; once the roster had been posted there was no way it could be changed.

My football career could have been over – just like that. Twenty months in the jungle would have done little for my CV. That said, I also knew I wasn't heading off to a five-a-side tournament here; this was serious. There was an actual war going on. This was real life and death.

When the unexpected happens, when you're totally unprepared, the physical and mental effects can be severe. This was certainly true in my case, as three days later I began to feel unwell. My temperature soared and I was sweating profusely. The local doctor, who also looked after PNE, swiftly diagnosed glandular fever. I was confined to bed with the necessary medication and told the fever would take 14 days, minimum, to clear. Departure to Malaya was 11 days away. The doctor duly contacted my battalion's medical department. Within 24 hours my mother opened the front door to two large individuals in full military uniform, one carrying a large black medical bag, who wished to see me. I vividly remember these two giants looming over my small single bed, so large they blocked what little light was available through the box-room window, inspecting me as if I was a piece of infected meat. They even insisted my mother wait outside the room as if she was merely my landlady. No action was required on my part, but I couldn't do anything anyway (I could barely even talk – quite handy, actually, as in the military keeping one's mouth shut was often the wisest option). My visitors completed their examination before departing swiftly and silently, offering no indication of their thoughts or findings to my mother or myself. (I suspect I was viewed as one of the countless individuals trying to avoid being drafted abroad; as such, my two visitors were only carrying out their duties.) Little did they – nor I – know the effect those findings would have on my career and, indeed, the rest of my life.

Shortly afterwards the military confirmed my condition before granting me the two-week recovery period. My amended report date was now after my unit's departure date. The army wouldn't let me wait another two months to join the next intake, that was simply not done, and I'd already passed out so there was no point in repeating ten weeks of training. Back at the barracks a job had to be found for me. Once again, my pal Dave Kerry played a crucial role. He knew the commanding officer's batman would shortly be stepping down and would need to be replaced. (The batman would ensure the commanding officer's everyday uniform and full military regalia were always pristine and be readily available to him around the clock; in essence, a full-time butler.) Naturally, this was a much sought-after position, not least because of its perks, one of which was being excused from morning parades and guard duties. Somehow, my opportunity to be interviewed for the role arose, whether due to my football connections, my pal having a word or both or neither of these. I don't know, but I suspect I did benefit from knowing the right people at the right time, people who could, and did, nudge me in the right direction.

Colonel C.E. Knight was my boss for the rest of my military service. A wonderful man, vastly experienced with a quiet presence that, considering his significant responsibilities, impressed me enormously. I was more grateful than ever to have landed the job; I knew how fortunate I was. The colonel enjoyed his football too, which inevitably helped our relationship, and he attended Preston home matches with his wife Sally, a friendly and intelligent lady who from the outset made me feel like one of the family – a far remove from the squaddies on the parade ground.

My responsibilities included hoovering the colonel's residence, cleaning the windows, lighting fires and generally keeping the house tidy. I'd found myself in the right place at the right time, with the added good fortune of being permitted to continue my football career alongside my military service, allowing me to train whenever I could. During my two-year service I managed to play more than 70 times for Preston. Furthermore, every season there were three or four representative army fixtures. These were wonderful respite from military life, with players permitted to leave their postings for a week. You could almost call it a football camp! Such occasions were terrific opportunities to meet up with and play alongside top-level internationals. Unless you already were or would become an international, such occasions would never come your way.

Colonel Mitchell, in charge of our team, was a complete football nut, so these gatherings and matches were always great fun, yet always competitive, and the football always of a very high standard. In one such fixture, against Glasgow Rangers at Ibrox, I must have done something right, as one journalist wrote: 'Milne, of Scottish parenthood, is eligible to play for Scotland.' It was the first time my nationality had been raised, in a football sense, but was no more than one brief line. I was indeed eligible to play for Scotland (both my parents were Scottish) but as I was born south of the border I was also eligible to play for England. Perhaps if the matter had been pursued there and then I'd have played for Scotland. At that time, if you were offered an international cap by anyone you'd jump at the chance. But that never happened, so when England eventually called, I had no hesitation in accepting. All this was still five years away, mind, but thanks to that journalist I began to think I might be good enough to play at that level. And that may never have happened but for the army.

From that very first day walking through the gates of Fulwood Barracks, military life had a profound effect on me; I just didn't realise it at the time – although after reading the above many of you may well question, understandably, whether I was in the army at all! I have so much to thank the military for and will be forever grateful for how National Service shaped me as a person: the lessons learned, the values instilled in me and the huge part it played, not just in my career, but in my life. And although this sounds bizarre, I also owe an enormous debt of gratitude to my glandular fever. I'd never wish this illness upon anyone, but knowing what I know now, and having experienced what I have, without contracting the fever when I did, I'd undoubtedly have a very different story to tell. In fact, I may not have had a story at all.

* * *

My education had begun in earnest at the local secondary school, Deepdale Modern, but had nothing to do with academia. Football was the only subject that truly captured my imagination, concentration and commitment; everything else was sheer torture. On the school field I must have been doing something right though, as I was selected for the representative Preston Schools team. The next step saw me reach county level with the Lancashire Schools team, which led to the attention of Preston North End. I was now 'in the system' – what an opportunity. It was up to me now. By my mid-teens I'd advanced to the Preston B team. Home matches were usually played on Saturday mornings at Willow Farm, the pleasant rural training facility three miles from Deepdale. I soon passed through the A team and by 18 was playing regularly for Preston reserves. And if you were playing for the reserves, you knew you were doing alright.

Reserve team football meant more travel and more commitment (and consequently – unfortunately – the end of my lucrative cycle parking business). Being part-time, lining up alongside and against those who were older, much more experienced, and full-time – more men than boys – was a major challenge. You had to earn your stripes, as the old saying goes; you had to have some mileage on the clock before you could earn any recognition, before you could ever hope to progress in such a tough environment. Clubs had large playing staffs, and with salaries in other fields of employment generally quite low (not that a footballer's salary was high), there was intense competition for places, even in the reserves, a genuine hunger to 'make it'.

Training on Tuesday and Thursday evenings offered a tremendous insight into what was required and was the ideal scenario for gaining experience and knowledge. The Preston North End senior team still had a group including Tom Finney, of course, Tommy Docherty, Frank O'Farrell, Tommy Thompson and Willie Cunningham; breaking through was never going to be easy so experience and maturity were imperative to be ready for first-team action. Most clubs were the same: the reserve teams I played against in my teens consisted of players in their mid-20s who had 'been around the block', were vastly experienced, hardened competitors, yet who remained hungry. They'd fight for their lives every single minute. It was extremely aggressive and competitive, an environment that meant everything to all involved. I had to learn quickly.

Some senior professionals that I played alongside in the reserves offered guidance and advice. Others, more selfishly, seemed to play only for themselves, thinking of their own welfare and little else. I found such a mindset difficult to understand and even more difficult to accept. Consequently, I was drawn towards, and bonded with, those who were prepared to give their all in the interests of the team and for the benefit of others.

Some of these players weren't always the most talented but their enthusiasm, commitment and downright honesty were qualities I admired and tried to absorb and emulate. This was as far as many careers went but the dedication and professionalism of these lads stood out for me. I quickly realised that without these qualities, I'd be going nowhere.

The reserve matches would attract a thousand or so loyal supporters, although at grounds such as Deepdale, able to hold upwards of 30,000, the terraces looked extremely sparse. What's more, many were only there to hear the half-time score of the first team (playing away), which was announced as the reserves re-emerged for their second half. A positive scoreline would lift the fans, who in turn would lift the players as much as they could in an almost deserted ground. The half-time scores of the day's other First Division fixtures were displayed on scoreboards, usually placed near the corner flags on opposite sides of the pitch. These matches were labelled alphabetically (A: Arsenal vs Blackpool / B: Everton vs Notts County, etc.) in the matchday programmes, and duly corresponded with the letters on the display boards (A: 2-2 / B: 0-1, etc.)

There was always great anticipation when the two elderly gentlemen in flat caps and long brown coats appeared pitchside before proceeding in opposite directions towards their assigned corners. Clutching their treasure troves of eagerly awaited information, enjoying but ignoring the buzz of the crowd, they single-mindedly strode past supporters desperate to know how our nearest rivals were faring. 'What's the Bolton score?' 'How are Arsenal getting on?' 'Are Wolves losing?' 'Just bloody tell us!' It all fell on deaf ears. Nothing was revealed until the boards were in place.

At times it felt like an eternity as the flat caps, deliberately taking their time I'm sure, moved from one board to the next. I'm convinced that to have been a scoreboard operator you'd have needed to be over 65, very thick-skinned and hard of hearing. Spectacles would help too – displaying an incorrect score would cause uproar. And woe betide any player taking a corner during this process, thereby blocking the view of the scoreboards; he'd have no choice but to listen to the 'advice' of supporters (with no interest in the match in front of them, only with eyes for the other scores), full of disdain and never complimentary. 'Get on with it!' 'Move out of the way!' 'Hurry up and take the bloody thing!' Or words to that effect. Unsurprisingly, corners weren't dwelt upon, and most certainly not by visiting teams. Such interactions meant no one was particularly keen to take a corner in the first place.

When the match finished many supporters would remain in the ground, waiting patiently for the first team's result. This was announced over the PA system – the two flat caps were spared the ordeal of running the gauntlet a second time – and would send the fans out into the Lancashire evening with a smile on their faces and a spring in their step, or anticipating a miserable rest of the weekend. Or somewhere in between.

* * *

Throughout my entire apprenticeship my dad was on the Preston staff, having played for the club in the '30s alongside, among others, Bill Shankly. Two consecutive FA Cup finals were reached. Preston lost the first, in 1937, defeated 3-1 by Sunderland. My dad was on the losing side that day and unfortunately missed the 1938 final (coincidentally, I'd suffer a similar fate in 1965), which Preston won 1-0 against Huddersfield, due to a broken collarbone. The following year, the outbreak of the Second World War brought an end to many a playing career, including those of my father and Shanks. Post-war, Dad had brief spells playing for and managing Wigan Athletic (again, I'd emulate my father many years later) and Morecambe, and following a short stint at Doncaster Rovers he returned to Preston in 1949 as first-team trainer, while also studying physiotherapy and general health (he had a passion for both all his life).

This meant he was always present during my Tuesday and Thursday training sessions. As I progressed, I'd get one free morning off work to train with the first team; my dad was involved in those sessions too. I can honestly say I never once felt uncomfortable with, or in, his presence; not once did I feel I was only there because I was the trainer's son. There was no favouritism; in fact, the very opposite is closer to the truth. I felt I had to work harder than anyone else to make sure everyone knew I was there on merit. And that was entirely due to the personality and principles of my dad.

My dad was from a different era. One of 16 children (although four of his siblings died during infancy), born in Dundee, he was the son of a railway signalman and as a young man worked as a railway porter at Lochee station in the west of Dundee. An enthusiastic cyclist, he once travelled to London (discounted train fares were available to him) to buy a chrome-framed bicycle he'd seen advertised in a magazine. Back in Dundee, nobody had seen anything like it; to the locals it was like something from outer space and my dad was incredibly proud.

Always a keen footballer, he'd rush straight from work to training. He didn't own any football boots so simply played in his work boots – not exactly designed for football! Despite the cumbersome footwear he was still good enough to earn a trial for Dundee United. The scout who arranged the trial was aware of my dad's predicament but advised him not to worry, a selection of boots would be available to all trialists in similar situations. On the day of the trial my dad arrived in good time, but the choice of footwear was limited; he found the correct size for his left foot but not for his right. As the trialists were called to the pitch, the only remaining boot in his size was another leftie. He quickly slipped it on, laced it and ran down the tunnel where the sharp-eyed scout shouted, 'Jimmy! You've got two left feet!'

Despite the handicap, Dad was invited for a second trial a week later. Having described the footwear shenanigans to his own father, he was told in no uncertain terms to go into town first thing the next morning and buy his first pair of real football boots (the funds would be made available). The new boots did the trick as his second trial was a resounding success, and he was immediately offered his first professional contract. Prudent as ever, his first reaction was, 'I have to discuss this with my father.' That's how it was in the Milne family. When he did sign for Dundee United, with his father in attendance, who else was at the ground but the scout who had helped him on his way and who greeted him with a huge smile: 'Jimmy, son! Well done! Amazing what you can do with two left feet!'

Dundee will always have a place in my heart, especially the fond memories of childhood holidays there. With so many aunties, uncles and cousins, I was always flavour of the month – it was like Christmas! It was also exciting to see my grandparents, especially my grandfather (my dad's dad), a big man, strong and mostly silent, but when he did speak, you listened carefully and acted accordingly. And you never questioned him. As a father to 16 children, he was a figure of authority and remained so his entire life. Even as adults, my aunties and uncles would stop what they were doing and pay close attention whenever he spoke. His mere presence could be intimidating, but he was a good man. He once gave me a battered old pencil case bearing the inscription 'Better do it now than wish it done'. The pencil case is long gone, but never the memory of the words. The message was 'Don't leave for tomorrow what you can achieve today'. It's an attitude that stayed with me. My father was very similar to my grandfather; what you saw was what you got, and no one was spared, even Sir Tom Finney, who once said, 'The trouble with Jimmy is that sometimes he says the right thing at the wrong time.'

My dad was constantly observing my burgeoning career but always remained at arm's length. It was up to me to find my own way. I'd been playing inside-right (football language and a position long forgotten now) for the reserves but rave reviews were few and far between. I wasn't progressing, so wasn't enjoying my football. The manager, Cliff Britton, decided to move me into midfield – right-half to be precise, into the No. 4 shirt. Immediately, a whole new world opened up. I could see the whole pitch and all the options available. I could attack and defend, although had to learn – the hard way – how to marry those two vital disciplines together. Nevertheless, the straitjacket was off and I was on my way.

I made my first-team debut aged 19 away to Portsmouth on 22 September 1956. Pompey had a strong team and were captained by Jimmy Dickinson, one of the era's finest defenders. The match finished 2-2, although for me most of it passed in a blur. Two memories stand out, however. The first is the tempo – every thought, decision and action took place at breakneck speed.

This truly was life in the fast lane. The excitement of the occasion brought such an adrenalin high that I had the legs for the entire match and finished in quite good spirits, largely thanks to the encouragement and support of my team-mates. I felt protected and, more importantly, accepted in this wonderful new world, due to the attitudes, efforts and effects of the players around me, none more so than Willie Cunningham playing directly behind me at right-back. Willie, a coal miner, was hard as nails and took no prisoners, yet for all his physicality and aggression there was also a quiet demeanour about him (off the pitch you couldn't wish to meet a nicer, more humble man). He never stopped talking for the entire 90 minutes, his surprisingly calm and reassuring voice seeming to pump oxygen into my lungs. 'If anything comes past you, son, don't worry … I'll deal with it.' It didn't take long for the message to get through to me; not many left-wingers enjoyed venturing into Willie's territory, and they all enjoyed it even less the second time!

The second stand-out memory? Being selected in the same team as Sir Tom Finney. I'd shared a training pitch with him many times, but this was different; joy, pleasure, an honour, and a privilege, all rolled into one. I talked earlier of the unhelpful attitudes and selfishness I'd experienced in the reserves, but this was the polar opposite. I'd graduated to a whole new level and even if it were to happen only once I'd have been happy. I played alongside my hero, and it was just how I dreamed it would be.

* * *

Today, players often play on their 'wrong' sides, but this was a rarity in the 1950s. Willie, though, was a left-footed right-back so when defending an attack coming from our left side,

Willie covered the back-post area. When the ball came across the danger zone he'd swivel on the spot before sweeping it left-footed away from danger, usually directly to Tom Finney out on the right wing, instantly turning defence into attack. The pair had a natural understanding, a simple combination, a notion that deeply resonated within me and would accompany my entire career.

Most teams employed wingers who loved to get at full-backs and whose managers encouraged them to do so at every opportunity. Defenders were encouraged to keep things simple but Joe Walton, our right-footed left-back (like Willie, also playing on his 'wrong' side) was proactive rather than reactive. He'd frequently dictate to his opposite number how the next 90 minutes would pan out. If his winger was right-footed (as most were), Joe would stay as wide as possible, hugging the touchline, offering the winger only one way to go – inside. This would force his opponent on to his own weaker left foot, bringing Joe's stronger right side into play. He'd also determine how the action would play out by often making the first move, kidding on to challenge before stopping short; playing the winger at his own game, Joe was writing the script.

This was an early lesson on the mental aspect of the game: a defender dictating to an attacker – would the attacker be clever enough to solve the problem? Many had problems with Joe, including the great Sir Stanley Matthews. Everybody knew Stan would feint to come inside before going the other way, but not everybody could stop him. (By contrast, if Tom Finney was shown only one way, that's the way he'd go, although he had the ability to go either side if he chose to do so.) But even Stan struggled against Joe, never truly comfortable against him. Watching and learning this proved invaluable to me, highlighting the tactics involved in, and the art of, defending. Alongside 'combinations', another of my mantras was 'square pegs in square holes' (more of which later), but Cunningham and Walton, our 'wrong-footed' full-backs, blew that one out of the water.

With a slightly different take on this theme was the great Blackburn Rovers and England winger Brian 'Dougie' Douglas, a diminutive bag of tricks, always difficult to contain. When playing against Bolton Wanderers in a fierce local derby, Dougie faced a Wanderers defence comprising Derek Hennin, Roy Hartle, John Higgins and the redoubtable Tommy Banks, a defensive unit commonly known as 'the wall of steel', the creeds 'no prisoners' and 'thou shalt not pass' firmly embedded in their collective DNA. A favourite line of Tommy's, delivered in his broad Lancastrian accent, was, 'Thee might come past, lad, or the ball, but not thee and the ball together.' Such chat was common. Lines such as, 'Hello Mr Douglas, nice to see you. Are you aware of what you're in for this afternoon?' were commonplace; all part of the fun, but not always so polite. 'What are you doing here? Who f***ing told you that you could play?'

Behind the wind-ups and industrial language, though, was always the sense of competition. Everyone knew the easiest targets, who had a short fuse and could be 'got at', and who couldn't. Equally, everyone also knew who not to mess with. As Dougie recalled, 'I managed to kid Tommy, got past him, put a cross in, which eventually went out for a goal kick. Jogging back to position, quite pleased with myself, I was confronted by a less than pleased Mr Banks, full of threat, and sage advice: "Hey! Young fella! Don't ever think of doing that again. Because if you do, you and the f***ing ball will be down there." I got the message.' 'Down there' was the bottom of the distinctive Burnden

Park slope, where many an ill-fated winger had disappeared before re-emerging with the 'just been hit by a tractor' look.

Even Sir Tom wasn't immune. I recall he and my father talking in the Preston treatment room the day after facing Bolton. Sir Tom was sat upright, grimacing, as my father inspected the great man's black-and-blue legs. 'That fizzing Tommy Banks!' said Sir Tom. 'Fizzing kicked me from start to fizzing finish! Then, at the end, would you believe it – he wanted to shake my fizzing hand!' He rarely swore, Sir Tom, despite being a plumber by trade, surrounded by coarse language. But in those few short words he described, beautifully, the reality of the world in which he, one of the greatest players of all time, was living. But, continually kicked from pillar to post, Sir Tom always took it all in his stride.

* * *

On 30 April 1960, Sir Tom's final appearance for Preston brought the curtain down on an incredible career. A one-club man of outstanding ability and humility, it was a pleasure, privilege and honour to have known him as a person and to have played and trained alongside him. That afternoon versus Luton Town at Deepdale was a sad occasion as players of both clubs, non-playing staff, officials and spectators all knew this would be the last time they'd ever experience, in the flesh, this most captivating of footballing thrills. For many, the tears flowed.

All too often, having watched the great man, my first thought – and my last as my head hit the pillow – would be, *I can't believe what I've just seen*. That's a true hero. That's an idol. I wasn't alone in my admiration for Sir Tom. The likes of Bill Shankly, Tommy Docherty and my dad all felt the same. Their respect for him was total. Shanks once said that Sir Tom could play in an overcoat and still no defender would get near him; and if Preston began to tire, they'd simply give the ball to Tom, and he'd keep it for ten minutes. In later years, when the Doc was regularly bringing the house down on the after-dinner circuit, he was asked how Tony Currie, a Sheffield United idol and QPR's talismanic new signing, compared to Sir Tom. The Doc paused to consider his response. 'I can see certain similarities,' he said, 'but you have to remember, Tom is 57.'

In my experience, education, in any profession, will have a lasting influence, and the earlier in life you're subjected to that education, the greater its influence will be. Furthermore, continued education means continued influence. My education and influence were established very early in my life – in large part thanks to my hero. As a youngster chasing the end of the rainbow, I believe it's vital to have a hero: someone to look up to, respect and admire; someone you wish to emulate, who will set standards and show you the way, with humility, honesty and good grace; someone with the character, temperament and ability to convey this by his or her behaviour (in a football sense, on and off the pitch); someone who makes you believe that one day you can, and will, reach the same heights yourself. These are special qualities to find in anyone, but to combine them with the most complete set of skills, pace and strength, you have someone truly special. Someone like my hero – my idol – Sir Tom Finney, who possessed all the above and more. I'm incredibly fortunate to have watched and learned from him; to have looked up to, respected and admired him in equal measure. To this day I remain utterly privileged to have known him, not only as a player, but more importantly as a man. A one-club man. A true one-off.

Chapter 3

AS SIR Tom's playing career drew to a close, so did my military duties. By the end of that season, I was getting noticed. Exciting times were on the horizon, and as the new season loomed, I was fully determined to push on. But where?

Tommy Docherty was by this time playing for Arsenal, having swapped Lancashire for London in 1958. The Doc had contacted my dad – discreetly of course – to let him know that Arsenal wanted to sign me. He also wanted to know my reaction to this news. There was little time for my dad to report back, though, as the very next day Bill Shankly made a similar approach: would I be interested in signing for Liverpool?

It was more than just two major clubs showing an interest in me. I had a personal connection to both, in Shanks and the Doc. My dad never mentioned to me how the chats went with his two old pals, nor did I expect him to; it wasn't in his nature. The other two were also no-nonsense ex-players from north of the border, so I knew any conversations would have been brief and bullshit-free.

My dad went straight to the point: 'What do you want to do?' It was extremely difficult. I was playing in the First Division for Preston North End, my home-town club that I'd supported since day one; Arsenal, also in the top division and with a beautiful stadium, was one of the biggest clubs in the country; Liverpool, though, were floundering in the Second Division, and their home ground Anfield was shabby and crumbling. If I were to move, the more attractive option seemed to be Arsenal. However, despite the general state of disrepair and air of decline surrounding Liverpool, it was a great deal closer to Preston than London and, even then, the cost of living in London was considerably higher than that of the north. Adding further to the importance of making the right decision, I was due to get married just one month later!

There were pros and cons attached to all three clubs. I loved Preston but was concerned about their immediate prospects, in particular how would we cope with the loss of Tom Finney? There were other senior players in the twilight of their careers too, which had to be considered. Maintaining our First Division status wasn't going to be straightforward so was in no way guaranteed. (Unfortunately, my fears were well founded: Preston were relegated the following year, 1961, and at the time of writing have yet to return to the top flight.) In terms of salaries, there was little difference between the clubs. The top money was £20 a week and was the same everywhere. The only way to squeeze out a little extra would be to 'play the game': ask for a signing-on fee, for example. But even if that worked it wouldn't have been a huge amount, £500 if you were lucky.

What followed, though, was a glimpse into the future, an indication of how situations would suddenly arise and develop throughout my career, and my first real insight into the psyche of my next manager. The day after telephoning my father, Bill Shankly appeared on my parents' doorstep (when it came to securing a player, he wasn't a patient man). I suspect he and my dad had been talking around the time Arsenal were first sniffing around but I don't know for sure and was certainly never privy to any conversations that may or may not have taken place. Either way, here he was.

'Hello, son. Has your father told you anything about Liverpool Football Club?'

'No,' I said, somewhat sheepishly.

'Well in that case, I will.' And the sales pitch began. 'Liverpool is a sleeping giant. There are 50,000 people desperate for a connection to the club they love. Loyal, hard-working people, just like you and me, son [this resonated deeply with me], who want to see a team with character, players to be proud of, players who will give everything on the pitch while the supporters give everything off the pitch. If you do that, they'll respect you, and we'll create an atmosphere where the crowd and the team are as one. Believe me, son: at Liverpool, this is possible. You will be one of my first signings, and there will be many more top players to follow. We are building something special. You have my word.'

I'd said nothing, just listened. Shanks clearly had a vision and was incredibly passionate. He had an image of what Liverpool could become, and how they could achieve it. Never mind the Second Division mediocrity, never mind the meagre Anfield crowds or the tired, old, decaying stadium. Shankly just *believed*. This was his message, his dream, his complete faith in what was achievable; a message delivered with the passion, fervour and energy for which he'll always be remembered. His sales pitch required no further reinforcements, but he wasn't quite finished. He himself had worn the No. 4 shirt at Preston – the shirt I now proudly occupied – during his most successful playing days; the number clearly meant a great deal to him too. So when he then promised I'd wear the No. 4 at Liverpool it was – *he was* – impossible to resist. I signed.

* * *

I'd completed my National Service, played my final match for my home-town club and signed for Bill Shankly and Liverpool. I was also due to get married! Professionally and personally, this felt like the beginning of the most important part of my life. I promised myself total commitment on all fronts.

Our training ground, Melwood, was situated in the Liverpool suburb of West Derby just a couple of miles from Anfield. Back then the players headed to Anfield first, changed into our training kit, before a coach took us to Melwood. Most of my team-mates would travel to Anfield by bus. Alighting on Walton Breck Road outside the Kop, they'd enter the ground through a small door next to a turnstile, then walk beneath the main stand towards the dressing rooms. The home dressing room was dominated by a large square table, centrally placed. There were benches against the walls and pegs above those to hang your clothes. The far wall of the dressing room was topped by a long, narrow window, maybe ten feet wide but only a foot high. The window was covered on the outside by heavy wire mesh. This gave the impression we could be in some kind of penitentiary, and the room's lighting and ventilation did nothing to convince us otherwise.

On my first morning there were two large cardboard boxes on the dressing room table containing shirts (various sizes and colours), socks and shorts, and long heavy woollen sweaters, which would conceal you completely if you were less than 6 feet tall and 15 stone. There was no evidence of the essential briefs or jockstraps, items that immediately jumped to the top of my shopping list. At that stage I'd no idea who was allowed in the dressing room, but it was clear there were more bodies than pegs on the wall or socks and shirts in the boxes. Fortunately, though, there would be no 'two left feet' scenario here, as I'd sensibly brought my trainers and boots with me. Once everyone was kitted out, we made our way to the coach for the short journey to Melwood.

It all seemed a bit ramshackle and was a real eye-opener for me, coming as I did from an environment of professionalism, organisation and cleanliness, all of which I'd taken for granted. This was an immediate reality check. I was no longer at Preston, in the First Division; I was at Liverpool, in the Second – so get on with it. Training sessions were naturally different but, of course, the manager's enthusiasm, drive, energy and constant dialogue all stood out, all alluding to where Shanks was convinced this club was heading. His own demeanour allowed players to express themselves just as he did, and enjoy hard work with a purpose. And it all rubbed off on us. The power of his approach can never be underestimated and was simply contagious. Training became keenly anticipated and was enjoyable and satisfying – not always the case in professional football.

* * *

My Liverpool debut arrived at Anfield on 31 August 1960 against Southampton. I'd replaced Johnny Wheeler, whose Liverpool days were winding down after nearly 200 appearances. The match also saw the one and only Billy Liddell make his final appearance for the club. With no time for preparation, not even a training session with my new team-mates, I didn't know

Billy at all well, although his reputation and ability preceded him. He was to Liverpool what Finney was to Preston. I got to know him well enough to recognise how similar he was to Sir Tom. Ability-wise, I'd say Sir Tom just edged it, but I'm biased of course! In terms of personality, though, there was nothing between them. Billy, too, was humble, modest, a wonderful man and a true gentleman. A crowd of almost 40,000 paid tribute to the great man but, on a damp, miserable evening we failed to give Billy the send-off he merited (after more than 500 appearances), deservedly losing 1-0.

My introduction to Second Division football and to Liverpool had been, at best, ordinary (although even that may be too complimentary). I struggled to have any influence on the match and drifted through the 90 minutes without effect. The full-time whistle brought a sense of relief and an end to the agony. It wasn't what I'd anticipated. And what the manager, my parents (watching from the stand) and the Anfield faithful made of the new recruit, I dread to think: 'What a waste of money,' would be a fair and reasonable assessment.

I left Anfield with my parents and, in a nearby side-street, discovered my dad's car was blocked in. We stood in the rain, scratching our heads, when four big lads approached. They'd obviously been to the match. 'Alright, Gord! Don't worry, we'll get you out.' They then bounced the car out of its predicament as if it were a toy, and we duly set off on what felt like an extremely long journey. I remember muttering, 'Well that wasn't a great start.' My dad said no more than, 'I agree with you.' Then my mum, trying in vain to dry off on the back seat, chirped up, 'Those lads recognised you straight away, Gordon, and were pleased to help you. I think you'll be fine.' Typical words of support and comfort, at the perfect time too. What's more, they turned out to be true.

* * *

After half a dozen matches I was dropped, Johnny Wheeler regaining his place. It would be Christmas before I played again. How it was conveyed to me revealed a facet of Shanks's management style that I was unaware of: despite his ubiquitous vim and vigour he was never a lover of confrontation, or encounters that could become argumentative. Surprising, given that in public he was bubbly, confident, occasionally aggressive and never afraid to offer his own opinions. Most would have thought a one-to-one with one of his own players would have presented no problem, but that wasn't the case; he simply didn't like it.

I experienced this for the first time one Friday afternoon at Anfield. I was in the boot room – not yet anywhere near the institution it would become – cleaning my boots under the watchful eye of Albert Shelley. Albert was a club stalwart, having joined the training staff in 1936. The original Boot Room Boy, he was extremely popular and highly respected. In his brown overall and collar and tie, Albert always kept the boot room pristine; it was his domain, and everyone knew it. With years of experience Albert had acquired a degree of wisdom few could match, with a remarkable capacity to ensure players kept their feet on the ground, with just a few short words: 'No room for Flash Harrys here.' That was a favourite of his.

That Friday only he and I were present when Joe Fagan appeared, closed the door behind him and immediately addressed me. 'Gordon, the boss thinks you've been finding it hard to settle. He thinks a wee break will help, so you won't be involved tomorrow.' This was clearly not good news, but delivered by

Joe, a lovely man who I grew to respect tremendously, in such a gentle manner (his natural personality anyway) that I had no trouble accepting the decision. With Albert quietly nodding his agreement I felt I had two experienced football men on my side; they understood how I felt but also knew that, in the long term, this was in my best interests. I also knew I couldn't argue. My form had been poor. As the 'meeting' ended, Albert rubber-stamped this notion with typical words of encouragement: 'Get your sleeves rolled up, son. This has happened to better players than you.' This was Shanks using his senior staff in different ways to achieve his own objectives. And for me, it most definitely worked.

The wake-up call intensified my desire to turn things around. Top of my list was the need to find a new home. I duly accelerated my efforts to do so. On the advice of Dick White, Liverpool's captain, Edith and I decided on a lovely semi-detached house in a leafy area of Lydiate, less than ten miles from Anfield. Dick and his wife Josie were just around the corner, and Ian St John and Ron Yeats would also soon move to the area. The village was on the right side of Liverpool for visiting our parents in Preston, and the commute to Anfield was easier still. The family mucked in, all under the supervision of Edith, of course, and the house was ready to move into as soon as we returned from our honeymoon in Jersey in June 1961. Settled and comfortable, I was ready to go.

Like me, Dick had served his time as a joiner, and one day in late August asked whether I'd help him with the odd jobs he was doing on the side: a new window here, a side gate there. These jobs would be undertaken in the afternoons after training. We tackled a couple and were paid cash in hand. Promising. But not for long. Within a week Dick was summoned to the manager's office; a rarity, but his status as captain meant the rest of us weren't overly concerned. Dick usually kept most things to himself but did offer me an abbreviated post-meeting report consisting only of some of the manager's words. The 'some' were more than enough, though, and the message was clear. 'They tell me you and Milne are out doing building work in the afternoons when you should be resting. You, Dick, are the captain of Liverpool Football Club. You are a professional footballer. You should be living like one. You should know better.' Pause. 'And you most certainly shouldn't be fixing any windows for Evertonians.' We'd never thought of that one. Our new business enterprise had come to a juddering halt before it had even taken off. Perhaps I should have stuck to parking bicycles.

Shanks never mentioned my commuting, but I suspect he was pleased and relieved when I moved closer. I know I was. My life changed considerably for the better, and it was the simple things that made the difference. Two of my team-mates, Jimmy Melia and Johnny Morrissey, were local lads who seemed to know everyone, with 'contacts' all over the city: dockers, butchers, bakers, you name it. All these boys together, it was like Ali Baba and the 40 thieves! There was a butcher's shop in Liverpool near the Adelphi Hotel, and you'd get a nudge from one of the lads at training: 'Fancy it?' And if you did, you'd be told to head to the shop at a particular time that Friday (it was always a Friday, although not every week – we didn't murder it). The place was always packed; you'd stand at the back and wait your turn.

The staff were predominantly Liverpool supporters and soon enough one of the lads would give you a nod: 'Two minutes, Gordon!' Sure enough, two minutes later he'd come whistling through the crowd and hand over a carrier bag. 'Here you go, Gordon, take that! And good luck tomorrow!' And that was it – you were away! You wouldn't know what was in the bag, and it might not be what you'd want, but that's how it worked. Choice never came into it; you'd get what you were given and there were no questions asked! (Edith never went in with me, she was too embarrassed. Plus, she'd want to pick what she wanted!) There were never any grounds for complaint because it didn't cost a penny, but someone somewhere was losing money. I think back now: how did they do it? But that's how it was, a footballer standing on his own at the back of a crowded city centre butcher's shop, waiting for his complimentary carry-out.

Something so simple as shopping in the city made me feel part of something more. I accept that because I was a footballer it was different for me; I was in the public eye more than most, but it was never a problem, not even with the Everton fans. The mickey-taking was great, the humour and mentality fantastic, and both Edith and I loved it. Everyone was so friendly to us, we felt accepted, we felt we belonged.

* * *

In 2020 Liverpool closed the doors on Melwood, their iconic training ground in West Derby, as the club moved their daily operations to Kirkby. Melwood had been Liverpool's base for 70 years, during which the site had grown in both significance and standing; for many supporters and players, this patch of grass in a Liverpool suburb has taken on almost mythical status. But the state-of-the-art facility it had become by the 21st century was a far cry from its origins.

Acquired from St Francis Xavier's College in 1950, Melwood (named after the two priests, Fathers Melling and Woodlock, who oversaw the ground and the pupils as they played football there) was little more than a large field with a wooden pavilion (little more than a glorified shed) more suited to cricket. By 1959 the site had been neglected and, according to the new manager, was 'a sorry wilderness'. Shanks soon persuaded the board to invest in Melwood. Prior to this training took place at Anfield, but to protect the turf there the decision was made to make better use of Melwood. Players and staff would now gather at Anfield before travelling by coach to the training ground. Over time, the camaraderie and bonding that took place on these journeys became integral to what became known as 'the Liverpool Way'.

Central to much of what we did at Melwood were the four big upright wooden boards introduced by the manager, each the size of a goal, laid out in a square facing each other around 30 yards apart. Painted on the edges were goalposts and crossbars. When you were in the middle with the ball, you'd have all four to shoot at. The ball would rebound towards you; control, swivel, shoot again. And so on. Given their size and how close the boards were it was quite a job to miss them, but these drills were really about building up the confidence to give the ball a whack, anticipate, change position and do it again. How long could you go? All aspects of finishing were worked on. The forwards, natural finishers such as Roger and Ian St John, loved them.

There were also four smaller boards, around 6 feet wide and 9 feet tall, in exactly the same layout but closer together, perhaps 20 yards apart; a tighter set-up used for quick-passing drills. All this was basic stuff really, but Shanks loved it. 'The boys are always on the move, twisting and turning, getting it, giving it, getting it back ...' These were his basic principles of how to play the game and could make for an intense session. If you did it right you were knackered after a couple of minutes, then you'd have a breather before starting again. It was hardly state-of-the-art stuff – it became known as the 'sweatbox' – but the boards were part and parcel of Melwood for years. Before training we'd whack a few balls off them to warm up, so they quickly became an integral part of our preparation. So simple, yet extremely effective.

Team meetings were held in the pavilion, although were extremely uncomplicated. We'd sit on the wooden benches and Shanks would have his 'tactics' board covered with red and yellow counters. He'd talk generically – a reflection of how simple he believed football was. 'We'll move the ball like this, and you'll move about like that.' Equally generically he'd be shifting the counters randomly around the board; no patterns of play involved here. 'Then we'll push up, then we'll sit back.' Standing alongside his board, gesticulating, all his actions and words were centred upon the team; no player was singled out, no counters ever isolated, it was always about the collective.

There would always be 11 red counters on the board, but never – ever – 11 yellows. Regardless of the opposition, the most he'd ever have were eight, so, at least on his board, we always had room to play – no wonder he thought we'd sweep the opposition away! This disparity was rarely questioned but I believe Shanks was practising his own psychology. One Friday before a trip to Old Trafford, Shanks began: 'We'll have 5,000 supporters with us tomorrow – 5,000! And they'll out-shout that lot! Think of that! 5,000 of them, all getting behind you! The pitch will suit us, we're in good form, we're fitter than them, sharper than them …' It was Shanks in his pomp. All the while he was moving the counters here, there and everywhere. The way he pitched it, we couldn't lose! Then suddenly, that was it, all done. We trooped outside for our usual Friday sprints (we'd put on old-fashioned running shoes – the spikes made us feel quicker) and a couple of stretches. Following the sprints, Ian St John – the Saint – approached Shanks.

'Boss, can I have a word?'

'Aye, son, what is it?'

'Well, in the meeting just then, you never said a word about Bobby Charlton, Denis Law or George Best.'

'Aye, that's right, son, but there's a reason for that.' A pause. 'Do you think I want to frighten everybody to death?' In fairness, anyone, including Shanks, could frighten himself to death while talking about that trio. He had the greatest admiration for them all, particularly Denis Law, who he'd managed at Huddersfield Town, and he knew they could cause chaos at any given moment. Nevertheless, the most we'd ever get from him tactically, even concerning such lauded opposition, would be something as basic as, 'We'll keep it tight for the first 15 minutes.' And he'd push the red counters closer together.

Much of our training consisted of small-sided matches, five- or six-a-side. These were always played at full tilt, an attempt to replicate the tempo of a real fixture. Simultaneously, Shanks, Bob Paisley, Joe Fagan and Reuben Bennett would take on the apprentices in their own six-a-side match (two unfortunate youngsters would have to make up the numbers on the staff team). After finishing, we'd often watch the old men vs the kids. Shanks would play as we all imagined he had years before, and his running commentary never stopped. He relished these moments and loved us watching him. These matches were as competitive as any due to the hatred of defeat embedded in his team; if they were losing, they'd play on, and on, and on – until they were winning. And as soon as they took the lead, Shanks would declare, 'Full time!', pick up the ball and march off the pitch. The poor youngsters had no choice but to accept defeat.

There were no refreshments after training, and we wouldn't even shower at Melwood. Different groups would finish at different times, leading to a staggered end to the session, five or ten minutes while the separate groups wound down before eventually coming together. There'd be another five or ten minutes to board the bus then a 20-minute journey back to Anfield. This was a natural cooling-off period in which Shanks was a great believer. Sometimes training produces friction: handbags, fallouts and the occasional full-on fisticuffs. There was never any real malice involved, no real animosity, but these games were certainly not friendlies. By the time the coach reached Anfield, however, tempers would no longer be frayed, temperatures would have dropped, and everything would have calmed down. And because we wouldn't shower until we were back at Anfield, we'd be cooling down physically in that period too (although if wrapped in the enormous training sweaters the perspiration continued for quite some time – there was nothing refined going on here).

Shanks also introduced what's now the standard practice of having lunch together as a squad. Previously, many would be straight off the training ground, into the shower, get dressed and be gone; not everyone, but there were plenty who couldn't get away quickly enough. The culmination of all these innovations proved the strategy and foresight in Shankly's thinking: now, by the time we'd had lunch (and nobody left the canteen without express permission to do so) we'd all had that extra couple of hours of settling down after what were, in many cases, heavy-duty training sessions. That extra time helped to forge stronger bonds and fortify relationships, even if we didn't realise it. Shanks himself would pass comment, discussing 'tempers calming, muscles relaxing, the lads getting on ...' 'Method in the madness' isn't the correct phrase because it wasn't madness; it was all very straightforward, and thc method was undeniable Those coach journeys, particularly the return legs, meant a lot to Shanks. We could see that, and we could also see it worked.

Simple. Basic. Straightforward. Uncomplicated. All this alongside honesty, passion, unity and belief, was 'the Liverpool Way', and is encapsulated in a single photograph. At Melwood, we're all lined up against a concrete wall as Shanks addresses us. Sitting on top of that wall are nine or ten kids listening to the manager just as intently as we are, but there's no way Shanks was going to move them on; they were interested in Liverpool – they *were* Liverpool – and had the right to be there. And if anyone tried to shift them, he'd insist they stay. There's nothing flash about the photo, or what it portrays, nothing false or staged. The content is simple, basic, straightforward and uncomplicated. It's honest, passionate and believable. Because the photo portrays the truth.

Chapter 4

IT WAS the saddest of occasions, yet one of celebration too. In March 2021, I attended the funeral of my old pal Ian St John – the Saint. Ahead of the funeral itself, the cortège approached Anfield, pausing at the Bill Shankly statue outside the Kop. A wreath was laid there before the cortège moved on. Following the service, we gathered to mourn, remember, celebrate and commemorate one of the most important figures in the club's history. While we were doing so, Betsy, the Saint's widow, said to me, 'At least we were there at the beginning, Gordon.' Betsy was right. Looking back, all of us would say the same thing. We didn't know where it was going to go – how could we? Thinking back to 1961, even if we did reach the First Division, we didn't have a bloody clue what would happen the next season, never mind the next five, and certainly never mind the next 50-odd years! But for Liverpool that summer proved pivotal, and the following season, 1961/62, was arguably *the* most important season ever. Because you've got to start somewhere.

Shanks had been around as a manager for a while already, beginning at Carlisle United in 1949. Spells at Grimsby Town and Workington followed, before a three-year stint at Huddersfield Town. A decade in football management had brought plenty of experience but little in the way of success. It was at that point,

December 1959, that he arrived in Liverpool. In describing Shanks, Tom Finney's book and my father's diaries are in many places identical: enthusiasm, energy, drive. His attitude had remained the same, but what had he learned? Should the previous decade be viewed as his apprenticeship? Was he readying himself for what was to come? Who knows? But for some reason, at Liverpool, it clicked. And it clicked big.

Three months after his arrival, Shanks's first signing was Sammy Reid, a young inside-forward from Motherwell. The 20-year-old struggled to make the grade though, failing to make a single appearance and leaving almost as quickly as he'd arrived. Three months later Shanks brought in Kevin Lewis from Sheffield United for £13,000. It proved to be an astute move. When you're a player you don't necessarily analyse your team-mates' abilities but you do know instinctively who you're comfortable playing with. Kev was most definitely one of them and fitted easily into Shanks's jigsaw.

I should have got to know Kev better really (he signed just before me) but my early struggles weighed heavily on me, and I was concentrating more on myself. I knew him well enough, though, to recognise he was a decent player. About 5ft 10in, with two great feet, he could play on the left, right and through the middle; he could go past people and finish too, with a hell of a shot on him. His track record proved it: 44 goals in only 82 appearances. Many still argue that two of his goals were *the* most important in the club's history: Kev scored both in a 2-0 win over Southampton in April 1962 that clinched promotion to the First Division. Despite this, a year later he returned to Yorkshire, to Huddersfield Town, which surprised me as he seemed to have everything Shanks would look for.

Success was far from instant but after 18 months Shanks discovered a major piece of his jigsaw. He'd never got on with directors, often fighting losing battles, but when it came to Ron Yeats and the Saint he wouldn't back down. On being told by the board, 'We can't afford to buy them,' the reply was swift and sure: 'We can't afford not to.' When he believed in a player, Shanks would push, and push hard; he'd build players up because he truly believed in them. In the case of the Saint, Shanks was right. Ian was arguably the most important piece of the entire puzzle, and Liverpool more than doubled their previous record transfer spend, paying Motherwell £37,500 to bring the 22-year-old to Anfield. The Saint's arrival in May 1961 was the foundation stone of a soon-to-be-built dynasty, the beginning of it all.

The Saint had a natural aggression; it didn't take much to light his fuse, but we needed that. He'd never shy away from confrontation. If he thought he was hard done by, if he wanted to get something off his chest, he'd do so – and even the manager wasn't immune. If the Saint didn't agree with Shanks, he'd let him know. And he'd let the rest of us know too.

Ron Yeats – Big Ron – joined two months later. My old pal Jimmy Armfield was present when Big Ron, having been signed from Dundee United, was presented to the media. 'Jimmy, Jimmy, come here!' Shanks enthused. 'Have you seen my new signing? This is Ron Yeats. He's my new centre-half. He's a colossus! Come and have a walk around him!'

As Jimmy told it to me: 'So I did! Ron was six foot two, his head was way up in the sky. He was that big I felt like I was assessing a block of flats!' Ron was indeed a big unit, but with two distinct sides to him. On the pitch, he had that air of menace about him. Physically, he'd frighten the opposition to death (mentally too, no doubt, when they found out that he used to work in a slaughterhouse in Aberdeen). He was quick, strong and he wanted to win. But off the pitch, Ron could barely have been more different. He was very softly spoken, a calm, quiet, gentle giant, just a lovely man. Ron was completely different to the Saint, but the pair became the best of pals and remained so throughout the years.

At times we'd deliberately put Ron in awkward positions: firstly, because he was our captain, we believed it was his responsibility to represent us (and we trusted him to do so); secondly, whenever he was put on the spot he squirmed with embarrassment, and we all loved to see that! During Ron's first season we went on the occasional Blackpool trip after a home win – leave on a Saturday, back on the Monday morning. After the first time we badgered Ron relentlessly: 'Ron, go and have a word with the boss, we're due a Blackpool trip.' Ron wouldn't fancy it: 'Oh no, I can't do that.' 'Come on Ron, we're due a trip! You have to ask him, you're the bloody captain!'

Ron most certainly didn't want to ask Shanks, but he also felt duty-bound to us so would stand tall and stand up for us. 'Boss, the boys are thinking we've got a chance to have a little break next weekend … we're on a bit of a roll … our form's good … a little bit of team bonding never hurts … it'll do us all good …'

Shanks knew exactly what was going on, of course, but frequently concurred with the skipper. During the week leading up to the game, he'd say, 'I've been speaking with the captain, and I agree with him. So, after the match this Saturday, the boys are going to Blackpool, to the Norbreck Hydro. For rest and recuperation. And sea air. And massages.' That's what he'd tell the board anyway, and the press too. To us he'd say, 'Right, this weekend boys, you're going to Blackpool,' as if it was his idea. 'It'll do you all good.' However, subconsciously, we'd now increased the pressure on ourselves and it was now more important than ever to win the match. To lose would be unthinkable; the party would be over, and we wouldn't see Blackpool again. Shanks knew this too. If memory serves, we never lost a match on a 'Blackpool weekend'. Ron made sure of it.

We'd arrive in Blackpool about eight o'clock on the Saturday evening, have a (very) quick dinner then be out on the town. Responsibility was left to Bob and Joe – Shanks would never come – who knew what went on and knew what worked. They'd say, 'Twelve o'clock curfew. We think that's about right.' They were telling us they'd thought about it properly and were passing the responsibility to us. On the odd occasion, you'd get back at midnight and Bob and Joe would be sat in the foyer with their slippers on, having a little whisky. They'd go to bed around one o'clock, even if they thought some of the lads were still out. We'd drift back in twos and threes, never as one big mob.

We all knew we might be late, we would be late or we were already late. But we knew to be late quietly. If there were any complaints from staff, residents or other holidaymakers, there would be major trouble; complaints would simply not be tolerated. We knew that only too well, and that it would spell the end of our R 'n' R getaways. But we all had far too much respect for Bob and Joe. Any trouble caused by us would reflect badly on them; they'd have to carry the can, and none of us wanted that, although neither Bob nor Joe would ever report back whatever had gone on. It was an unspoken agreement, but one we'd never abuse; we knew who was in charge. And the whole point was, we wanted to come again.

Without fail, Sunday mornings in Blackpool meant blowing the cobwebs away with a stroll along the seafront. Although it was Shanks's mantra of 'fresh air for the boys', it was Bob and Joe managing the situation as they saw fit; in other words, remembering the previous night's curfew, or the breaking of it. And under their control, the penalty could hurt. At 10.30am on the button, no stragglers, we all assembled on the front steps of the hotel, fully kitted out in tracksuits, heavy sweaters underneath, waterproof tops, some of us wearing woolly hats, trying to hide eyes that were barely open. We were presented to the Blackpool promenade and the elements, usually pouring rain, blowing a bloody gale, with not a soul in sight, just the empty trams passing us by. This motley crew would set off looking like a group trekking the Arctic Circle. There was never so much as a peep from the lads, and not much from Bob and Joe either. No one dared complain; this was time that had to be served. We all knew it, and there was nothing we could do.

But really – three points won on a Saturday afternoon, manager and fans happy, a night out with the boys, a walk along Blackpool prom, a steam and a massage on the Monday, no training, a nice lunch – not bad that, is it? We'd troop on to a lovely warm bus for the leisurely drive back to Anfield, and you could guarantee that before we reached Blackpool Tower, barely two miles down the road, most passengers would be fast asleep. I wonder why?

* * *

By Christmas 1961 we still hadn't achieved anything. We could easily have missed out on promotion, could have slipped back to crowds of 20,000 or less, and godness knows where that would have led us. Shanks was aware of this, of course, but had no option other than to evaluate and utilise those resources already available to him. Fortunately for him, one of those resources was Gerry Byrne.

Gerry was a tough-tackling defender in his early 20s, a local lad who by this point hadn't had much of a look-in. He'd made his debut in 1957 but Ronnie Moran and John Molyneux had kept him on the fringes ever since. But when Ronnie got injured not long after my own debut, Gerry came in, proved himself immediately and was practically ever-present that season. He was that good and that important that he'd go on to play well over 300 matches for Liverpool.

Gerry was very much like Big Ron: tough, uncompromising, courageous, no nonsense. He wasn't hot-tempered by any means, but was utterly committed, all the time. So natural and constant was Gerry's aggression that he was simply incapable of playing without hurting people, even in training. A bump here or a nudge there was never deliberate but a bump or a nudge would hurt. Gerry, though, would be completely oblivious. It led to the occasional flare-up – 'For Christ's sake, Gerry!' – but gentleman that he was, he'd always apologise: 'Sorry Gordon, didn't see you coming.' Bless him. Gerry would kick his granny and not know he'd done it.

Off the pitch, again like Ron, Gerry was softly spoken, meek and mild. He and Chris Lawler were the quietest individuals you'd ever wish to meet. We'd be on the train playing cards and we wouldn't even know they were there. It was an unusual characteristic for a pair of Scousers. That said, when Tommy Smith broke through soon afterwards, he generated enough noise for all three of them!

Another local lad was Jimmy Melia. When Shanks arrived, Jimmy was already well established, having made his debut aged 18 in 1955. Jimmy played a lot of matches for Liverpool and was a very highly rated and skilful midfielder; another Scouser, not heavy duty, but much chirpier than Gerry and Chris. And, of course, Jimmy had his network of contacts from all walks of life, many of whom came in more than handy for us over the years.

It looked as if Jimmy would play more of a part in the bigger picture given how he was performing, the type of player he was, the ability he had. He was a true footballer, but perhaps a bit fragile; he didn't put his foot in really, but could play, no doubt about it, and was easy to play with. But with the emergence of Tommy Smith and the arrival and impact of Willie Stevenson, Jimmy began to feel the squeeze and soon moved to Wolves. I didn't quite understand it at the time but with hindsight (and my ex-manager's hat on) I do now: the force of nature that was Tommy Smith was already on the way to becoming unstoppable, and Shanks wanted him in the team.

Alan A'Court was another ready-made resource and had also long since proven himself. He too counted as a local really, as he was born in Rainhill, just ten miles east of Liverpool. 'Accy' had made his debut in 1953 (only he and Ronnie Moran remained from the team that was relegated in 1954) and would go on to make nearly 400 appearances for Liverpool. He lived in Culcheth, near Warrington, in the same area as his best pal and room-mate, Roger Hunt. The pair were thick as thieves. Accy was a great lad, always laughing and joking, and always with chubby rosy cheeks. He was a great all-rounder too, one of those annoying sods who are good at all sports: tennis, water sports, paddle board, golf, a good runner; he'd have a go at any sport and be good at it.

Staying over after an away match one night we all went out for a few beers. Accy returned to the hotel before the rest of us and, when we returned, Roger said, 'Come and look at Accy.' We went into their room and there he was, flat out and rosy-cheeked, lying on his back with his hands folded neatly on his front as if he was laid out on a slab in a bloody morgue! Unknown to any of us, Accy suffered from eczema and as he slept was wearing a pair of mittens like something his grandma had knitted for him! Horrible, woolly, itchy things, he used to put these on to stop him from scratching himself. I thought, 'Christ! If you put them up to his face, they'll only make him scratch more!'

Roger himself, of course, requires little introduction. He too was already on the books when Shanks arrived, having signed in 1958 from Stockton Heath (then of the Mid-Cheshire League). Roger would go on to score 285 goals for the Reds, a figure surpassed only by the extraordinary Ian Rush (hard as it is to believe, Roger's goals to games ratio is actually better than Rushie's). Famously, Rog was also the only Liverpool player to appear in, and win, the World Cup Final for England in 1966. (Gerry and Cally were both in the squad – Cally appeared in the group match against France – although neither played in the final. Both would eventually receive winners' medals in 2009.) Roger was a manager's dream. He came in, trained hard, scored on a Saturday, went home. No fuss. Strong as an ox, very rarely injured despite getting clattered every week, a brilliant goalscorer but no ego whatsoever, just another humble, unassuming, down-to-earth character with a great sense of humour. It was a pleasure just to know him. His dad owned a haulage business and during the summers Rog and his brother would help out by doing a bit of driving. Yes, he was playing for Liverpool but there was no reason he couldn't drive a truck! Roger was as low-profile as a (future) World Cup winner could ever be!

Tommy Leishman was another Scot, another great personality. Every other word was 'f***ing'. It was his natural vocabulary and he used it well, so often in fact that eventually we wouldn't even notice. His tone wasn't aggressive, it was just how he spoke, from first whistle to last. I always thought Tommy was best suited to playing at the back. He and Big Ron formed a formidable partnership, but he played a lot in midfield too, and I played in there with him. Tommy was more defensively minded than most of us, which proved vital to the team's balance. He was an uncompromising ball winner, another no-nonsense lad who took no prisoners. A proper player.

Another top-class character, and another Scot, was our goalkeeper Bert Slater. He was small for a goalie, 5ft 9in at best, and he knew it. He couldn't escape it to be fair, not with the highly original 'Shorty' as a nickname. Bert relied on his wits, intelligence and anticipation. He was tough as teak and brave as a lion, widely respected by supporters and his fellow professionals, and particularly within the Shankly family: in 1962 Bill sold Bert to Dundee, then managed by Bill's brother Bob. I'm sure Shanks wouldn't have sold his own brother a pup, so that was a little pat on the back for Bert.

One famous story concerns Bert being knocked unconscious during a match and Bob trying everything to revive him: smelling salts, cold water, magic sponge. Nothing worked. In desperation, Bob knelt close to our stricken keeper's ear and said, 'Bert, give us a kiss.' Bert suddenly sat bolt upright, looked Bob in the eye and told him to 'f**k off!' before clambering to his feet and jogging away. Even then, way before he showed his genius as a manager, Bob proved he could work miracles.

With a third of the season remaining, however, Bert was replaced by Jim Furnell. He was a good lad, Jim, and he and I got on well (he was from Clitheroe, just down the road from Preston). Jim was a good six inches taller than Bert and a more than competent goalkeeper, but just as Shanks was never completely convinced by Bert, neither was he by Jim. Two months into the following season, a broken finger saw Jim replaced by Tommy Lawrence, who would prove to be the long-sought-after answer to Shanks's goalkeeping conundrum. It ultimately signalled the end of Jim's Anfield career, and although he was only a Red for 18 months or so he proved to be another top-class character as well as a top-class keeper. He went on to play more than 160 times for Arsenal, and you don't do that if you're no good.

And then there was 'Cally' – Ian Callaghan. At the risk of being boring here, he was another local lad seemingly made from the same Scouse mould as Gerry, Jimmy and all those before him: unassuming, ego-free, a great lad who loved his football. Still very young when he first broke through – he'd just turned 18 when he made his debut in 1960 – Cally was championed from the outset by the great Billy Liddell. With the talent he had there was no way Cally could be stopped. Coming through at such a young age there was no fanfare, but we could all see how special he was. He came in, he played and he stayed – for 16 more years! The fact that no one has ever played more times for Liverpool, 857 – and no one ever will – tells you all you need to know about Cally.

* * *

Battling to escape our Second Division exile, eight of us would each go on to play at least 40 league matches that season. The Saint was one, while Big Ron, Roger and Tommy would only miss a single match each, and Accy, Gerry, Jimmy and I would be ever-present. It was some core and meant we'd only ever shuffle personnel in three or four positions, and when those personnel included my old pal Dick White (24 appearances), Cally (23), Kev (21) and Ronnie (16), with Tommy Smith and Chris Lawler in the bushes as well, we knew we were on to a good thing. And not just in terms of ability.

In any squad, personalities will clash. When it happens it can have a serious detrimental effect on what the manager is trying to achieve: 'He doesn't do this, he should be doing that ...' But we had none of that. We had good lads, all genuine, all pulling together, all knowing what needed to be done. That doesn't happen by chance. The manager was big on character, and Shanks had built a team suited to its circumstances, a team to escape the lower division doldrums.

Having joined as a 15-year-old, Ronnie Moran knew more than most what needed to be done. He was club captain and had been at Anfield for a decade by the time Shanks arrived. Throughout his entire time at Liverpool – he eventually left the Boot Room in 1998 – Ronnie never changed: he was in your face, 100 per cent Liverpool and another of those lads who couldn't play friendlies. He didn't even enjoy six-a-sides, it seemed; for Ronnie, there was always something not quite right, not quite good enough, so he was always moaning.

He played behind me at right-back and he and I had a little throw-in system. 'When I stand here, you throw it to my head. When I stand there, you throw it to my feet.' It was basic, but it worked, and it was Ronnie all over. We even practised this in training, years before a 'throw-in coach' was heard of! He used to say, 'You'll always hear me. I'm always talking so you'll know exactly where I am.' And when he was playing behind me, I always did. It sounds obvious but sometimes the bloody obvious is genius in a way. You didn't always have time to look over your shoulder to see if your right-back was in the correct position, but if you heard his voice, you had a fair idea of where he was.

Ronnie was old-fashioned, a real family man. He'd say, 'You get home and put your slippers on, you sit down and you've got your family around you. You ask for a cup of tea and a biscuit; you *get* a cup of tea and a biscuit. It's great!' Such a mentality – simple, basic, grounded – meant Ronnie's eventual move on to the staff was inevitable, so well-suited was he to the inner circle of Bob, Joe and Reuben. Even in later life, with Liverpool flying, and regardless of his job title, Ronnie was never flash, something I picked up on and would use in my own managerial career. When the likes of Ronnie spoke, the words of wisdom came so naturally you wouldn't even notice. But if you listened properly, you'd think, *Christ, why didn't I think of that?* They made so much sense.

Reuben Bennett came from the same pot. Yet another tough Scot, he was already on the staff when Shanks arrived. In essence – and I'm not being disrespectful here – he was the warm-up man. We'd get to Melwood, Reuben rounded us all up and off we went, all under his watchful eye. But he offered much more. He was hard as nails and didn't believe in pain. He was always in shorts, nearly always in short sleeves, no matter how cold it was. Even in the depths of winter he'd dress as for the beach. And Shanks being a great believer in fitness overcoming any impediment, Reuben's message was always the same: 'Good morning boys, isn't it great to be alive!' The theory of repetition was at play here: the same bloody greeting every day! Reuben was hammering home what became second nature to us, and integral to who we were. The words he used, albeit very few, were always the same, the warm-up was always the same and subconsciously we were all repeating ourselves, building up the belief in what we were doing. We kept it simple – the early days of 'the Liverpool Way'. After the jovial greeting, however, Reuben's tone would change: 'Now, off you go. Get on with it. And don't you dare feel sorry for yourselves, you're lucky to even be here.' The message was repeated, time and again.

Reuben was quieter than Ronnie, but then everyone was. But like all of them, Reuben didn't say much but what he did say made sense. After training had finished, he was easy to talk to, approachable and always had time for anyone. He wouldn't offer much advice because he felt it wasn't his job, rather the responsibility of the assistant manager, first-team coach, reserve-team coach, or whatever titles were attached to Bob and Joe at the time (although nobody was bothered about job titles back then) and would never tread on their toes. They all knew their own responsibilities and Reuben was no different. The manager listened to all of them and collectively they covered all avenues. And the message, from all of them, always remained the same: repetitive and consistent. In short, they drilled into us what was required to play for this football club and what was required to be successful. All we needed to know, really.

Reuben travelled to and from training in the manager's car, discussing all aspects of the day's work and whatever else came into Shanks's head. Reuben could really make us laugh, especially if he himself found the story funny. One such anecdote concerned Shanks taking delivery of a new club car, much bigger than his old one. (Driving wasn't Shanks's strongest suit – he was bloody awful.) Returning home from Melwood one rainy afternoon, Shanks drove the car directly into his garage. His shiny new car, however, was much wider than his previous one and once inside the garage neither Shanks nor Reuben had room to open their doors. As Reuben told it, 'We drive in, but we can't bloody get out! It's p***ing down with rain, we're sitting in the car, in the garage, the engine still running, the car steaming up and the windscreen wipers going at full pelt. Shanks is steaming up too, losing his temper and soon in full flow, ranting.' To make matters worse the gearstick was attached to the steering column, which was new to the manager. Chuckling away, Reuben went on: 'Shanks could never work that gearstick. He's revving the engine, a lot, but we aren't moving! Desperately trying to find reverse, he nearly rips the gearstick right off the column! Eventually he finds it and we shoot backwards out of the garage like a rocket, nearly ending up in the road. Shanks brakes hard, stops the car, switches off the engine, turns to me and says, "Reuben, this is no good, son. I'll have to change the f***ing car!"'

I suppose Reuben had to put up with Shanks (if that's the right phrase) more than others as he spent more one-on-one time with him than anyone else, but his role was as vital as any other. Shanks always needed someone to talk to as he always had his opinions, which he always needed to share. Reuben was the perfect foil.

Chapter 5

SHANKS HAD been making all the right noises, to anyone who would listen. The manager's fervour had convinced me to sign in the first place, and the Saint and Big Ron arrived the following year. (Shanks had said, 'There will be many more top players to follow.' He kept his promise.) Their mindset matched my own: neither had left Scotland to remain in the English Second Division.

We were searching for the promised land, although we never used words like that. We'd finished third in the Second Division the previous season but our form and performances hadn't lived up to the billing bestowed upon us by the manager. The reality was, we're in the Second Division here. Perhaps we're not as good as we think we are. We weren't talking about the Manchester Uniteds or Arsenals, we were more concerned with Leyton Orient and Lincoln City.

The importance of the coming season couldn't be underestimated. For me it was personal. I'd come from the First Division to the Second, and I didn't like it. My debut season had fallen well short of my own standards; I'd proved next to nothing and wanted to put that right. Shanks's bullishness left us under no illusions: 'We've got to get out of this league.' On occasion, however, his dynamism could be a double-edged sword. He filled us with confidence and belief, but that led to hope, expectation and pressure: 'He's been telling all and sundry how good we are – what if we don't live up to it?' Shanks kept pushing, while we remained ever conscious of the potential reward. But it was still one match at a time. It always was. We knew where we wanted to be but we weren't there yet. We weren't in the First Division, we weren't where Everton were.

Everton. It was always Everton. We weren't saying we wanted to be where Tottenham Hotspur were, or Wolves, or Manchester United or Arsenal. It was always Everton. And Shanks, having to live with that, took it harder than most. Being in the same city the gulf between us was exaggerated even further, and we were never allowed to forget it. They called themselves the School of Science, which was always thrown at our supporters, and us too. My first season saw us miss out on promotion while Everton finished fifth in the division above us. Two years later they were crowned First Division champions. The bragging rights were blue. The Evertonians mercilessly took the mickey out of the Liverpool fans, who didn't have a leg to stand on; they literally *weren't* in the same league.

We had to get amongst them. Shanks was continually talking up our potential but the gap between us and Everton was vast. Sir John Moores, the head of Littlewoods Pools, was the chairman of Everton. Whether he was 'operating in the bushes' (as they say) or not, he was certainly supporting Everton financially. Theirs was a well-run, well-managed club, with stability (Harry Catterick would be the manager for more than a decade) and a competent board. The gulf between the teams was mirrored by the quality of the board members at each club. Credit for the Liverpool board was in short supply: lower division, tatty stadium, struggling team, poor training facilities, mix and match kits – we were second best in all areas.

There was no real escape. Writing about Everton (and their next lauded opponents), the *Liverpool Echo* produced what always felt to me like newsflash moments that, instead of lauding Everton's achievements, only highlighted our failings. Us winning never had the same impact as an Everton victory. It couldn't, because the comeback never changed: 'Come back and talk to us when you're in the same league!' All this bloody stuff went on, every day. And every evening in the paper there was always something else. It was always there, rammed down your throat from the moment the milkman dropped his wares on your bloody doorstep of a morning. In a place like Liverpool, you just couldn't escape the football. (It was the magic of the city – and still is.)

In football terms they were streets ahead of us. Everton had an exceptional team with a strong Scottish core: Bobby Collins, Jimmy Gabriel, Alex Parker and Alex Young were friends with Big Ron and the Saint, who would hear all about how it was at Everton and what they were doing, how they trained, what the training ground was like, and so forth. Such chat was standard. There was never anything untoward in it, but statements such as, 'We've got United away, Wolves at home, then Arsenal away,' would merely fuel the Liverpudlians' fire. Bloody Everton were off to play the likes of Arsenal, and we weren't! It was never arrogant or big-headed, simply the glamour of the top tier filtering down yet remaining tantalisingly out of our reach. It was natural for us to think, *Hang on, we want a bit of this.*

The Saint, particularly, was naturally feisty. 'What are we doing f***ing about in this division?' He was pragmatic, although vociferous with it. He made his Liverpool debut against Everton in the final of the Liverpool Senior Cup – a bit of pre-season local spice – which saw him score a hat-trick in a 4-3 defeat, but the match revealed to him the level at which Everton existed, the team they had, the publicity surrounding them – and it bugged him. He was always restless about that, but in fairness he was always restless about the next match, whoever the opposition. Being in different divisions meant, cup ties apart, there were no derby matches – further motivation. We wanted to play Everton (and the rest) more than we had been, so that season they provided that extra stimulus for us on a weekly basis. We saw everything they were doing and we wanted the same, but the only way we could have a proper go at Everton would be to step into the same playground as them. All this kept Shanks on his toes more than ever. Everton were the yardstick. He, Bob, Joe and Reuben were all very close, they all felt it, and they knew the situation at Anfield was, by comparison, a mess. Everton finished fifth, then fourth, then went on to win the thing. If we ever wanted an example of what could be achieved, we needn't look any further – it was on the bloody doorstep.

* * *

We began meaning business, winning ten of our opening 11 matches. Our form then slipped, six wins from 13. One of those six did, however, bring personal satisfaction. I returned to Deepdale. Preston were managed by my dad, we won 3-1 and I scored one of only two goals I managed all season. Still, this one was against my dad and helped us to victory. He called it a 'fluke' – and it probably was! It was at the Kop End, a volley from the right-hand side of the box. That makes it sound quite good, but in truth it was a mishit. I cut across the ball – sliced it, really. The ball looped into the air, spinning madly and dropped into the far top corner. The goalie had no chance. It was a genuine attempt on goal but nowhere near how it had played out in my mind! I knew it, and so did my dad. As for celebrating? Well, today I imagine a player in the same situation might think of celebrating in front of the opposition bench. That was certainly not for me.

The season developed into three distinct chunks. Come October our fortunes changed so we dug in right through into the new year. After losing to Rotherham on Boxing Day we only suffered three more defeats all season. Unfortunately, one of those saw my dad exact his revenge. After two 0-0 draws, our FA Cup tie against Preston went to a second replay in the snow at Old Trafford. We lost 1-0 thanks to Peter Thompson, who Shanks would sign the following August. I particularly remember the second match at Deepdale. The 7.30pm kick-off was delayed because there were so many Liverpool fans en route to the match that the roads were blocked, traffic jams everywhere. At around seven o'clock our team bus crawled past my mum's house, and she and Aunty Grace were in the window, giving us a wave! Eventually, 90 minutes couldn't separate us, nor could extra time, so as was the form in those days we went to a second replay. And that was my dad (and future team-mate Peter) knocking me out of the FA Cup. But if we couldn't score a goal in three matches (plus all the extra time), what more did we deserve?

Despite this, we generated some momentum again, but there were still plenty of rocky days along the way. But on 12 April 1962, it all proved to be worthwhile. With half a dozen fixtures remaining, Southampton came to Anfield. We knew a draw would be good enough to ensure promotion. We also knew, however, that a win would mean the Second Division title. Two goals from the much-underrated Kevin Lewis secured both. Liverpool – champions of the Second Division! And at long last we'd be back at the top table!

You can imagine the scenes: sheer jubilation, on and off the pitch. We made it back to the dressing room but the supporters wanted us back out on the pitch. We tried to oblige them. Hoping for a lap of honour, we trooped back out of the dressing room but as soon as the fans glimpsed Big Ron at the top of the tunnel they swarmed on to the pitch and he and the Saint immediately disappeared, swallowed by the masses, engulfed by a sea of red. The security lads took one look and sent the rest of us back to the dressing room for our own safety! It was a good job really as Ron and the Saint returned battered and bruised – still smiling though.

Players are all different. At such times some are completely knackered, emotionally and physically drained, sitting quietly and soaking it all in; others go mad, popping champagne and jumping up and down. At some point comes the time for contemplation. For me it was an enormous sense of relief. The mantra 'We've got to get out of this Division' had dominated the entire season; it was a burden we'd put upon ourselves, and it was a massive relief to get shut of it. I'm sure there was a big cheer in the dressing room, then a photograph or two, but half an hour later came the calm after the storm. The dressing room was very different and if you'd walked in then you might have even thought we'd lost.

For me it sank in maybe a day or two later. But there were still five more matches to play and we wanted to win the title with as many points as we could. The job had to be completed.

We didn't finish brilliantly, but it wasn't too bad either – three wins, one draw, one loss. Still, one of those wins was away against Plymouth, a memorable fixture for two reasons. The first is that we flew (pretty novel in those days) to the south coast and stayed over after the match, which we won 3-2, for a bit of a night out. Secondly, this was the trip when we found out Accy wore mittens in his sleep!

When you're a player, you don't really consider what the manager is thinking, or the staff – you're thinking about yourself. Now, I know it meant just as much to them and that we were all in it together. Shanks believed our fitness was the key to success. Vital victories in those opening 11 matches – two each against potential rivals Sunderland and Newcastle United – had set us on the right path, and Shanks believed we never looked back from there, although conveniently – and typically – he chose to ignore the slip-ups we'd experienced along the way!

Shanks was never one for celebrations. Besides, for him, escaping the Second Division wasn't a true reason to celebrate. He wanted to be where Harry Catterick was at Everton, challenging for and winning the First Division title. He wanted to be judged on the big stage, so winning promotion wasn't that big a deal, at least not publicly. In private he'd have been happy, but unfinished business remained, which perhaps accounts for the end of that season being so low-key. Winning the Second Division was nowhere near 'job done'. It was just the beginning.

I'm still surprised that it was Leyton Orient who were promoted with us. That's no disrespect to Orient, who were a bloody good team; it's the thought that the so-called 'bigger' teams of the day, the likes of Preston and Newcastle (both had been relegated from the First Division the previous season), or

Sunderland and Southampton, had lost out to Orient and us. This was proof, if it were needed, of just how difficult a division this was to escape. Escaped, though, we had. Now it was about what lay ahead. Pre-season training couldn't come soon enough.

Chapter 6

FOLLOWING PROMOTION, the name of the game is survival. Having reached the First Division, we were under no illusions regarding the challenge facing us. It had been hard enough to win promotion, but the following season in a higher division was certainly not going to be any easier. Initial results proved this: we won only four of our first 16 matches and by November were in 19th place. However, nine wins in a row saw us climb into the top five. Like our previous campaign, this season was also a three-parter: indifferent start, fantastic mid-season and a poor last couple of months (winning only one of our final nine matches).

Perhaps our shoddy late-season form was down to the weather. In England and Scotland, December 1962 saw the onset of the Big Freeze. This wasn't a brief snap, it was one of the coldest, longest winters on record, lasting until early March. More than 500 fixtures were postponed. Between 22 December and 16 February we only managed to play two FA Cup ties. We couldn't even train properly; all we could do was run. The local greyhound track, covered with straw laid out for the dogs, was one of the best options. Nearly everywhere else was just too bloody dangerous! The winter went on ... and on. A fixture pile-up was inevitable.

CHAPTER 6

When the thaw began it did so in Ireland. While Liverpool remained frozen, the milder temperatures across the Irish Sea meant that, after a few enquiries, a playable pitch was located, as well as some opposition: Drumcondra FC, in north Dublin. We were jumping for joy at the thought of playing an actual match, and no one was more excited than the manager.

As I recall, we arrived on a Tuesday with the match scheduled for the following day. Unfortunately, on Tuesday night the rain came, and come Wednesday afternoon the pitch was waterlogged. There was no option but to call off the match. We were all gutted, but it was out of our hands. With no other immediate commitments, we remained in Ireland, hoping to play the following day. That evening the opposition's social wing invited us to their home ground to have a quick drink and say hello to the fans. Most of us did just that, before drifting back to the hotel. However, Big Ron and the Saint stayed a bit longer, until around one o'clock in the morning. The next day, Shanks, already under a cloud because the match had been called off, summoned them both. Ron went first. When Shanks asked him what had gone on, Ron replied, 'Boss, you know how it is, they were so chuffed that we came over to play them. They're lovely people, Boss, you should have heard them – "Imagine it! Liverpool coming to play us!" They loved it! And we didn't want to appear rude. We just had a little drink, played darts, snooker, you know how it goes. It was really nice, nothing too serious. I suppose we just lost track of time, Boss. Suddenly it was, "Christ! It's one o'clock in the morning!" We just didn't realise. I'm sorry, Boss.' Shanks had listened intently to every word. When Ron finished there was an awkward silence as the manager paused for thought. Eventually, Shanks looked Ron square in the face, waved him towards the door, and said, 'Go!' Ron didn't need telling twice. But as he was leaving, he turned back to Shanks and said, 'Shall I send the Saint, in Boss?' Shanks looked up at Ron dismissively and replied, 'Don't f***ing bother. He'll only tell me the same pack of lies you've just told me.'

We weren't alone in this, of course, but after the thaw, fulfilling our fixture obligations felt relentless. In April we beat Spurs 5-2, then beat Manchester United – the following day! Two matches in two days quickly became three in four, as 48 hours after defeating Manchester United we met Spurs again, although this time were trounced 7-2 at White Hart Lane. We ended up playing six times in 13 days – and people moan about fixture congestion today! Being walloped by Spurs was the beginning of our decline. We lost six of the last nine matches of the season, winning only one. Somehow, though, we managed to hold on to a top-ten spot, eventually finishing in a respectable eighth place.

It wasn't the worst return to the top division, nor was it the best, as we were 17 points behind the champions – Everton! That didn't help, of course. Any respectability we felt we may have salvaged was ground into dust by our neighbours' triumph. But it was all part of the learning curve, an indication not of where we were, but of what we had to learn. I think we needed to go through that to get where we wanted to be; it's essential to learn from going up, down and sideways, and we seemed to be doing all three. In a strange way it did us good to finish the season so poorly, as we could go away, lick our wounds and come back with the benefit of experience, ready and raring to go again.

Our league form was offset by a good FA Cup run, defeating Wrexham, Burnley, West Ham and Arsenal, before succumbing 1-0 to Leicester City in the semi-final at Hillsborough. Gordon

Banks was in spectacular form that day. He always was against us it seemed; he'd kept two clean sheets against us in the league that year, as Leicester beat us 3-0 and 2-0. Banksy was a major reason in the Foxes becoming a bogey team for us. After the full-time whistle at Hillsborough a photographer snapped a disappointed and disconsolate Saint. In the background was a delighted Banksy showing his great big, wonderful smile. Unfortunately, there was a suggestion from the newspaper in which the photo was printed that Gordon was actually laughing at the Saint. Nonsense! He wasn't even conscious of him, but unfortunately it led to Banksy being booed by some Liverpool fans when Leicester next visited Anfield. That was unfair. Gordon had won an FA Cup semi-final, he was entitled to be smiling, especially given some of the saves he'd pulled off that day! His display made the defeat even worse in a way, as it had been one-way traffic for most of the match, but we just couldn't make the breakthrough. To get so close to Wembley before falling at the final hurdle was a real hammer blow: so near, yet so far. And, of course, at that point Liverpool had still never won the FA Cup.

It had been a mixed season but arguably the most significant events took place on the personnel front, in particular the emergence of two local lads who would go on to become Liverpool legends: Chris Lawler and Tommy Smith. The pair were already close, both having been at the club three or four years before making their debuts. Nowadays it's well recognised that Tommy was a hard man, but if you asked the 1960s Liverpool squad if there was anyone who may have intimidated him, the answer would have been Chris. He was quiet as a mouse, Chris, but with 14 siblings (there were 11 boys) he'd learned to fight his own corner and could look after himself. Tommy would never start something with Chris. As young pros he and Tommy once – to put it mildly – had words. Nothing serious developed but to say that in this skirmish the so-called favourite came second best would be an understatement. There was more to the quiet man than met the eye, something that Tommy always respected for the rest of their careers.

One of the most famous stories about Chris concerns a six-a-side match between the staff and the kids. One day after training, many of us stopped to watch the action. They were using pegs for goalposts, only about three feet high, and to score the ball had to remain below the top of these pegs. Shanks had a crack, the ball flew hard and fast between the pegs – but high. The manager, though, saw it differently: 'Goal.' The dispute duly began.

'No chance! That was high! No goal.'

'No, no, no,' said Shanks. 'Nothing wrong with that, that was low. Goal.' And on it went. Shanks saw us all watching and picked Chris as a potential ally. 'Chris! Chris is a good judge. He'll tell you that was a goal.'

Chris considered his options for a moment before delivering his verdict: 'That was high, Boss. No goal.'

Shanks was apoplectic. 'Jesus Christ, son!' he bellowed. 'You never open your bloody mouth, you don't say a word for years, but when you do, the first thing you do is tell a bloody lie!' It was a brilliant line and had us all in stitches. Chris, though, wasn't particularly amused. As Shanks had rightly pointed out, Chris was indeed quite reserved – but he had an edge about him.

The team was evolving. The two silent assassins, Chris and Gerry Byrne, alongside the colossus and captain, Big Ron, and his sparring partner, Mr Angry, Tommy Smith – two turbocharged combine harvesters always on full throttle, much more pleasant to play with than against! Marshalling this group calmly and quietly, never flustered, never flying out of his goal trying to play like a sweeper, was Mr Reliable, Tommy Lawrence, by now well established as Liverpool's goalkeeper. Modern-day goalkeepers jump up and down, shouting and screaming when the ball's not even in play, creating uncertainty and panic when neither is needed. Tommy was the exact opposite: 'Don't worry about this corner son, we'll deal with it.' He was a top man, a top keeper who handled responsibility with dignity and class and who was loved by us all, but especially by the four amigos directly in front of him.

It wasn't just the team that was evolving, either. I wouldn't call it tactics, more the style of play: being close to a red shirt, never being isolated, playing the simple pass. All of these were preached to us day in, day out, until they became second nature. (Now I think about it, never being left on your own sounds uncannily similar to what became the club's anthem, 'You'll Never Walk Alone'. Perhaps there's a subconscious link there – or perhaps I'm being a bit romantic!) All this became part of 'the Liverpool Way', the beginning of how they went on to play for the next 20 years and more.

Another part of what became the natural order of things was the bedding in of players. Chris and Tommy were great examples: they didn't walk straight into the first team, there were years spent learning the ropes first. In a way, you needed a year or two to amass the required football intelligence, and only then would there be a sniff of the first team. It's something that continued throughout the decades as players such as Ray Clemence, Ronnie Whelan, Ian Rush and Andy Robertson all went through the same.

Arguably the most effective element of this entire period was how these lessons were delivered: simple repetition. Shanks said the same things every day, as did Reuben, Bob and Joe. Before we knew it, we were all saying and doing the same things every day. If you watched us train, you'd probably say, 'I didn't learn anything there.' Today, coaches are often lauded due to the variety of their sessions. That wasn't us. Success and stability thrived on repetition – time would prove this – and although they may have appeared basic, we took these principles on board. And because Shanks was a great believer in principles (rather than rules, which he knew would be broken), it was nigh-on impossible not to be swept along. He believed in the basics: living right, sleeping right, eating right, training right. Shanks was no fool, though, knowing that one or more of us may veer off track, and not always unintentionally either. But this was where the repetition came into play. If we did stray off the beaten path, we'd always find a way back to it simply by what was being repeatedly drummed into us. The reality was that there was no escape from it. To paraphrase Albert Einstein: simplicity is genius.

* * *

Liverpool's connection with Preston North End was reinforced by further signings. The link had been established by the arrival of Shanks himself, who signed me in 1960. Peter Thompson followed in 1963, Dave Wilson in 1967. (In later years Mark Lawrenson and Neil Mellor shared ties with both clubs.) Shanks was clearly comfortable dealing with Preston, but not every transfer worked out. Dave, unfortunately, made only one appearance, as a substitute when he actually replaced me in my final Liverpool appearance, a 3-1 loss at home to Blackpool, before returning to Deepdale a year later. There was, however, one Preston player who Shanks did miss out on.

In 1964 my dad led Preston to the FA Cup Final. Unfortunately, they lost 3-2 to West Ham United but there was plenty for me to be proud of. Preston had a wing-half called Ian Davidson. A couple of weeks before the final his grandmother sadly passed away, so he asked my dad to be excused from the final league fixture to attend the funeral. Reluctantly, my dad agreed. He wasn't convinced by Ian's story and was right not to be. Ian's grandmother hadn't died at all. Ian had lied. He didn't want to risk injury in the final league match and thereby miss the cup final. But his plan backfired as my dad found out and left him out of the team. Instead, he picked a 17-year-old by the name of Howard Kendall. On that day at Wembley, Howard became the youngest player to ever play in a Wembley FA Cup Final, a record he held until 1980 when it was broken by Paul Allen.

I'm very proud of my dad for what he did. It took some doing to leave out such a good player, especially one so experienced and who had played all season. But Howard seized the day. It wasn't his debut but was still some feat. Howard would remain at Preston until 1967. Shanks was desperate to sign him, but Liverpool simply didn't have the funds and, to make matters worse, the beneficiaries of Liverpool's financial struggles were Everton, who signed Howard just before his 21st birthday. His subsequent career would have eaten away at Shanks as he went on to become an Everton legend, not only as a player – and what a player he was, one of the midfield 'Holy Trinity' alongside Colin Harvey and Alan Ball – but in later years as a successful manager who built one of Everton's greatest-ever teams. For Liverpool, and most certainly for Shanks, Howard was the one that got away.

* * *

The city of Liverpool was already well known, having been one of the biggest ports and shipping hubs in the world. Now, in the early '60s, the football clubs were beginning to attract attention. But although I'd like to say we were the top draw, we weren't, as the city's main attraction was the music scene, and in particular, of course, The Beatles.

It was a great time to be young in Liverpool. The Anfield crowd didn't really sing in the early '60s (that would soon change), but while the weekdays saw the city swinging with the music, the weekends bounced to the beat of music *and* football. And both, at their best, were truly inspirational to those of us lucky enough to be involved. I was in my early 20s, part of a generation who were just as keen on the music scene as they were on football. The city was jumping, and as the music took off, football too was on the up. It was nigh-on impossible to separate the two, a truly magical time. Everything felt connected. And the Kop began to find its voice.

In May 1963 we were already preparing for the next season: head-to-head, hopefully, with our local rivals, the champions. The Beatles, however, had a higher calling – they were about to conquer the world, a campaign that began that same month with their first number one, 'From Me to You'. In Liverpool that whole scene was kicking off and there were so many other bands involved. Gerry and the Pacemakers was one of the most famous, which is hardly surprising, particularly in the world we're talking about. Their version of 'You'll Never Walk Alone' became synonymous with Liverpool Football Club and remains the supporters' anthem to this day – and in my view it will remain so forever. What's more, the song was released in October 1963, pretty much at the start of what would become a momentous season for Liverpool. Now, is that a coincidence?

You couldn't help but get caught up in it. We were in the spotlight, with everyone looking at us. The pressure was on and I'm sure Shanks felt it more than most. He'd already worked wonders but was nowhere near finished. This was the season when he went into overdrive; this was the season when the Bill Shankly that everyone knows today truly emerged.

Shanks had long seen the potential of Liverpool, and everything he did related to that. We all bought into it, as did the fans. You couldn't help but think, *This guy truly believes this.* And he did, absolutely; with Shanks it was never an act. It wasn't propaganda (as some thought). Even the music, Shanks loved it all. He saw it as an extension of everything he believed in, a common cause bringing people together, all looking in the same direction, all seeking the same goal. It was a philosophy drummed into us and, for him, the fans – the people – were at the heart of it all.

Before a match he'd open the dressing room door as part of his team talk, saying, 'Can you hear them? Can you hear them? It's twenty to three and they're going bloody mad!' Of course, we could hear them! He'd go on: 'Listen to them! How can you let these people down?' He constantly reminded us we were at one with the fans. If we lost, we knew we'd let them down, and him too; he'd now be answerable to quarter of a million supporters, because of us. 'You've let them down today. How can you do that? They're in the ground half an hour before kick-off. The ground's full! And you've let them down.' No individual was ever the target, though; it was always about the collective.

For Shanks, the supporters were one side of the coin, the directors the other. Shanks rarely had anyone round the boardroom table supporting him. He wanted to sign Jack Charlton and Dave Mackay, for example, but the board refused to sanction either transfer. There was so much work that needed doing, but the board's reluctance to fully support the manager remained an issue. However, that changed with the arrival of Eric Sawyer, an accountant with Littlewoods Pools who was chosen for a position on the board by Sir John Moores himself. Something of a kindred spirit to Shanks, he became a welcome ally for the manager. In fact, it was actually Sawyer, not Shanks, who back in 1961 informed the board they couldn't afford *not* to sign Big Ron and the Saint. Like Shanks, he'd seen what was needed and wasn't afraid to go after it.

All this butting of heads led to an 'us and them' mentality. In the dressing room Shanks would often take the mickey out of the board, have a laugh and a joke, doing his James Cagney bit – he loved that – with the directors often on the receiving end. There was always the sense that he didn't handle them with any diplomacy – deliberately so.

Shanks knew what he was doing, always. Rather than address us directly he'd often use the third person, usually when talking to Bob, but always loud enough for us to hear. We'd be on the coach, having lost, and he'd be at the front with Bob, deliberately raising his voice. 'How many times have I told them, Bob? How many f***ing times?' Sometimes it would concern an unnamed individual: 'I've told him, haven't I Bob? I've told him!' Half a dozen of us would think, *Is he talking about me?* But we'd never know. He'd never single out or name an individual. But when he said, 'They don't f***ing listen, Bob.

They don't f***ing listen,' you can bet your bottom dollar that we were all listening.

We rarely lost at Anfield, but if we did, Shanks would put on another show. The expected bollocking rarely came. Instead, he'd turn to Bob and, again, loud enough for us all to hear: 'Bob, that's the worst f***ing team I've seen in my life. They'll be relegated, Bob, I guarantee it. They'll go down!' And they'd just beaten us 3-1! He'd keep going: 'They haven't got a player! Not one single player! None of them would even make Skelmersdale reserves!' He'd march around the dressing room, always – on the surface at least – talking to Bob. But we knew everything he said was for our ears. The flip side of this was the scene after we'd won. Talking about a team we'd just thrashed 5-0, Shanks would strut around the dressing room. 'They're not a bad side, Bob, not bad at all. They won't get relegated. They won't go down; they've got nothing to worry about.' Classic Shanks.

Prior to a match there was never any fear. Any need for wariness would be dismissed before it got through the front door, often with a quip. Reuben once tried to discuss the all-round ability of an opposing player due at Anfield that coming Saturday. Shanks gave Reuben and the player equally short shrift.

'He's a threat, this lad, Bill. He's got everything ...'

'Aye, Reuben, he's got everything alright. He's got dandruff, bad breath, spots on his face ...'

Another firm favourite was his pre-match set-up. At Anfield, to reach their dressing room the visitors had to pass ours. Shanks would watch them. When West Ham arrived late one day, Shanks opened the dressing room door by just a hair and was peeping through the gap like a schoolboy. 'I can see them, Bob, they're coming.' As West Ham filed past, Shanks provided a running commentary – all for our benefit. 'Here's Bobby Moore. Christ, Bob, he doesn't look well. He's pasty-faced, Bob, white as a sheet. And here's the goalkeeper. Look at him! I never realised he was so small!' We heard it all, just as we were supposed to. 'Look at them. They're all nervous, you can tell. They look like a bunch of part-timers. They're up against it now, Bob. They'll be rushing. They won't be ready.' West Ham were actually out on the pitch before us and, after following them, my first thought was, *They don't look nervous at all! They look ready alright!* I sought out Bobby Moore; Shanks's description was way off the mark! He didn't look pasty-faced at all, he looked great, as usual. And there was Geoff Hurst, also resplendent, smashing balls at their goalie, Jim Standen. I looked at Jim closely. *He's not that small, is he!* I thought. Because he wasn't. They beat us 2-1.

Shanks also liked the surprise appearance at your own front door. During the close season he and Reuben would turn up at your house with no warning. Edith once went to answer the doorbell. 'Oh, Mr Shankly. Mr Bennett! What a surprise! Come in, please.' There was little else she could have said.

'Aye, we'll come in, thank you.'

'Cup of tea?'

'Oh aye, we'll have a cup of tea, lovely.'

Immediately Shanks would be looking around, making no attempt to hide what he was doing. He'd come to check up on me, to see how I was living. Is the house clean? Is it tidy? What's the wife like? And so on. They never stayed more than 15 minutes. Reuben never said a great deal (he was more circumspect), but on this occasion, fortunately for me, Shanks said all the right things. It was as much as you could hope for.

'Nice spot here, Gordon. I like it.' He paused. 'St John's around the corner, isn't he?' he said. 'I'll go and see him in a minute.' And then just as quickly as they'd arrived, he and Reuben disappeared. Such visits were rare, but I know he did the same to several players, especially those who were married. We'd discuss it among ourselves. 'Shanks came to see me, so be careful. It might be you next!' His own little semi-detached house was all he desired; what Shanks really wanted to know was if our living conditions and home life were as satisfactory as his own – are they living properly?

Having been a manager I fully understand his logic, but it's not something I could have done – indeed, I didn't; I'd have felt as if I was intruding. But he looked at things differently. His mentality was unique. Perhaps that's why my managerial career didn't quite match his!

* * *

Easter fixtures are crucial in any season. They always were. In 1964 we had three matches in four days: Spurs away on Good Friday, Leicester City away on Easter Saturday, then Spurs again at home on Easter Monday. With Manchester United to follow five days later we were certainly not the bookies' favourites to come through this run unscathed, particularly as Leicester were a bogey team at that time. It was a daunting programme, and more difficult than anything our rivals faced.

We began well at White Hart Lane, winning 3-1, thanks to Roger's fantastic hat-trick. It was a hectic and bruising encounter, most of us feeling the after-effects immediately. It was a relief to all when we arrived at the hotel in Leicester later that evening. Our instructions were to have a good long soak in the bath and get as much rest as possible. As the kick-off was at three o'clock the following afternoon there were no dissenting voices; we were all knackered.

My loyal room-mate Peter Thompson took the responsibility of filling the bath. Easier said than done as both hands were required to turn a single tap. After much puffing and panting there was enough hot water to just about cover our weary legs when we both climbed in. Being the youngest (and less experienced), Peter found himself at the tap end – obviously. I can picture him now, his head resting on a towel carefully placed between the two gigantic brass taps, eyes closed and a slight smile on his flushed face. We both believed this was doing us good and the aches and pains were easing. We were fully relaxed and feeling much better by the minute. Half an hour later it was straight into bed – no rocking required. We'd be ready for Leicester.

Memories of their heart-breaking victory in the FA Cup semi-final less than a year earlier were still fresh and, looking at the fixture list prior to the Easter programme, you'd have thought this would be the trickiest of the lot. But on a Filbert Street mudheap we won 2-0 thanks to Roger and Alf Arrowsmith. It felt like a marker, an indication that we might be on our way here.

We returned to Liverpool in high spirits with the luxury of nearly 48 hours until our next tussle: Tottenham again on Easter Monday. A second 3-1 win duly followed. Maximum points from our Easter programme, and a convincing 3-0 win against Manchester United five days later meant we'd met the challenge head-on. It was a crucial period in which to do the business and was a huge step – four steps, actually – towards achieving our goal.

At that point we felt turbocharged. That winning streak meant we were all on a high, and you just couldn't see us not winning – convincingly too. The crowd were obviously up for it as well, and everything came to the boil. We were unstoppable. Our seventh consecutive win, 5-0 against Arsenal. Liverpool – league champions! It had a nice ring to it – still does! I can't remember whether it was one of our best performances (although it must have been pretty good), but the result spoke for itself. And once we got to maybe 3-0 up it was carnival time.

The corks were put back in the bottle after that – we lost two and drew one of our last three matches – but that was, to an extent, natural and understandable. Until the job is done, the pressure builds – until it blows. But once you've achieved what you set out to achieve, human nature takes the foot off the pedal. That certainly applied to us. Such a run of fixtures, performances and results, culminating in the victory over Arsenal, was a direct consequence of all the hard work and concentration we'd put in, not just over the previous three or four weeks, but throughout the past few months or, dare I say it, the last couple of years. And it had been hard … bloody hard.

Incidentally, I always thought the win over Arsenal was the match featured on the first-ever *Match of the Day* highlights broadcast, but I was wrong.

The first *Match of the Day* did indeed feature Liverpool vs Arsenal, but it was the opening fixture of the following season. We won 3-2, a real ding-dong affair, but the match is most fondly remembered for the appearance of a black cat on the Anfield pitch. It was a great win for us, but the bloody cat got more publicity than we did!

* * *

When things had calmed down a little (although the red half of Liverpool was still an inferno), an informal player gathering saw Liverpool's skipper informed by his team-mates that a few days in the sun would be a nice reward and help strengthen the strong bond we'd undoubtedly developed. The instructions were clear: seven days in Majorca would be acceptable. Poor Ron wasn't great in these situations, and Shanks knew it. Another meeting, slightly more formal this time, took place. The attendees were 11 of us players, Bob and Shanks, and the meeting took place in the manager's office, barely big enough to accommodate us all.

Shanks began: 'I've been carefully considering the captain's request and I can immediately see a major problem. I've heard on good authority that the club across the way tried something similar last year and it was not a success. In fact, it was a disaster. So why should we risk it?' I never knew the details of Everton's trip but, for Shanks, a precedent had seemingly been set.

Big Ron replied, 'Ah, but boss, their problem was with the players' wives. They couldn't get on. It caused friction in the camp. We talked about this with Alex Young and Alex Parker.' Ron was playing the game here, as he knew full well that, despite being Evertonians, Shanks respected both players enormously (nothing to do with them being fellow Scots, of course).

'So, what are you trying to tell me, son?' asked Shanks, looking Ron squarely in the eye.

'Well boss,' began Ron, straightening his back and shoulders, expanding to his full, massive frame, dominating the room as the rest of us squirmed on wooden benches like mini choirboys, 'we don't want to make the same mistake as Everton, so we thought it should be a "players only" trip.' Deadly silence. Ron began to flush a little. There was an awkward pause, as if he'd been speaking Swahili.

Shanks came back full throttle: 'Players only!?? Am I hearing this right? Players only? I've never heard anything like it in my life! Are you telling me, players only? Bob, are you hearing this?' He was in full flight: loud, animated, dancing around, waving his arms as his captain's face turned ever more red. Ron was now shrinking, it seemed. The room became more claustrophobic and stifling; blank faces looked at one another, like errant schoolboys. Even the Saint was speechless.

Shanks was now dominating proceedings: 'We have a dilemma, Bob, we have a dilemma ...' Whenever Shanks discussed a non-football matter, it was always a 'dilemma'. Bob hummed, hahed and mumbled, but actually said nothing. For the rest of us the mood was: *Let's get out of here. We're wasting our time and suffocating while we do it!*

Then suddenly ... bang! The mood changed. The manager was now cool, calm, collected. In an extremely composed manner, Shanks said, 'Right. I would like those of you who think a "players only" trip is the right thing to do to raise your arms.' Big Ron's arm shot up, nearly punching a hole in the ceiling as perspiration ran down his now smiling face. The congregation duly followed suit, some with just a thumbs-up, others as if they were asking to leave the room (many undoubtedly were). But there was no question: the vote was unanimous. The manager had clarity.

I've always been convinced that Shanks co-stage-managed that entire performance. He was one step ahead of us from the minute we entered the dungeon of his office until he released us back into natural daylight and fresh air. We'd all danced to his tune. He was in no way surprised by the request and, I believe, totally comfortable with the outcome. He'd been a player himself, of course, so fully recognised our mindset. Yet he still orchestrated the entire performance beautifully, keeping us all in suspense yet knowing all along the eventual outcome. What none of us had considered, though, was part two: how to explain this to the wives. Somehow 'we're all off to Majorca; sorry, but you're not invited' wouldn't quite cut it. There must have been some interesting conversations in the homes of those involved …

A few days later us players, Bob, Joe and Reuben arrived in Can Pastilla, 20 minutes from Palma. One day we decided to hire a boat, get a few drinks on board and head to a little island for a nice change of pace. At ten o'clock in the morning we gathered on the jetty. Willie Stevenson was on the beach talking to a young couple on their honeymoon and, somewhat misguidedly, invited the lad, a Liverpool fan, to join us. His wife was very understanding, more so than some of the lads. Willie was far from flavour of the month.

Off we went. Nothing had been said about where we were going, or for how long, so at about one o'clock the lad was beginning to panic. 'When are we going back?' 'Not 'til this evening,' said Willie. Three or four hours later we arrived back in the harbour to be greeted by two police vans with lights flashing, and the young lad's distraught wife. She thought he'd gone overboard! He staggered off the boat, she jumped into his arms and the police disappeared. No harm done, and an international incident was happily avoided.

The following year we were back again. They'd looked after us so well the previous year, everything was within walking distance, so it was an ideal spot. This time, though, it was Tommy Smith at the centre of another Spanish escapade. Tommy and

I were quite close, despite him being the youngest and me the oldest. He could be quite aggressive, Tommy (understatement of the year, perhaps?) not least when he'd had a few drinks. In the evenings the lads would disappear in twos and threes. We'd come off the beach at five o'clock, meet in a particular bar, then have our dinner before heading off out. At about two o'clock one morning I was fast asleep (me being a goody two-shoes of course) when there were several knocks on my door. 'Gordon! Gordon! It's Tommy!' Bleary-eyed, I opened the door, and there he was, even more bleary-eyed than me and flanked by two large policemen. 'I'm in a bit of trouble here, Gordon, you've got to help me.'

I soon found myself in the back of a police jeep, a policeman either side of me. Sitting opposite was Charles Bronson – if you ever saw Tommy when he hadn't shaved, he reminded me of the film star – with a policeman either side of him, and two more up front. My only thought was, *We're in serious trouble here.* On top of that, Tommy was continually pleading his innocence. 'Gordon, I haven't done anything ...' But I wasn't having it. 'Shut up Tommy! Just be quiet! Don't say a word!' After three or four attempts, the message finally hit home.

The road to wherever we were heading eventually became an extremely rough and bumpy dirt track. The jeep was bouncing all over the place, like we were going across the bloody Rockies! The situation became increasingly uncomfortable and intimidating; even more daunting was the thought of what might lie ahead. We arrived at the police department in total silence at about four o'clock. But Tommy started up again: 'Gordon, it wasn't my fault, I was ...' Again, I stopped him in his tracks: 'Shut up Tommy! Not another f***ing word!' He kept starting, and I kept stopping him. The officer who had made the arrest had to call his boss at home; clearly, we were going to be there some time. At that point I was sober enough to fear the worst: we're going to get hammered here. The press will get hold of this, and it'll be something we're not going to get out of. I was anything but optimistic; switched on but panicking. I kept telling Tommy to keep quiet. If he kept going, he'd only make things worse.

A senior officer appeared, far from pleased at having been called from his bed at such an ungodly hour. He joined the arresting officer and his colleagues, listening carefully to them while casting his eyes over Tommy and me. Thankfully, he understood English, so I took a chance and stepped into my ambassadorial shoes: 'My name is Gordon Milne. Of the two of us here I'm the senior member of the Liverpool football team. We're here on holiday. I'm very sorry about all of this but I'm sure there's been some sort of mistake. Tommy here is the youngest player in our group, it's his first time with the team and he's very inexperienced. I apologise for any misunderstanding. He's just a young lad, but I apologise on his behalf for his behaviour.'

The senior office was extremely irritated, but to be fair he listened patiently. When I'd finished, he looked at Tommy, looked at me, thought for a moment, then suddenly said, 'Go. GO!' We went! And we went bloody quickly, fairly flying down the stairs. Thankfully, the senior officer had seen this 'incident' for what it was – nothing, really. I think his own staff came off worse as he was more annoyed by the early wake-up call than anything Tommy might have done.

At that point, I still didn't know what had actually happened. I didn't want to discuss it on the way over, and certainly not in the police station. As it turned out, when Tommy had returned from his night out there was a night porter on duty at the front desk. What you generally had to do to keep the peace was throw the night porter a few pesetas to keep him happy. Tommy, however, decided he wasn't going to do that, telling him to 'eff off' along the way, so the night porter shopped him to the police. It really was nothing. But ever since the knock on the door I'd been anticipating the worst, fearing Tommy had stuck one on someone, or something like that. I knew it wouldn't have taken much for him to do so.

On the unnecessarily expensive taxi ride back, I was more relieved than anything else. So was Tommy. Like me, he'd feared the worst, no doubt about it. Now he was like a little mouse. 'Sorry, Gordon, I'm sorry.' I spoke to him quite gently but hoped my message was blunt enough to hit home: 'Christ, we've got away with that one. For f***'s sake Tommy, stick to the bloody rules. You could've cocked it up for everybody. We set standards, you know that, and you don't step out of line. This could have been the end of our trips, d'you realise that? And you wouldn't have been too popular with the lads then, would you?' Tommy sat sheepishly in the back of the cab like a little boy lost, sobering up and realising how close he'd come to making a balls-up of it. It's hard to picture, I know: Tommy Smith all contrite, feeling sorry for himself. But the fact remained that we all knew the rules, Tommy included. Nobody caused trouble, nobody did anything daft. Bob and Joe, they knew everyone was different, and they knew all the lads were doing their own things. But as long as there was no bother, we'd be okay.

When we reached the hotel, maybe half past six in the morning, Tommy gave me a big hug and a kiss. Imagine getting a kiss from Charles Bronson! That morning, for the first time ever – and I'm sure the last – he and I were the first to make it into the restaurant for breakfast. We both needed a strong coffee, that's for sure – and probably more than one.

As far as I was concerned, Bob and Joe were completely unaware of our meeting with the authorities. But that said, what do I know? Maybe they knew everything. It was never discussed though. Sometimes, when you're a manager, players think you don't know something, but you do. It's how you handle the knowledge that counts.

Chapter 7

'YOU'VE COME the wrong way.'

Believe it or not, these were the words preceding Liverpool Football Club's first-ever European fixture. Now, 60 years later, with more than a dozen European trophies to their name, these words seem laughable. When they were said, though, we were all laughing.

The 1964/65 season began with a 2-2 draw at Anfield against West Ham United in the Charity Shield, in those days played at the league champions' home ground (Wembley was only used for special occasions such as the FA Cup Final and England internationals). We'd begin our league title defence at Anfield too, against Arsenal a week later. Between those two games, though, was a landmark occasion: Liverpool's first-ever European tie. Winning the First Division meant qualification for the European Cup, so in August we set off on the club's first continental adventure; yet another new beginning, and we were there at the start once again. None of us realised it, of course – how could we possibly know that this would be the first chapter in what would become the biggest success story in Liverpool FC's history?

It began in Iceland. The preliminary round pitted us against KR Reykjavík, hardly a household name, but being so unfamiliar with them – scouting networks didn't stretch to the Arctic Circle – meant this really was a journey into the unknown. Adding to the novelty was the concept of flying abroad to play competitively. The odd pre-season match in Ireland was our only real experience of travelling overseas and even then, such fixtures were only friendlies. All of this was new.

For reasons long forgotten, we had to fly to Iceland from Prestwick Airport, 30-odd miles south of Glasgow. For some reason a bus first took us to Speke Airport just outside Liverpool before we flew south – the wrong bloody direction – to London Heathrow. At Heathrow we boarded another flight, north, to Prestwick. And from there, eventually, to Iceland. The logic behind this route baffled me then and still does now, although I'm sure there must have been some method in the madness.

When we reached Prestwick, we learned that our next flight was delayed, and would be for several hours. Kicking our heels in the airport terminal (for who knew how long) wasn't the most attractive proposition. Fortunately, a couple of miles from the airport was a holiday camp with a few leisure facilities where we could kill a few hours. We commandeered a coach from somewhere and were soon faced with a long, straight approach road leading to the camp itself. Halfway down was a barrier across the road, next to a little cabin. It was too small to be called a gatehouse really, although patrolling this area – his domain, clearly – was a little old guy in his security uniform with an official-looking cap perched on his head: the gatekeeper. It was obviously up to him as to who was, and wasn't, allowed into this pleasure palace, and he clearly took this responsibility very seriously.

The coach pulled up at the barrier, which remained perfectly still. Shanks rose to his feet as the gatekeeper stepped out of his cabin, straightened his cap, then raised his palm in the air, instructing us to stop. I'm not sure why; we were stationary already. Shanks stepped out of the coach: 'Hello, son,' he said. Son! Brilliant – the guy was older than him!

'Yes, sir, can I help you?' replied the gatekeeper politely.

Shanks straightened up his posture and puffed out his chest. 'Liverpool Football Club!' he announced. In fact, he almost bellowed it. 'We're on our way to play a European Cup tie,' he said, his Scottish accent strengthening with every syllable, which somehow seemed to emphasise the importance of our mission. 'We're going to play KR Reykjavík.' Pause. 'In Iceland.' Shanks had plenty more to say and looked set to do just that, but the gatekeeper got there first, raising his palm once again.

'Let me stop you there,' he said. Pause. 'You've come the wrong way.' As Shanks looked at him, he carried on: 'What you want to do is turn around, go back up to the end of the road, and …' The rest of what he said was drowned out by the entire coach bellowing with laughter! He was giving Shanks road directions – to Iceland!

When the hilarity died down and the confusion had been sorted, we were allowed in. The gatekeeper was a little embarrassed but he and everyone else at the camp made us feel very welcome. The delayed flight hadn't been the greatest start to our first European foray, but that little exchange certainly lightened the mood!

Iceland wasn't at all like I'd imagined. I'd pictured mountains, lakes, icebergs, and I'm sure all that stuff was there somewhere but we never saw any of it as we were staying in the city. The people were fantastic, however, extremely kind and very accommodating. We were made to feel so welcome, and their hospitality was magnificent.

The match itself was straightforward, and we chalked up a 5-0 win. That was to our credit, and the management too; we applied ourselves properly and took our task deadly seriously. We wouldn't have been allowed to treat the match any other way, nor would any of us have dreamed of doing so. Some might say that we were fortunate to have been handed an easy starting fixture, but I don't go along with that; that's much more of a modern-day concept and, in actual fact, that didn't matter. What did matter was this: it was the beginning – again; the start of something special – again. And nobody – none of us – could possibly have anticipated how that story would unfold. And it's still unfolding today. With hindsight I think it's fair to say that 'you've come the wrong way' was misleading to say the least. But they were the opening words of the opening chapter of an ongoing story, a story still being avidly read by Liverpool supporters all over the world. And they all remain desperate to find out what happens on the next page.

* * *

Dining at the top table of European football meant extra exposure via the TV coverage accompanying such a competition. In turn, the side effect of such coverage was the (hopefully) enhanced image of the clubs participating. We were all in the spotlight, so had to look the part. And in all areas too.

One such area that changed for the better just as rapidly as it seemed to grow was the medical department. In particular, for Bob, this meant the acquisition of a new matchday medical kit. This box of tricks was very big and bloody heavy! A big handle on it, chrome clips everywhere, quite posh really, but more suited to an actual treatment room than a pitch. There were numerous small drawers, all of them stuffed with potions, pills, dressings, sprays and who knew what else. Unsurprisingly, Bob was more than happy to take delivery of this medical marvel, not least because it represented such an upgrade on what had previously sufficed; the old bag with a wet sponge and smelling salts was no longer enough. And as Bob was chief medic, assistant manager, masseur, trainer, coach and knew how to pour a Guinness in the boot room, no one could challenge his authority to take full control of the new piece of equipment and its magical contents.

In its early days of competition, March 1965, we were playing away in the European Cup quarter-final. It was our third match against Cologne, the previous two legs having been unable to separate us, and this third would be no different, finishing 2-2. We were playing in Rotterdam, a neutral venue, on a swamp of a pitch, but after 300 minutes of football there was still nothing between the two teams. Penalty shoot-outs were yet to be conceived so the referee called the two captains to the centre circle. Incredibly, the result would be decided by a flip – not of a coin, but of a plastic disc more akin to a poker chip, red on one side, white on the other, specially made for the occasion, I'm sure.

The referee was firmly in charge of which side of the disc represented which team (presumably we were the red half), very definitively pointing at it before pointing to the respective captains. With us all craning our necks to see what was going on, the ref flipped, and the disc landed – vertically, on its edge, stuck in the mud! He promptly picked it up to go again. The tension was unbearable, red and white mud-splattered shirts alongside a gaggle of press men, all jostling for a view, surrounding, crowding and nearly suffocating the referee. With the steam rising from the entangled bodies, how was this titanic battle going to end?

For the second time the disc flew into the night sky and, on landing, lay not quite flat, but most definitely red side up! I was in the mix but not close enough to see it land. What I did see, though, was Big Ron shoot up like a red rocket launched, a signal to all those watching from afar who couldn't possibly know what was happening. Either way, the reds had it! We were through to the semi-final of the European Cup!

Big Ron always told the story of Shanks's reaction. 'Well done, son. What did you pick?' asked the manager. 'I picked tails, Boss,' said Ron. 'Yes,' replied Shanks, 'I would've picked tails too.' And he walked off. I think Ron was expecting a bit more …!

When the dust had settled, as delighted as we were, there always remained the feeling that this was no way to end a football match, and certainly not one of such importance. It was more than a damp squib; in fact, it was disrespectful to the players who had given their all over three epic matches, and we most definitely understood how we'd have felt had the disc landed white side up. It was an extraordinary way to settle a tie, and nobody should have had to go through such an amateurish conclusion. What did come out of it, thankfully, was the need for an improved solution, and I suppose a penalty shoot-out is as close as you can get to producing a fair outcome. (A nice post-script to this story, though, is, thanks solely to that epic trilogy, the clubs developed a close relationship, and a few years later some of the Liverpool boys went over to play a friendly against some of the old Cologne stagers.)

Prior to all of that, though, during the first leg in Cologne, Willie Stevenson went down injured. The referee beckoned on Bob, who duly made his way to Willie, although he was in no rush, shuffling across the muddy surface in the murky light with what appeared to be his new suitcase in hand, looking for all the world as if he was going on his holidays. By the time Bob reached Willie the mood of the crowd had darkened, the referee too. Bob remained unmoved. After two attempts he managed to open his magic box and eventually got Willie sorted.

Helping Willie to his feet, however, Bob stumbled over his new kit, scattering its contents everywhere. The referee and the crowd reared up once again but Bob remained the calmest person in the stadium. Slowly – very, very slowly – and carefully – very, very carefully – Bob picked up his displaced medicals one at a time and very methodically returned them all to their correct drawers. He then left the scene of the crime as if nothing had happened and, again, in no rush.

What *had* happened, though, was the pattern of play had been severely interrupted. Cologne had lost any momentum they'd had and struggled to get it back, failing to re-establish the authority they were enjoying before Willie's injury. The situation had affected them all mentally, no question. This was something we were all continuously reminded of by Bob and the rest of the staff: when you're speeding along, it doesn't take much to nudge the train off the tracks. So, did the man with the suitcase have something to do with Cologne's derailment? Yes. Bob knew exactly what he was doing, and despite the inevitable added time, we saw the match out 0-0. Mission accomplished.

Chapter 8

WHEN I think of our back four, I can't help but think of Leeds United. Not the Leeds defence (although big Jack Charlton was hard to ignore), but the character of that team and the characters in it. And the parallels with the Liverpool team of that era were as difficult to ignore as Big Jack.

Don Revie was building something special in the Second Division (Leeds wouldn't be promoted until 1964) along the same lines and with similar principles to Shanks's Liverpool. This was arguably not surprising as Shanks and Revie used to talk regularly on the phone. It may have just been just two guys having a catch-up, but that's doubtful. Shanks didn't really do niceties, although there was a mutual respect there, each recognising and respecting what the other was doing. The chemistry of the two teams was remarkably similar. Each had a nucleus of players who seemed to play in every match. They had Big Jack and Norman Hunter, and Billy Bremner and Johnny Giles were two of the smallest in the team but, to put it mildly, were a real handful. Little Johnny, in particular, could mix it with the best of them. Then there was Willie Bell (a good pal of mine), Paul Reaney, and the rest of them. Leeds had their own band of brothers doing what they did probably better than anyone else, square pegs in square holes, players who were perfect examples of each position. In midfield

Giles and Bremner was as good a pairing as you'd find, and then what about Bobby Collins! Bobby, even smaller than me, was heading towards the twilight of his career but what a player. Collins, Giles and Bremner – Christ almighty! Three lads who could all bloody play but didn't mind a bit of the naughty stuff when it was required.

The whole team could play, but they could also cause trouble. Wherever Leeds played, flare-ups were common. To me though, that's where the similarities between the two teams ended. We weren't goody two-shoes by any means, but we didn't go as far in the darker arts as they did. Traditionally we always had a bit of needle with Manchester United but, once Leeds got their feet under the table, Leeds/Liverpool became much more of a tinder box. On one side you had Big Jack and Norman, Bremner, Giles and Collins, while on the other you had Tommy Smith, Ron Yeats, Ian St John, Gerry Byrne and Chris Lawler. You could put them all in the ring together just to calm them down – and then send them out to play! The competitive nature, individually and collectively, meant that out on the pitch you just knew: *Something's going to happen today.*

Following their promotion, our second match of the 1964/65 season saw them beat us 4-2 at Elland Road. We immediately knew how good they were, and how seriously they needed to be taken. Later at Anfield, we won 2-1, but Leeds were clearly a force to be reckoned with. And that year, all roads led to Wembley. For us both to reach the FA Cup Final – well, you couldn't have had a spicier occasion. This was box-office stuff.

Our cup run took in victories over West Bromwich Albion, Stockport County (via a replay), Bolton Wanderers and Leicester City before a semi-final at Villa Park against Chelsea at the end of March. We won 2-0 to book our spot at Wembley for the FA Cup Final on 1 May. It could all have been so different though. Against Stockport at Anfield on a cold, frosty day, a rare Milne strike had given us the lead before Lenny White equalised. In the last minute, from a Stockport corner in front of the Kop, Lenny White, again, crashed a header against the underside of the crossbar. The ball bounced down on to the goal line, Gerry Byrne hooked it clear and the referee blew for full time. We'd earned (if that's the right word) a replay by the skin of our teeth; if Lenny's header had dropped an inch or two lower, that first-ever cup win wouldn't have happened – at least not that year.

Interestingly, Shanks wasn't at Anfield that day. He'd gone to Germany to watch Cologne, our next European Cup opponents. (Obviously he had full confidence in our ability to beat Stockport!) On his return he approached one of the airport porters. 'FA Cup today, son – any surprises?'

The porter shook his head. 'No, nothing really.'

'What about Liverpool?' Shanks continued. 'How did they get on?'

'A draw. 1-1.'

Shanks was incredulous. Staring dead into the porter's eyes, he said, 'Liverpool 1-1? A draw? And you're telling me that's not a f***ing surprise?' The poor lad must have been thinking, Who's this I'm talking to? He's a bloody headcase! I'm pretty sure Shanks never missed another match after that.

Two weeks before the cup final we met Chelsea in a league fixture at Stamford Bridge, a momentous occasion for me, although unfortunately for all the wrong reasons. Perhaps fatigue got the better of us (it was our sixth match in 16 days) as we were trounced 4-0, our fourth consecutive loss. This was no time for our form to be slipping, and for it to be slipping so dramatically only made things worse.

But it was a single moment, rather than the whole match, when it all unravelled for me. The Saint played a short pass to me – a little *too* short as it turned out – which I stretched for. Eddie McCreadie, Chelsea's left-back, came in on my blind side. With a chance to win the ball he did what any defender would have done – won the ball and clattered me into the bargain. I never saw it coming. Eddie cleaned me out completely and my leg twisted the wrong way. Knee ligaments gone. I'd never been seriously injured before but as soon as it happened I knew. It was no-nonsense from Eddie, a hard tackle, but a fair one. My injury wasn't Eddie's fault. After the match the Saint was very apologetic: 'Gordon, I'm so sorry. It was rubbish, that pass, I didn't do you any favours there.' But it wasn't his fault either. These things happen in football.

I'd gone a few seasons barely missing a match so, considering where injuries can take you, physically and mentally I'd been very lucky. Unfortunately, my luck ran out just at the wrong time. Afterwards, people said, 'Don't worry, you'll be back; this team is too good not to reach Wembley again.' As it happened, we'd get close, but not close enough.

The final was only two weeks away. I'd done my ligaments and there was never going to be a quick (enough) fix for that. Still, I carried on kidding myself, trying to get fit. At Melwood, maybe ten days before Wembley, Bob and I were at the sprint track when Shanks appeared and asked Bob, 'How is it then, Bob?' This was classic Shanks, he'd always ask Bob's opinion ahead of the player himself.

'Not much better, Boss,' said Bob.

'Well, if that's the case,' replied Shanks, 'it's f***ing worse isn't it! If it's not better, it's f***ing worse!' And off he went.

Now, I'd like to think he was hoping I was going to be fit. I like to think that but, once you've been a manager, you realise that's not necessarily the case. He just needed to know: is he going to make it or not? I knew I was never going to make it, there was just no way. I could have said it was a wee bit better, but I'd have been kidding myself, and everyone else too. And the situation was far too important for me to say that. I was sick that I wasn't going to make it, but there was nothing I could do. Perhaps I should have told Shanks my grandmother had died, and asked to be excused from that Chelsea match?

The worst part was still to come, however, not just the big day itself, but the build-up. In a city like Liverpool that begins as soon as the semi-final has been won. In 1965 there was, as you'd expect, a solid fortnight of unavoidable cup final fever. Knowing I wouldn't be part of it (I'd be involved, just not how I wanted to be) hung over me the entire time. The build-up seemed to last forever. I'd keep hearing, 'You've still got two weeks. You've got time.' But I knew I didn't. And every day there were more reminders: shops and houses decked out in red, fans approaching us, photo-shoots, and so on. It wasn't easy.

What did help, though, was that I wasn't just a player, I was a fan. Players all start out as supporters, and for a short while that's what I became again. The only real way I could relate to missing out was from a fan's point of view, an extremely excited fan whose mates all have tickets, but he hasn't, and he's bloody sick about it. But once the game kicks off, he'll be wherever he needs to be, watching it as passionately as anyone else. That was me.

'Special Training at Morecambe. (Harry) Lowe, (Jimmy) Dougal, (Bill) Shankly, and a Golfer' (circa1939). Footballers have always loved golf, it seems, though I'm not sure just how good the 'Golfer' – my dad – actually was. Courtesy of Gordon Milne

Smile for the camera – or don't! Winners of the 1950 Dawson Cup, a Preston schools' competition, in 1950. I'm middle row, far left, aged 13. How could I possibly imagine I would go on to be photographed in similar poses, representing my country? Courtesy of Gordon Milne

Ten-shun! Passing Out Parade in 1958 following ten gruelling weeks of National Service training. Initially a ramshackle, shambolic bunch of individuals, we were now one single, slick, coherent unit; one battalion in perfect harmony, testament to what can be achieved with dedication, pride, and determination – much like on a football pitch. Courtesy of Gordon Milne

One of the proudest and most humbling moments of my life as I receive the award of Best Recruit from my intake. I couldn't have won that without the support of all the other lads; to this day I remain in their debt. Courtesy of Gordon Milne

I daren't take my eye off the ball – especially with my hero watching over me! The great Tom Finney is on my right, Derek Myers next to him, and Sammy Taylor on my left. All caked in mud and loving it! Courtesy of Gordon Milne

A trio like no other: Paisley, Shankly, and Fagan. Four European Cup wins between them yet, remarkably, none for Shanks. (Bob in 1977, 1978 and 1981; Joe in 1984.)

Shanks always said, 'Never mind the player, speak to the wife first.' I took his advice. Edith and I were married on 17 June 1961; unquestionably the best – and most successful – signing I ever made.

Back in the big time … though you might think from the photograph it was Liverpool's directors rather than the players who won the 1962 Second Division title and promotion. Perhaps that's why Shanks (bottom left) looks so nonplussed – directors were never his favourite people!

Celebrating our first First Division title under Shanks in 1964 after beating Arsenal 5-0 at Anfield, with the Saint in charge of refilling my glass. We still played in white shorts then.

Fun in the sun! Not sure if this was the year of Tommy Smith's troubles in Majorca, but his absence here suggests not! I'm bottom right with a very young-looking Cally resting his hand on my shoulder.

I was desperate to prove my fitness before the 1965 FA Cup Final but unfortunately, I always knew I'd fail. Still, there's something magical about an empty football stadium

The Lonely Man. With my team-mates inspecting the Wembley pitch I took myself off for some quiet reflection. Just like my dad, I was destined to miss the FA Cup Final

English football's Wembley showpiece, the FA Cup Final, in 1965 – yet only one bench for the two management teams (and a ball boy)! Bob, Reuben, myself, and Shanks; Syd Owen, Don Revie, Les Cocker. Bob and Les didn't bother trying to stay dry: they were up and down like yo-yos, on and off the pitch every two minutes dishing out treatment after yet another 'tackle' – Liverpool v Leeds was always a feisty affair

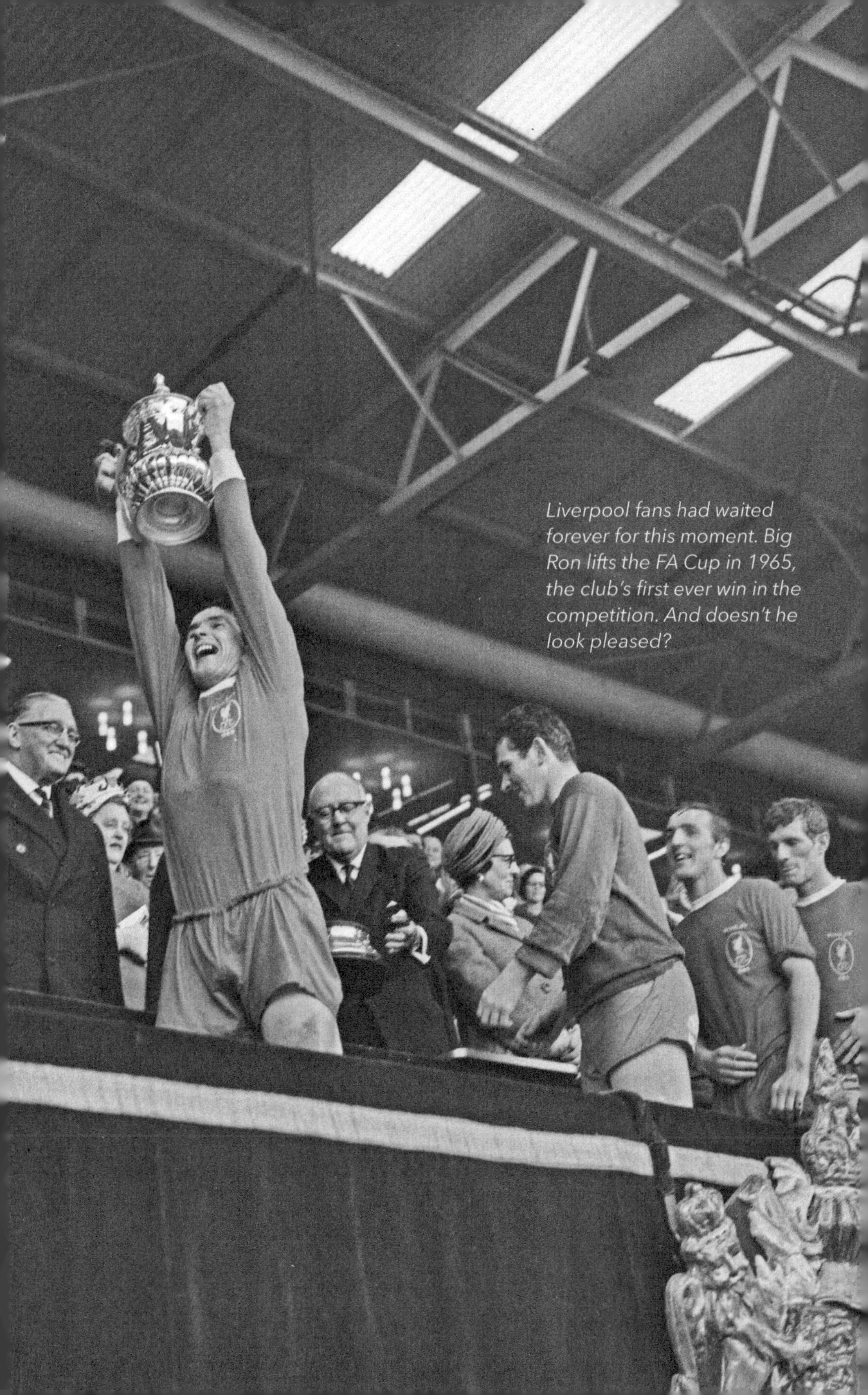

Liverpool fans had waited forever for this moment. Big Ron lifts the FA Cup in 1965, the club's first ever win in the competition. And doesn't he look pleased?

Although I was never going to be fit enough to play, there was no way the lads would see me miss out, but it was a bittersweet afternoon; I had my hands on the famous old trophy but felt I didn't truly deserve it.

History-makers - plus me and a couple of policemen!

Excitement, disappointment, nervousness, self-pity, desperate for the lads to win – I felt them all. There was the Wembley factor too. In those days, unless you were going to play for your country (fortunately I'd already done so), the only way to play at Wembley was to reach the cup final. The grand old stadium, the home of football, was a massive part of the 'magic of the cup'. If you played at Wembley, you felt privileged. The day before the final we went to have a look at Wembley. There's a great photo I call 'The Lonely Man'. All the lads are out having a look at the pitch, and I'm sat in the stand miles away, on my own. I can't remember that picture being taken but, painful as it is, it tells a story.

Tickets were always an issue. Any final created a 'how many tickets do players get?' scenario. Many would flog their tickets simply because of their low wages; they'd make far more money selling their tickets than from playing football. Ticket allocation fell to the club secretary (and former player) Jimmy McInnes, but Shanks was heavily involved too. The allocation to the clubs was never enough; twice as many were always required. Pressure and stress were constant and tragically led to tragedy. Four days after the cup final, the morning after Liverpool defeated Inter Milan 3-1 at Anfield, the players reported to the ground for training as usual. Entering the stadium from Walton Breck Road, Alf Arrowsmith arrived in the dressing room white as a sheet. I don't know whether Alf discovered Jimmy, but he certainly saw him. Our secretary had committed suicide, hanging himself from the rafters of the Kop. I wouldn't like to speculate – I wouldn't dream of it – but there's little doubt in my mind that the ticket issue was a factor in Jimmy making the decision he did. He was a good man, and a loyal servant to the club. What happened was truly a tragedy.

Shanks too felt the pressure of this issue. The directors gave the players ten tickets each. Shanks never got on with directors, but he'd go into battle with them for his players (strong characters like Big Ron and the Saint would push hard, but ultimately it was Shanks who would take the fight upstairs), and he did, telling the directors a little white lie, something like, 'The Leeds players got 120 tickets. Each! My boys should have the same!' Incredibly, he managed to get us each 100 tickets, but for the likes of Chris Lawler and Tommy Smith, with so many relatives, even that wasn't enough! If you gave Aunty Brenda two, you had to give Uncle Jack two, and so on – it never stopped! No matter how many you got, tickets were always a bloody nightmare.

Because we'd played for England with Jimmy Greaves, Roger and I knew a lad called Johnny the Stick who was quite close to Greavsie. Johnny was a Londoner with a dodgy leg, needed a stick (hence the nickname), long coat, cap ... a typical spiv, although I suppose these days you'd call him a straightforward ticket tout. Quite the character, Johnny always had the best patter, the best prices and pockets full of cash. He was only too happy to take tickets off your hands, and he did just that. Tommy Lawrence sold Johnny the lot, saying, 'These bloody tickets are more trouble than they're worth! If I give X to so and so, I've got to give Y to such and such! But if I tell everyone from the start, "I'm sorry, I haven't got any," it stops it all, just like that!' I think most of the lads flogged some and kept a few back for family, but dealing with the family was the hardest part. And remember, Liverpool had never won the FA Cup, so demands and expectations were only heightened further – the world and his wife were after you!

The tickets were all different colours (I think purple were the top level). When our bus arrived at Wembley, we were surrounded by Liverpool fans, banging on the bus, shouting, 'Bill! Bill! Got any spares?' Shanks, sitting at the front, said, 'Driver, open the door!' He began pulling tickets from his jacket pocket and handing them out to the fans! It was amazing. We were going, 'What's he doing? He's just given two purple ones away! Those lads are gonna be sitting next to the Queen!' Some may have sold them on immediately, I suppose – where there was money to be made, the Scousers knew how to make it. The fans were pleading, 'We've come all this way, Bill!' Stuck in human traffic, Shanks must have given a dozen or so tickets away. They weren't all purple, I'm sure, but even if they were, that didn't matter to Shanks. He was genuinely trying to help the fans. It's simply what he did.

During the match I sat on the bench on the touchline, desperately wishing I was out there. It wasn't the best view, and the benches were quite far back from the pitch in the first place. There was no shelter either, and it was a filthy day. For some reason I'd just put my tracksuit on over the top of my suit – I've no idea why! My tracksuit was soaked, but I suppose it kept my suit dry!

It was a great final, extra time and all. And, given the opposition, much of what went on was probably to be expected. We'd barely kicked off when Bobby Collins clattered Gerry. Watching the challenge now, you think, *Bloody hell!* If Bobby didn't get him with a high foot, he got him with his shoulder instead. It all meant Gerry played the best part of 120 minutes with a broken collarbone – can you imagine that happening today? It was an incredible effort and too often overlooked. He was a proper hard man was Gerry, no doubt about it. Not long after that, Big Ron went straight through one of their lads, Jim Storrie, I think. The ball ran loose, and the referee waved it away, shouting, 'Play on!' as if nothing had happened. It was a bit of retribution, I suspect, for what had happened to Gerry.

But even without those two challenges it was still a spicy affair. The physios (or trainers as they were called then) were on the pitch four or five times in the first ten minutes! These were two of the best – and toughest – teams in the country, a showpiece occasion on the best pitch (albeit rain-sodden and very heavy), in the best stadium in the country, and no one let themselves down that day. It was a bloody hard game, 0-0 after 90 minutes, but we got there in the end. Roger gave us the lead early in extra time before Billy Bremner equalised. Then with seven minutes left Cally whipped in a cross and the Saint headed home from five yards. Liverpool had won the FA Cup for the first time!

We were soon running round Wembley with the cup and, like everyone else, I was swept along by the emotion of it all. But it was bittersweet. During the lap of honour, I did feel part of it; I'd contributed because I'd played in all the other rounds. But I also felt like an outsider because I hadn't contributed that day. And there was no getting away from that. Geoff Strong, bless him – a lovely bloke and great player – tried to give me his medal. He knew if I'd been fit, he wouldn't have played. But there was no way I could have accepted it as he'd given blood, sweat and tears. It was an amazing, lovely gesture though, one I've never forgotten. (Sometime later – I don't recall how, or when – I unexpectedly did receive a medal. I always thought it was just the starting 11 who were eligible. But when it did arrive, it meant the world to me. It still does.)

Dinner that night at a Park Lane hotel was difficult. That feeling of detachment hovered over me all evening, but thankfully the lads saw things differently: 'We're all here together; we've all won this together.' Had I played I'm sure I'd have felt the same but, looking at Gerry with his arm in a sling, it was hard to agree that I deserved the same medal as him. The evening, which predictably ran into the next morning, was lost in music, dancing and drinking, with everyone – quite rightly – having a great time. It had been a day of ups and downs, highs and lows, adrenaline, euphoria – and too much drink!

The train journey to Liverpool was something else again – surreal. Big Ron and the Saint were playing cards, nothing unusual in that, only this time the FA Cup was sat right beside them. That certainly hadn't been seen before. And when we arrived at Lime Street station it was just bloody mayhem! The number of people was staggering, and that was just in the station itself. When we made it on to the streets, we were all knocked for six. We knew we had great support, but this was like nothing we'd ever seen before. I remember saying to myself, 'How many were at Wembley?' And then, 'How many are here?' We were all suddenly conscious, again, of what our victory really meant, and it really hit home. The importance of the club's first FA Cup couldn't be overstated. Hundreds of thousands packed the city, many, I'm sure, like us, nursing hangovers. It was an incredible sight but, again, for me tinged with regret. I couldn't shake the thought that this reception was for the 11 players who had done it on the day. They'd won the cup; they deserved the acclaim.

The disappointment didn't linger too long, thankfully. You move on. You have to. What was done was done, what was won was won. And then you went again. I remember Roger, after winning the World Cup in 1966, reporting back to Anfield and bumping into Shanks, who said, 'Hello son, nice to see you. Go and get ready, we've got important work to do.' No handshake, no congratulations, not even a mention that Roger was a World Cup winner. In my view that was because: firstly, Shanks was Scottish so not remotely interested in England (even less so in them winning); secondly, and I think more importantly, he was, genuinely, only concerned about Liverpool and what lay ahead for the club. And in one way he was right, the past was just that. We all had to move on, and that included World Cup winners.

* * *

Those homecoming scenes live large in the memory, but Wembley was already history. Two days later was another massive occasion: Inter Milan at Anfield, the first leg of the European Cup semi-final, no less! Mentally, we were on a different planet, and so were the supporters. The Anfield gates were opened at three o'clock – four and a half hours before kick-off!

Gerry and I, both injured of course, were in the dressing room trying to keep out of the way. The FA Cup was sitting on the big table surrounded by teacups, bandages and bottles of liniment. Nobody took any notice of it. Suddenly, the boss said, 'Boys, we think it would be great if Gerry and Gordon take the cup out to show the crowd before kick-off. I think the Kop would like that.' That last sentence must surely rate as the biggest understatement Shanks ever made as the manager of Liverpool Football Club! Bob gave the cup a quick rub down with a towel, found the lid among the teacups, placed it in position and we were ready to go. A couple of stewards guided Gerry and me down from the dressing room door to the steps leading to the pitch.

On exiting the tunnel (unannounced, I think, but such was the noise any introduction would have been pointless) we weren't initially spotted. There was a little last-minute sorting-out required: Gerry had to be positioned on his good side to get a decent grip on the trophy and, as soon as we moved off towards the Anfield Road stand, the entire ground erupted. Photographers and cameramen appeared from nowhere, swarming around us. By the time we reached the corner flag, the noise was electric; I felt I could touch it. Thousands upon thousands of smiling faces, many with tears in their eyes, were glued to us and the gleaming trophy. Passing behind the Anfield Road goal we felt we were walking on air, propelled along by sound and emotion. It was as if we were somewhere else, somewhere we'd never been. Halfway round, the strain began to tell. The FA Cup is bloody heavy once you've held it above your head for so long! And the longer you hold it, the heavier it gets.

On reaching the Kop we were entering God's country, the very heartbeat of the club. We were bringing them the FA Cup for the first time ever – by special delivery, right on to their doorstep. In front of the Kop, we stopped behind the goal for two reasons: one, this was right in the middle of 26,000 swaying bodies paying homage to the achievement of their beloved football club and respecting the proof in front of their very eyes; and the second reason? We both needed a breather!

Having watched and waited patiently for our arrival in front of them, the Kop's response that night was unprecedented. The volume went up several notches, how, I don't know, because it was ear-splitting to begin with.

It was impossible not to be affected by it all. We struggled along the final stretch in front of the Main Stand, lifting the cup high again for one last time before disappearing down the tunnel.

We all know there have been numerous massive occasions at Anfield since then. But that night was different. What we did was completely unexpected; the fans certainly had no inkling we'd be showing off the cup – 20 minutes earlier, nor had we – but the fervour was already building long before we appeared. The supporters were still on a high after Wembley, Anfield was jam-packed and Inter Milan were in town. The scene was already set without Gerry and me doing what we did. But when we came out, the night jumped to a different level.

Back in the now deserted dressing room (the lads having headed out into the cauldron), Gerry and I looked at one another. We were both exhausted, looking like two rag dolls, shirts wet through with sweat, our suit and tie approach in complete disarray. We were a sorry sight. The fact that the dressing room was empty only enhanced the sense of mystique. It all felt so unreal. Neither of us showed any urgency to go out to watch the match. We were sitting in wonderland.

Gerry looked at me, with his one good arm on the cup and a smile on his face as big as the moon. In his lovely quiet way, he said, 'Listen, Gord, you missed the cup final, and we're both missing this one tonight. But I'll tell you something: what we've just done is a first. Never been done before, ever, in the history of this football club.' He paused. 'And there's only you and I who have done it, Gord. You and I. Nobody else.' Gerry was never a great talker, but his words were perfect. He and I were the chosen ones. And what it did for me, having missed the cup final and about to miss the two Inter matches, was cancel out those disappointments. It's now part of Liverpool folklore, and was very, very special. I've met so many supporters who talk about what Gerry and I did but can't remember much about the match. It was a masterstroke by Shanks, but I don't think even he fully realised the effect it would have.

I've talked throughout this book about beginnings, and where the club subsequently went, and that evening was another: the very first magical European night at Anfield. It set the standards for all such nights to follow and was incomparable to anything else I ever experienced. I won my first cap for England, against Brazil at Wembley. You might think, *Christ almighty, you can't get any bigger than that! 100,000 at Wembley, and against Brazil too!* I played for England in the FA's Centenary match against the Rest of the World, again at Wembley, again in front of 100,000 fans, against players such as Lev Yashin, Ferenc Puskás, Josef Masopust, Denis Law, Eusébio, Di Stéfano … There was Scotland at Hampden Park in front of 134,000, the biggest crowd I ever played in front of. And Brazil at the Maracanã in Rio, against Pelé and the rest of them. If I'd only experienced one of those four occasions I'd count myself very fortunate, but to feature in all four, all leaving lifetime memories, remains something to treasure, truly unforgettable. All that said, though, compared to walking around Anfield lifting the FA Cup with Gerry – well, that night outstrips all those occasions by a million miles.

Who would have thought my greatest memory would be an occasion when I didn't even play? When people ask what I remember most from my career I don't say playing in front of thousands, I don't bring up a crucial goal I scored, or when someone stuck a medal in my hand. I always come back to that evening at Anfield, and the most memorable of pre-match strolls.

To this day I can't remember where we sat to watch the match (probably due to exhaustion) but I do remember the noise. Shanks had released the atom bomb by sending us out first. You couldn't hear yourself think, and if you were playing you wouldn't have been able to hear your team-mates, that's for sure. But, swept along by the supporters, the lads did the club proud once again. Goals from Roger, Cally and the Saint meant we'd take a 3-1 lead to the second leg in Milan. Our first European Cup Final was, hopefully, just 90 minutes away.

* * *

The second leg in Milan is also now part of Liverpool folklore, but unfortunately for all the wrong reasons. There's no sugar-coating it: we felt cheated.

Arriving at the San Siro stadium was cold, hostile, unwelcoming and lively. You'd expect that, of course, and in fairness I don't know what reception the Inter players received at Anfield, so who knows – a bit of touché, maybe? But before the match, and most certainly throughout it, there was the constant nagging feeling that it wasn't going to be our night, that whatever we did wouldn't be enough. If we scored, they'd always score next. A 3-0 win would have done for Inter (the away goals rule was yet to be introduced in the competition). And that's exactly what they got. There has long been a conspiracy theory surrounding this match, that it was fixed from the start. True or not, it certainly felt that way.

To put it mildly, the referee was dodgy. The first Inter Milan goal came from a free kick just outside the box. Firstly, it wasn't even a foul. Then the referee pushed the Liverpool wall further and further back, much further than it should have been. Finally, it's widely thought – at least by Liverpool fans – that the free kick should have been indirect, but when Mario Corso belted it in at the near post the referee happily let the goal stand.

The second goal was even more controversial. Again, Liverpool fans remain convinced of wrongdoing, that Tommy Lawrence had the ball kicked out of his hands. I was in full agreement, but the mind plays tricks. I can almost see the incident now, and in my mind's eye it was a definite foul. However, having recently seen the footage it's clear the ball wasn't in Tommy's hands when Peiró nipped it off his toes before scoring. It's disappointing: more than half a century's belief wiped out by a couple of mouse clicks on a computer! Our two-goal lead had been wiped out and there was still 80 minutes left. Giacinto Facchetti gave Inter the aggregate lead in the second half, after which the Saint had a goal disallowed, allegedly for offside, I think, although I still don't know for sure. And that was that. We were out.

For Gerry and I, high up in the gods behind the goal, watching this was horrible. There were plenty of Inter fans nearby, and a sense of discomfort hung over us both. I'm pretty sure we sat still all night without exchanging a single word. We were so far from the dressing rooms that we stayed in our seats during half-time, too. And at full time, let's just say the stewards weren't the most helpful. It wasn't a pleasant experience, none of it, and losing just made it worse. But remember, this was all new to us. We'd never experienced anything like it before, so in Europe we weren't battle-hardened. In such situations we were horribly inexperienced. You'd never call the likes of the Saint and Big Ron, or Roger and Tommy, naive, but we all lacked familiarity with such tactics and gamesmanship.

However, in the long run, the experience helped. Bob, I'm sure, benefitted tremendously from such encounters, and a decade or so down the line used all the knowledge he'd gained to conquer Europe three times. That night in Milan was a 'welcome to the real world' moment. This was what European football was all about. But as we'd never been in such a situation before we shouldn't have been too hard on ourselves. The only way to gain European experience is by playing in European competition. As the referee and Inter went about their business that night in Milan, perhaps we were on a hiding to nothing from the start? Perhaps we never had a chance in the first place? Either way, we weren't clever enough to shut it all down because we'd simply not learned how to. If we'd had the knowledge, the experience, the know-how, I think it would have been different. The likes of the Saint, Tommy Smith, Ronnie Moran and Big Ron would never have taken any shenanigans lying down; they'd have been right into the opposition, and the referee, and wouldn't have given a s**t about it.

The lesson was eventually learned. But that night, we learned it the hard way.

* * *

On 28 December 1965, we travelled to Elland Road for the second leg of a double header. Leeds had already beaten us in the league ... the previous day! Incredibly, we faced each other home and away on consecutive days. Peter Lorimer scored the only goal at Anfield but 24 hours later we reversed the scoreline, G. Milne truly doing the damage from a corner (I like to think of it as a towering header ...). At only 5ft 6in, for me to even get my head on the ball, with all the giants in there, was a bloody achievement! For it to end up in the back of the net obviously gave me even more satisfaction, and when it turned out to be the winner, I was on cloud nine! Certain things stick in my mind and that goal is one of them. And whenever I watch a match from Elland Road, I find myself looking at the left-hand goal and always remember. (Similarly, at Stamford Bridge, today I could stand within a square yard of where I got injured prior to the 1965 FA Cup Final.)

Back-to-back fixtures were a throwback to my childhood. Christmas Day and Boxing Day always seemed to involve double headers, although they were rarely festive; two teams kicking the shit out of one another on the 25th, then doing it again on Boxing Day at the other ground. They were often high-scoring affairs. One Christmas Day, Newcastle United lost 4-1 at home to Nottingham Forest, then won 3-2 away the next day; Chelsea beat Portsmouth 7-4 at Stamford Bridge but lost 3-0 at Fratton Park 24 hours later. The festive programme was a huge part of the season, and back-to-back fixtures were special. Years later we'd play three times in four days: Good Friday, Easter Saturday and Easter Monday, a time of year when league championships were won and lost. The matches were so close together and you just couldn't call them. Magic.

Following my Elland Road triumph, the following match on 1 January was against another huge rival, Manchester United. At 1-1, in the 88th minute, who should pop up with the winner but yours truly again! (You couldn't make this stuff up!) Again, it was a header, and again came from a corner. The ball fell to Gerry (Christ knows what he was doing up there) and he smashed it towards the goal. Standing in the six-yard box I literally stuck my neck out. The ball flicked off my head and flew into the net

– in front of the Kop, too! Our two biggest rivals had been done, either side of new year, and 'Milne' went down in the record books as the scorer of both winning goals, rarities to savour that played a big part in us going on to win the championship. I wasn't always the man for the big occasion, but every so often … well, I had my moments. And it's nice to look back on them with a little bit of romance.

It was a fantastic season for the city as 1966 saw us clinch the First Division championship once again, and although our defence of the FA Cup was as poor as it could be, losing 2-1 at home to Chelsea in the third round, our neighbours Everton flew the Merseyside flag, defeating Sheffield Wednesday 3-2 at Wembley to ensure the famous old trophy remained in Liverpool for another year. The league title was sealed in our penultimate match, against Chelsea at Anfield, with a 2-1 win thanks to a brace from Roger. We rounded off the domestic season with a 1-1 draw away at Nottingham Forest with a certain G. Milne scoring the final goal of the campaign, ultimately finishing six points clear of Leeds United. Between those two fixtures, however, sat an historic occasion: Liverpool Football Club's first European final.

* * *

In 1964 I'd played for England against Scotland at Hampden Park in Glasgow in front of 134,000 supporters, the biggest attendance of my career. Two years later I returned for the European Cup Winners' Cup Final, Liverpool against Germany's Borussia Dortmund. It was a vastly different affair.

The semi-final had thrown up a 'Battle of Britain': us against Celtic. If that wasn't mouth-watering enough, the final would be played at Hampden Park in Celtic's home city of Glasgow. To say our opposition would be 'up for it' would have been an understatement. However, we were equally determined.

As 60,000 supporters welcomed us to Parkhead for the first leg, it's fair to say the Liverpool fans were outnumbered! It was hostile and aggressive, which we fully expected. We couldn't hear ourselves think. Yes, it was 'Scotland vs England' but both managers were Scots (Jock Stein and Bill Shankly was a real heavyweight collision) and we had four players from north of the border – Big Ron, the Saint, Tommy Lawrence and Willie Stevenson. None of that mattered to the Celtic fans, though. The gates closed long before kick-off, the atmosphere boiled and the hostility bubbled.

The match was played at a ferocious tempo, was incredibly physical, but never over the top. Celtic were a great team that went on to win the European Cup in 1967, the first British club to do so (the famous Lisbon Lions defeated Inter Milan, who had dashed our European hope two years earlier). They had some terrific players such as their captain Billy McNeill. I've been fortunate enough to cross paths with numerous greats of the game and Billy was right up there with the best of them. He knew how to handle every type of player, opposition or team-mate. After nearly two decades playing for Celtic, he's certainly worthy of the term 'legend' and is rightly recognised as such. He sadly passed away in 2019 but a statue of the great man outside Celtic Park ensures he'll never be forgotten. Our own captain, Big Ron, was so similar, as a player and a character, and theirs was a close contest, one that was replicated all over the park.

The match had all the ingredients you wanted, all of which were chucked into the melting pot: Celtic/Liverpool, Scotland/

England; two massive clubs, two iconic managers, two Goliaths for captains; both teams looking to attack, talented internationals all over the pitch … I don't recall too much, but it lived up to expectations, put it that way. The bruising encounter saw us lose 1-0 but didn't disappoint in terms of spectacle.

At Anfield the second leg was the same, but also different, primarily because of the invasion of Celtic fans. They travelled in huge numbers, which Liverpool had never experienced. Photographs taken the following day showed the terraces previously occupied by the 'away' supporters. The clean-up had begun but there remained rows and rows of beer bottles, cans, whisky bottles, you name it! They were six or eight deep on the steps, the walls, the track – we'd never seen anything like it! On the night itself they matched our supporters for noise, helping to create another phenomenal atmosphere. Thankfully, we got the right result, a 2-0 victory, thanks to Tommy Smith and Geoff Strong, although it took an hour to break Celtic down.

Both legs lived up to their billing, and then some. Any hostility was kept under control, but no quarter was given or taken. It's a pity it wasn't the final. Had it been, I don't know how you'd have picked a favourite. The fact that Celtic went on to win the European Cup the following year (I often wonder to what extent their defeat at our hands stood them in good stead) emphasised just how big a win it was for us. Two epic matches had taken us to the final and we'd denied Celtic the opportunity of playing for European silverware in their home city. Had they been victorious, you can guarantee the atmosphere for the final at Hampden Park would have been very different to the one we encountered.

With the final being played in Glasgow we assumed that would be to our advantage. We saw it as home soil, and our Scottish contingent would certainly have felt comfortable. Following the blockbuster tie against Celtic (and, in my case, recalling my last visit to Hampden Park in front of 134,000 people) we all anticipated a big turnout and a night of noisy expectation. The reality was quite different. On a miserable, stormy evening, a crowd of just over 41,000 filled around a third of Hampden's capacity, and with the fans spread at both ends of the ground, the cavernous terracing looked sparse and uninviting. The fans were so far back, through the mist and rain, that we could hardly see them! And despite most attendees being from Liverpool, there was a complete lack of atmosphere. We weren't kidding ourselves that the crowd would have matched that of Scotland vs England, but we certainly expected more than we got; after all, it was a European final.

That night against Borussia Dortmund we did little to stop the match sliding away from us and lost 2-1 after extra time. Shanks and Bob must have been bitterly disappointed with our performance. We all were. I'd be surprised if anyone watching thought any one of us had a good game. We were all a bit soapy, a bit in between, but there was no reason to be that way. The occasion required much more than we produced. Perhaps the subdued atmosphere rubbed off on us. Either way, we struggled from the very first whistle.

Aside from the atmosphere, there was still that naivety about us, echoes of what had cost us against Inter Milan, that basic lack of experience. It applied to the players, to Shanks, to Bob, to everyone at the club, and it cost us. It would take time to learn and, fortunately for Liverpool, Bob was a quick learner.

When he took the reins following Shanks's departure, Bob put everything he'd learned to good effect. By then he was no longer a novice, like we all were back in the '60s, like we all were against Dortmund.

Perhaps we were just so excited to reach a European final that we lost our focus. Nothing panned out as we'd hoped. We were as flat as the atmosphere. But the atmosphere is only created by the performance of the players … isn't it?

Chapter 9

MAY 1963. At home, in the hallway, the telephone rang. I was in no hurry to pick it up, assuming it would be for Edith (it usually was) but she was nowhere in sight. I lifted the receiver and a male voice said, 'Is that you, Gordon?' Before I could say yes, the voice continued. 'It's Frank McGhee here from the *Daily Mirror*. I just thought you'd like to know you've been selected to play for England against Brazil at Wembley on 8 May.' I sat down at the bottom of the stairs.

'Is that right?' I replied meekly. 'Are you sure that's right?'

'You'll read all about it in tomorrow's papers,' he said. 'Congratulations.' And he put the phone down. As daft as it sounds, that's how you found out in those days. I must have sat for three or four minutes before Edith appeared. 'Is everything okay?' she asked. 'Who was that? Is there a problem?'

'I've just been picked for England,' I muttered.

'Oh, that's alright then,' she said.

It was a moment never to be forgotten. If you think of the achievements of someone like Sir Tom Finney – capped 76 times, 30 international goals, the first player to be named Footballer of the Year twice, to name just three – at age 83 he could still articulate, clearly and precisely, the date and time he learned of his first-ever cap, and what it meant to him. I hope those values remain and are respected in the same way today. To wear the white shirt of England for the very first time meant so much to so many very special players – better players than I ever was. For me to achieve the same honour as such icons was overwhelming. I felt like I didn't deserve such an accolade; like I didn't deserve to reach the same level as those greats of the game; like I didn't belong in their company. To receive the same news as them was incredibly humbling.

Incidentally, there were no congratulations from Shanks. Perhaps it would have been different if I'd been selected for Scotland!

* * *

Joining any new team brings a sense of trepidation; as dictated by human nature, its presence is inevitable, unavoidable and uncontrollable. What can be controlled, at least to a certain degree, is the level of that trepidation. That's where an individual's character comes into play; that will see him sink or swim. A new team means a new manager, new tactics and new faces. Football will always be a team game, and without your team-mates, you're nothing. No matter how talented, skilful and committed, a player can't achieve anything on their own; success or otherwise will be shaped and defined by those alongside them. At international level, that sentiment is magnified.

My initiation to international football was as low-key as it gets, for which I was thankful. Alf Ramsey simply welcomed me to the squad and that was it. I was grateful there were no bells and whistles; I just wanted to get on with it. Don't get me wrong, I felt that trepidation in the pit of my stomach, but it was tempered by the excitement of what lay ahead. I was as thrilled and excited as any Englishman who had gone before me and couldn't wait to get started.

When I was initially selected it dawned on me – people said it to me, too – that, at that moment, I was viewed as the best No. 4 in the country. I felt I was under the microscope much more than at Liverpool and was more exposed than ever: 'Let's see how good this fella is.' You can't get a much bigger stage than playing at Anfield every other week, but this was a different level. I felt more responsibility than ever before. Every single time I pulled on the shirt I had to justify my selection. I tried my utmost to think of nothing beyond the 90 minutes; a challenge in itself, but one I relished and would never shirk.

There were lessons to be learned everywhere I looked. One of the first was how to flick the switch between club and country, not 'what was better' or 'what I preferred', but in terms of prioritising. I quickly realised international football, by its very nature, is a switch-on/off affair. It wasn't easy, but day-to-day life had to be put to one side and attentions turned to the matter in hand. Mental strength is a huge factor in football at the best of times but on international duty its importance is multiplied; the mindset must be different and must be right. If your club form isn't as good as it could be, you're conscious of that, and if you're picked for England after a month of mediocrity you can't just switch off that form and expect to play like a top international. Equally, your personal form might be okay but your club is in the doldrums. Such day-to-day trials and tribulations aren't easy to park.

My first England appearance felt blessed. Firstly, it was against the magical Brazil. If you had the choice, you wouldn't pick any other country to face on your debut. Secondly, this was the first match where the England manager himself selected the team. Previously, selection was in the hands of the FA Select Committee. However, on being appointed England manager, Alf insisted on, and received, total control over team selection. That was important to me, it was vindication. I'd been picked by a single selector, not a committee, meaning he rated and had faith in me, which boosted my confidence no end. My inclusion was an honour, a privilege and extremely humbling. And exciting.

Revisiting the names of my team-mates on that day, I must have been doing something right to be included in such celebrated company. Eight of that starting 11 would feature in Alf's World Cup-winning squad three years later, but I never felt overawed, despite the stature of the players in the dressing room. On 8 May 1963, against Brazil at Wembley, my first England appearance saw me line up alongside Gordon Banks, Jimmy Armfield (captain), Bobby Moore, Maurice Norman, Ray Wilson, Bobby Charlton, Bryan Douglas, Jimmy Greaves, Bobby Smith and George Eastham. Despite my inevitable butterflies, such illustrious company (and the opposition) gave me a lift. I did okay. We drew 1-1, although I should have scored after just 20 seconds!

Five months later I won my fifth cap, against the Rest of the World, as part of the FA celebration marking 100 years of Association Football. That day I shared a pitch with household names now recognised as legends: Lev Yashin, Ferenc Puskás, Djalma Santos, Uwe Seeler, Jim Baxter, Raymond Kopa, Josef Masopust, Denis Law, Eusébio, Alfredo Di Stéfano. Even now, as I write these names, I feel a chill and can't believe how fortunate I've been. England won 2-1 with Jimmy Greaves scoring the winner in the final minute.

I'd experienced Greavsie before, of course. One of our earliest encounters still shakes me to this day. In August 1959 we (Preston North End) drew 4-4 at Chelsea (I wasn't playing), with Greavsie scoring three. In December, at Deepdale, I was selected and received strict instructions from the manager Cliff Britton to man-mark Mr Greaves: 'Where he goes, you go.' I wouldn't say I was brought in to tighten up the defence, as that certainly wasn't my forte, but I knew I had a job to do. Another incredible match finished Preston 4 Chelsea 5 – Greavsie scored all five! And he was still only 19 years old! The words 'where he goes, you go' still ring in my ears today. I swear I was never more than a yard away from him, yet he still scored five! In the dressing room afterwards, trying not to look at Tom Finney, Tommy Thompson, Willie Cunningham and the rest, I was numb.

Playing against Jimmy was like playing against a ghost. He'd flit here, there and everywhere, and had the art of loitering and looking disinterested down to a tee. He'd let you get close, but would drift – quickly, if that makes sense – and if he got a yard on you, he was gone. Today, everyone talks about work rate and pressing but few mention the art of standing still (and finding space by doing so). My dad had an expression: 'Running like hell to get there last,' referring to someone running with no real purpose. Jimmy was the total opposite: loitering, but *with* purpose. He wouldn't move – seemingly – but would still get there first, knowing before anyone where and when the ball would arrive. And when he did get there first, he could finish. A cross would come in and before you knew what had happened the ball had hit the back of the net. Front post, back post, one-on-one – it didn't matter. He never panicked, he had the patience to wait; he'd pass the ball into the net (you rarely saw him have a blast), or maybe take it around the keeper first. Everything looked so easy. Greavsie: one of the best finishers of the English game. In one respect, how he played reflected his personality – the cheeky chappie cockney who, in every way, was just that bit sharper than you.

Jimmy didn't think too deeply about the game, he'd just go out and play. He gave the impression he wasn't too interested in training or tactics, a bit like George Best. Bestie lived a life, when he was young, that he shouldn't have been living, yet his exceptional ability simply couldn't be ignored. He lived the way he chose to, and although everybody tried to change him, nobody could, he was his own man. When you talk about a genius you often talk about his flaws; there's something in there that makes him different. That was Bestie, and for me, Jimmy too.

Perhaps that's what Alf felt. What happened with Jimmy in 1966 remains a talking point to this day. He played in all three of England's World Cup group matches before a nasty gash to the shin meant he missed the quarter-final against Argentina. Geoff Hurst replaced him and scored the only goal of the match. Greavsie was still injured for the semi-final against Portugal, so Geoff kept his place. And when England won that one, that's when it got tricky, because for many there was a history. The manager had a big decision to make.

I always felt – and I stress, this is my view only – that there was a hidden agenda between Jimmy and Alf. Alf knew all about Greavsie. He was no shrinking violet, however, so most people knew a bit about him! He liked a drink, yes, which Alf wasn't too keen on, but he wasn't the only one. It was much more prevalent than it is today, but there were certain ways of going about it. Bobby Moore, for example, liked a drink too, but did it quietly, out of the spotlight, whereas Jimmy would drink in the pub with the fans after a game, happy – and proud – to do so. I'm sure that was a factor in Alf keeping Jimmy at arm's length. They were never totally comfortable with each other, there was never any real warmth between them, although Jimmy was never openly disrespectful towards Alf. To me it was very noticeable, and during all my time with England it was something I never saw between Alf and any other player.

I suspect all that did influence Alf's final selection. Geoff kept his place, Roger was picked again and Jimmy missed out. Not an easy decision, I'm sure. Yes, Greavsie took a nasty one against France, but it was only a gash. He hadn't torn or broken anything and made it clear to the manager he was fit and ready. I wasn't in the inner circle, of course, but my feeling is that Jimmy was indeed okay to play or, at the very least, he wasn't unavailable as was widely reported, so I fully understand why he buggered off into town after the celebration dinner. England may have won the World Cup, but he was p***ed off.

All that said, you can't argue with Alf's decision. Given what happened with Roger and Geoff playing together it would have been difficult for the manager not to put them first, and splitting their partnership to accommodate Jimmy would have been equally contentious. Alf's team won in dramatic style on a day that will live in our memories forever. But so too will the genius of Jimmy Greaves.

* * *

International football requires a real leap of faith in one's own ability. Some embrace it, others are cowed by it. Some just 'get it' straight away – the likes of Jimmy Armfield, Martin Peters,

Alan Ball and Ray Wilson. Ray was a top left-back, very highly rated, who just went out and did what he did seemingly without thinking. Greavsie was another. Some had the ability to succeed but had to work harder mentally. Others had the ability but were never classed as top internationals, a category you could only fall into with a certain number of caps on the table. On the international stage you were judged on how many times you were picked, so realistically (and remembering there were fewer international fixtures back then) it could take three or four years before a player received the full recognition he deserved. It's a matter of experience, too: the player with more helps the team-mate with less. Bobby Moore was a great example. He had a nonchalance about him, strolling around like Cool Hand Luke. His natural persona rubbed off on others and, in my case, helped give me the confidence to be myself. Bobby Charlton played more instinctively, raising his game whenever it was required; again, that helped the rest of us to do the same.

The next step was one of education. International managers often say, 'Go and play like you do for your club,' but it's never that simple. I'd earned my call-up due to my form for Liverpool, but that form was a result of training and playing with the same lads, day in, day out. But with England, there was so little time. I was now the new boy, but my team-mates were new too. We all had to learn – quickly – how to play with each other.

I found international football to be much more of a mental test. Us new boys had everything to learn, whereas those who had played 30 or 40 times had an inner confidence simply due to their experience. Nevertheless, at its most basic level, we were still a group of individuals and fitting in was a challenge. I was now playing with strangers. I didn't know their inner workings:

where they'd be when I was on the ball; the runs they'd make (or not); how, when and where they'd want to receive the ball (or not); how they'd deal with difficult situations (or not). Jimmy Armfield played very differently to Bobby Charlton, who played very differently to Jimmy Greaves, and so on. Receiving the ball from those three was very different to receiving the ball from Gerry, Roger, Cally, or any of my clubmates. To play instinctively – always the best way – was the immediate challenge, but the ultimate aim. I had to learn on the hoof, in real time. Practice sessions were limited so where I'd have to produce – and where I'd be judged – would be out on the pitch in front of 100,000 people. Furthermore, there was no guarantee I'd be playing with the same team-mates in consecutive matches, so new relationships would need to be developed all over again. Does he want it early? Is he a give-and-go merchant? Establishing that telepathy is rarely instant and never easy. While studying my team-mates I'd also be considering my own game, trying to do the right thing, fit in, give a proper pass to somebody. These were things any player would think about but at international level you were more conscious of them; it became *too* easy to think *too much*.

Club versus country is an age-old discussion. At club level only local opinion really matters. That brings its own pressure, but one diluted by the volume of matches and familiarity with team-mates. We didn't have to prove ourselves to the supporters as they watched us every week, so knew when we were drifting, having a stinker or just having one of those days. At Liverpool, such performances would be absorbed by the group; they were never acceptable, but it's much easier to get away with a poor individual performance yet still end up on the winning team. At Anfield, making a mistake didn't come into your head, but if it happened you moved on so quickly that you didn't think too much about it. You couldn't do that at international level. If you gave the ball away for England the effect was amplified, regardless of the outcome, and weighed far more heavily upon you. The spotlight is bigger and brighter and shines from much further afield. You're seen and judged by the whole bloody country. I quickly became ultra-aware of not wanting to make a balls-up.

That can be daunting. At its most basic level my England debut was on the wide-open spaces of Wembley, in front of 100,000 people (at that point the biggest crowd of my career), alongside ten lads who I'd never played with in my life, all of which heightened my self-awareness and forced me to be more self-centred. And that was without considering the rest of the country watching! There was the opposition to think about too, although it's worth remembering even the great Brazil were in the same boat as us: a team of superstars, granted, but they too would come together from numerous club teams, and they too would have to find a way to gel.

'Switching on' immediately was also necessary to adapt to the opposition, their different styles, methods and tactics, something I'd soon come across with Liverpool in Europe. In the First Division, most teams played roughly the same way and the tempo of the matches remained fairly constant. But those early years in Europe were an eye-opener and took time to get to grips with. We'd play against teams who seemingly never wanted to get out of their own half but who would keep the ball forever. We'd soon realise they were going nowhere, but also realise we hadn't had a kick for five minutes. International football was similar: players and teams didn't act (or react) in the same way as in domestic football. This, though, was nothing new.

In 1953, England met Hungary at Wembley. A very good English team including Billy Wright, Stanley Matthews, Stan Mortensen and Alf Ramsey himself, were torn to shreds by a team playing a brand of football unlike anything ever experienced before. Led by Ferenc Puskás, the Hungarians won 6-3. It was a result and performance that shook English football to its core, leading to an in-depth and detailed review of our national game, and rightly so. Compared to what these lads had come up with, we looked as if we'd been playing in the bloody Stone Age!

Hungary's demolition of England pointed the FA towards a new footballing blueprint, but certain elements of international football were set in stone – like club rivalries. At Liverpool I was winning things but someone like Jimmy Armfield (a far better player than me and someone who could have joined any club he wanted) spent his entire career at Blackpool and didn't win a bean! Tom Finney played a different bloody ball game but, in terms of medals, had very little to show for it. I recall West Ham struggling but it wouldn't affect Bobby Moore, whereas us Liverpool lads would turn up, buoyed by success, yet not have anywhere near the same effect on the England squad as Bobby. Club success meant England supporters *expected* us to perform, just as we expected it of ourselves. More pressure.

Head-to-head records played a part too. We all have a natural inclination to prove our own worth, and players weigh each other up throughout a season – Bobby directly faced Roger, for example – but on England duty, any domestic altercations that may have occurred had to be put to one side. 'Suspicion' isn't the right word, but certain players watched others closely. I never felt that way, though. To use Bobby as an example once again, regardless of how good he was on the pitch or how nice he was off it, I wasn't concerned whether he'd had a good game or not against Liverpool. As far as I was concerned, with England he and I were team-mates and aiming at the same target. That said, it's only natural that cliques form, that Manchester United players stick together, that Liverpool lads do too. It's not cut and dried, mind, as certain guys from different clubs just gel, whether it's over football philosophies, the liking of a glass or two or a love of the horses.

As joyful as it was to represent my country, I was stepping out of my comfort zone. At Liverpool, familiarity took the pressure off, whereas with England, although I may have had one or two clubmates alongside me, relatively speaking I was on my own. And let's be honest here, there were egos involved. As ever, certain players were more self-centred than others – characteristics that ordinarily wouldn't be on show would suddenly appear on the international stage. What's more, England get-togethers were much smaller, more intimate affairs, so if a disagreement or confrontation took place, everyone knew about it.

However, regardless of any altercations that may have occurred, playing alongside such good players was only going to help me, and I knew it. I'd already had that with Liverpool, where alongside such talent I couldn't help but improve. International football was an extension of that. Having someone like Bobby Moore on the same team was never a hardship.

* * *

On the eve of the 1966 World Cup Final, Alf Ramsey famously took the England squad to the pictures (Alf loved it: I remember going to the cinema when I was involved). As they arrived, my pal Roger Hunt felt a tap on his shoulder: 'Roger, a little word with you please.' Alf took Roger to one side and whispered, 'I'd just like you to know that you'll be playing tomorrow.' No more, no less. At the time, Rog said it was the best thing that ever happened to him, although with hindsight was less certain: 'I wasn't sure if it was a good thing or not … I was so excited, I didn't sleep a wink that night.'

It was Alf's way: functional, practical, no nonsense. In 1963, against the Rest of the World, my captain was Jimmy Armfield who, at right-back, found himself up against the Real Madrid superstar and Spanish legend Paco Gento. Alf's instructions to him were clear: 'Stop Gento. Keep him under control. I know you like to get forward, but not today please.' Jimmy's instinct took over, however. England attacked and he was off, but when the ball was lost and Gento countered, Jimmy was stranded. Fortunately, it came to nothing. At half-time Alf approached Jimmy: 'Jimmy, did you not understand what I told you before the game?' His demeanour was quiet, but firm, and very, very, clear. 'If you do that again I will be very disappointed.' What Alf was saying, without actually saying it, was that if you disappointed the England manager twice you wouldn't be around for the next match. Like Shanks when he talked to Bob, the message was in there somewhere.

Sometimes, though, the message was delivered in a manner that left no question marks. Leaving the dressing room after one Wembley match, Gordon Banks shouted, 'See you next time, Alf!' Alf turned to face him. 'Gordon …' he said. The dressing room fell silent. The pause lasted a lifetime. '… if selected.' Banksy's big cheesy grin disappeared pretty sharpish! Another pause followed, much shorter, before the whole room burst into laughter. Everyone except Banksy, that is. His mouth fell open, still (sort of) smiling, but his eyes told a different story: 'I wish I'd just left and not said anything.'

Behind the humour, though, was brilliant management. In as few words as possible, Alf delivered his message: 'Don't take it for granted.' And not just to Banksy but to all of us; if Alf could say that to the brilliant Banks, none of us were safe – and we all understood that. Whereas Shanks would speak to the entire squad to make us think as individuals, Alf had picked on an individual to convey his message to the group. Clever. Diametrically opposed methods, yet strikingly similar and equally brilliant.

Unlike Shanks, though, Alf did speak individually to players. I can't really remember him addressing the group, other than generic welcomes at the beginning of a get-together, and there were certainly no great tactical discussions involving the whole squad. But being as we were all relative strangers, and didn't spend a great deal of time together, an international manager had to be a bit more one-on-one.

I mentioned that Alf wasn't particularly warm towards Greavsie but that sentiment wasn't exclusive towards Jimmy. When I first joined up, Alf said something like, 'It's a pleasure to see you, well done, you're here on merit,' and that was it. Alf came from that old school; he held selection for England in high regard, and as it was through him that you were there, that should be enough. Again, like Shanks, Alf never wanted to complicate the situation. I think back sometimes and wish I'd said more to him or asked him whether he was happy with what I was doing, but my view was that if he didn't say anything, you were alright; no news is good news. That said, if there was something he felt he needed to say, he'd say it, and have no problem in doing so.

The challenges of playing for your country are plentiful, but I imagine managing England is equally difficult, if not more so. The players aren't yours, you're only renting them, and not for long either. With Alf, it was square pegs in square holes. He picked players to do the same job they were doing for their clubs. 'Keep it simple.' In football terms, it's a phrase that still resonates today.

* * *

Having missed the FA Cup Final in 1965 through injury, you could argue I was unlucky. But missing out on selection for the World Cup squad in 1966 was a different matter. I had to accept I simply wasn't good enough. And as those who were selected went on to win the bloody thing, I couldn't really argue, could I?

The opening fixture, England against Uruguay, took place on 11 July at Wembley. Three months prior to that, Alf had named a provisional squad of 40 players. I was one of them. A month later, 40 became 28. Again, my name was on the list. Throughout this period Alf gave nothing away. During training I'd play with Geoff Hurst one day, Jimmy Greaves the next, and so on. Alf mixed the teams up all the time. He never gave any real hints, although there were certain players – the two Bobbys, for example, Charlton and Moore – who we all knew would make the team. On 18 June the squad was cut to just 22 players. I was invited to Alf's room.

'Come in, Gordon. Please sit down.' I sat on the sofa; Alf sat opposite me. 'Now, Gordon, I have information which I wish to pass on to you.' It was how Alf spoke, clipped tones and to the point. And certainly no emotion. 'I'm afraid you will not be a member of the final squad of 22. I'd like to thank you very much for all you've done for England.'

'Okay, Alf. I understand. Thank you.' I got up and walked out. There was nothing to say. Or do. I couldn't throw the bloody cushions at him, could I?

The news was devastating, of course, but his approach was the only way; like ripping off a plaster, it had to be done quickly. Years later I'd truly grasp the importance of his method: as a manager, the more you waffle, the bigger the hole you create for yourself. Brevity of execution is crucial for all involved. Deliver the news, receive the news, move on. Peter Thompson, my Liverpool team-mate, went through the same experience, although I never understood why because he was flying at the time; I thought he was a shoo-in. However, thankfully, Gerry Byrne, Ian Callaghan and Roger Hunt were all selected.

Now, picture the scene: the five of us from Liverpool, all sharing a car, leaving Lilleshall for the journey home. Roger at the wheel, Peter next to him, Gerry, Cally and myself in the back. We were listening to the news on the radio: 'The England manager Alf Ramsey has selected his final squad of 22 players for the upcoming World Cup. The following have all been selected ...' Before the newsreader named the first of the fortunate few, Roger leaned forward and gently turned the radio off. Nobody batted an eyelid. Nobody said a word. Because nobody knew what to say. I imagine Roger, Gerry and Cally were on cloud nine, but at the same time sick on our behalf. And as disappointed as Peter and I were, we were equally delighted for those three.

I do remember I didn't want to embarrass myself by saying anything daft, and I'm sure the others all felt the same. Five

Liverpool players on a two-hour journey together; you'd never believe how little conversation there was!

It was hugely disappointing, of course, but totally different to missing the cup final the previous year. I suppose I could have been picked by Alf but not played at all, which would have been different again. Several players experienced just that, Gerry for one, and Cally only featured in one match. Roger's contribution shouldn't be underestimated though, playing every match and scoring three times. Geoff Hurst scored just one more than Roger, but three of them were of course in the final! As it was, for me such achievements remained tantalisingly close but forever out of reach. I had to take it on the chin but have no regrets. I simply wasn't up to snuff.

However, representing my country was never a burden, never a chore. Every single appearance was, without fail, an honour, a privilege and a tremendous thrill. And when I look at the names of those former team-mates, it's hard to believe I was ever in their company. I must have been doing something right.

Chapter 10

IN SEPTEMBER 2021 my dear old pal Roger Hunt passed away. His funeral service took place at Liverpool's magnificent Anglican Cathedral where I was honoured to be asked to say a few words by Roger's wife, Rowan:

> Roger, when Rowan asked me to say a few words I searched for what to say about a friend, a team-mate, a pal. Very quickly I came to the conclusion that you have already said everything in your own calm way, in your own style, with no fuss; from where you always felt most comfortable and happy, and where it really mattered – out there on the football pitch, and especially at your beloved Anfield. It was there that you did your talking, Rog: action, not words; fact not fiction. The record books speak quite clearly on your behalf. It's there for us all to see, and always will be.
>
> The Kop also had something to say to you in their own special way.
>
> At Anfield on October the 3rd they sent a message to you from their hearts, for all the world to see how much they respected and truly loved you. And that message confirms quite clearly Rog, that your story will never

> go to sleep; Liverpool supporters all over the world will make sure of that.

As you'd expect there was a fantastic turnout. Kevin Keegan, Ian Callaghan, Jimmy Tarbuck and I all spoke, and Liverpool Football Club was of course well represented by the likes of Roy Evans, Ian Rush, David Fairclough, David Johnson, Gordon Wallace and John Aldridge. The Professional Footballers' Association's Gordon Taylor was also among the mourners. It was a sad day, of course, but also a day for smiles and reminiscing. We all had stories to tell – possibly even some that hadn't been heard before! Various tales from varied eras, all sharing the common ground of Liverpool Football Club. Likewise, the mourners themselves. Some attendees were at the club yesterday, others from back in my time. Rushie, for example, wasn't particularly close to Roger – their eras were 20 years apart – but his respect for him was there for all to see. (In fairness, it had to be: Rushie remains Liverpool's all-time top scorer, but he didn't net as many league goals as my old pal!)

Chatting to the legendary Cally (just the 857 appearances!) was Gordon Wallace. Gordon's a cracking fella, very popular in and around the club. He played nowhere near as many times as Cally (ironically, thanks in part to Roger being so good), but that doesn't matter a jot. No former player would ever be made to feel inferior to any other, in any way – that's the nature of the club – and nor should he be, of course. In death, as in life, all of us are equal. No superstars, no egos, no person better than the next. 'The Liverpool Way', quite rightly, still ruled. We were all there in mourning, of course, but also laughing, joking and winding each other up. We had a pie and a pint and enjoyed each others' company.

Prior to the service, we were sitting in the cathedral when Cally brought up the 1966 match against Ajax in Amsterdam against Johan Cruyff and company for the first time (I was injured so wasn't involved). That night, the stadium was enveloped in a thick, dense fog – a real pea-souper. As Cally recalled, 'It should never, ever, have been played. You couldn't bloody see! We were two down, early, and were bombing forward trying to get back into it. Shanks was going mad. He was actually on the pitch, five yards inside the line, screaming, "Calm down! Calm down! We've a second leg to play yet! Don't go mad!" He'd have settled for a 2-0 defeat, even 3-0. Because he knew if we weren't careful, we'd get properly turned over, and the tie would be finished on the night, never mind the second leg. And he was right as well. He never got through to us though. We carried on chasing and got trounced 5-1. And we only got the 1 in the last minute!'

The tie was indeed over. We only managed a 2-2 draw back at Anfield (for which I was back in the team; must have been why we had a better result). That was our first introduction to Cruyff, who was still only 19 but already making a name for himself. And then Cally wrapped it up perfectly: 'Cruyff was like a bloody ghost when we could see him! What chance did we have when we couldn't?'

* * *

In March 1967 we met our great rivals Everton in the fifth round of the FA Cup. It was an historic occasion, to this day still the record attendance for a meeting between the two teams – although with a catch. The tie was played at Goodison Park, and with demand for tickets far outweighing the supply, eight giant screens were erected at Anfield to broadcast the match live. All tickets for both grounds were snapped up, around 105,000 in total. For a certain G. Milne, however, this only meant double the pain: twice as many supporters witnessed my sloppy back pass, allowing the Blues to pressure Tommy Lawrence and, from the ensuing melee, Alan Ball rifled home. It remained 1-0 and we were out of the cup.

I remember it well. It's funny how disappointments, mistakes or failures often remain clearer in the mind than some of the good times. At least they do in my case, although it's hard to forget such an error in a city like Liverpool. Following the match I hardly dared to venture out beyond Melwood and Anfield but, when I did, there was, inevitably, always an Everton supporter on hand to remind me of my slip-up. It was the classic triple whammy: a mistake against Everton, knocked out of the cup and, thanks to the big screens, twice as many people saw it. I didn't know it at the time, but I wouldn't be at Liverpool much longer; make of that what you will!

* * *

The end of the season was in sight, and I'd heard from Jimmy Armfield that Blackpool's manager Stan Mortensen was interested in signing me. I had a great relationship with Jimmy. He was a Lancashire lad and we were friends already, having played together for England, so I knew him well. He was a proper football man, Gentleman Jim. It was a pleasure to have known him and his family, and to have called him a friend. So, when Blackpool came to Anfield for the campaign's final fixture, the thought of a possible move had been in my head for three or four weeks already.

Blackpool were a good outfit. Jimmy would say, 'We've got Alan Skirton, Tony Green, Tommy Hutchison – good young players, you'll be alright with us, Gordon. And Stan's a great bloke.'

After the match I was in the corridor outside the Anfield dressing room when I saw Shanks. 'Mr Mortensen wants to talk to you.' That's all he said, and then he left. I'd never met Stan before, but we had a brief word and he asked me to come over to Bloomfield Road on Monday (two days later) for more of a chat. I agreed. And that was that. When the season ends, all the players are in the dressing room, shaking hands. 'Blah blah blah, see you whenever,' and then they're off. And they never see one another until the start of the next pre-season. And that's just how it was that day. I got in my car and went home.

Later, it dawned on me: everybody had gone, and if I was going to sign for Blackpool, I wouldn't see them again. I spent the rest of the weekend thinking about this, that and everything else. On the Monday morning I rang Blackpool and said, 'I'll come over tomorrow.' I then went to Anfield to fetch my boots. I don't remember a conscious, definite, decision, but obviously I'd made one. I had a pair of boots and a pair of rubbers to pick up; they were falling to bits, but I went for them anyway. Dear old Albert Shelley was the only soul at the ground, although I never expected to see anybody else. Albert shook my hand and said something like, 'All the best son, you've been a good servant to the club.' He handed me my boots, which he'd cleaned, bless him, then I made for the exit. I didn't say cheerio to anyone else, as there *wasn't* anyone else to say cheerio to. I drove home, never to return (not as a player, anyway), never to say goodbye to my mates, the staff or the supporters. Thinking back now, it seems an awfully cold way to leave after such a wonderful period of my life, but I don't blame anyone for that; that's just how things were. It certainly wasn't a deliberate snub, or anything like that. I didn't want anything dramatic, of course, but this was the exact opposite. I don't think it would be unreasonable to call it a damp squib.

Shanks had long been interested in signing Emlyn Hughes from Blackpool. He'd actually got his man in February, three months earlier. And although Emlyn didn't directly take my position, I couldn't help but feel the writing was on the wall. I still suspect I was actually part of the deal, and that moving to Blackpool was inevitable; the transfer of Emlyn may have been done with the two clubs agreeing I'd sign for Blackpool a few months down the line. Either way, my days at Liverpool had come to an end. And although I have no regrets, and bear no ill will towards anyone involved, it was a finale that fell some way short of what I'd have wished for.

We finished fifth that season, nine points behind the champions Manchester United. My final Liverpool appearance saw me substituted ten minutes before full time, with Dave Wilson replacing me (his only appearance for the club). I wonder whether Shanks knew I'd be leaving and was offering me the (potential) ovation departing players all seem to be afforded these days? I very much doubt it. If that was the case, the 30-odd thousand fans in attendance that day must have known of my transfer before I did – and there was no ovation anyway! To top it all, we lost 3-1. What a way to bow out. It probably wasn't until the Monday morning, when I went to collect my boots, that things had properly sunk in. My Liverpool career was over.

It all happened so fast. There was nothing from Shanks, no communication at all, other than 'Mr Mortensen wants to talk to you.' As a Liverpool player, the last I saw of Shanks was when he told me Stan wanted a word before turning away and heading back towards the dressing room. But as one door closed, another immediately opened. There was never too much turmoil, and this was no different. I wasn't too happy with Shanks or the way the situation was presented to me but by then I knew his nature. I respected it too and recognised his behaviour as classic Shanks. I've wondered, though – of course I have – what would have happened if I'd said, 'F**k it. I'm not going to Blackpool. I'll turn up for pre-season with Liverpool in five weeks' time and see what's going on then.' I could have done that. But I didn't.

It was uncanny how my departure from Liverpool echoed my arrival. Back then I'd entered an empty car park; now, on my last day, I was leaving the same one, equally deserted. My debut was a home loss against Southampton on a miserable evening, a match in which I contributed very little; my swansong was another home loss in which I was dragged off with ten minutes remaining – an equally grim affair. I left the way I came in. History had repeated itself.

Have boots, will travel.

Chapter 11

JIMMY WAS right: Blackpool had a lot of good players. Glyn James, the Welsh international centre-half, had played 400-odd times for the club; Alan Skirton, ex-Arsenal, a big strong powerful winger; Tony Green and Tommy Hutchison, good young players who went on to bigger things (I actually signed Hutchie for Coventry years later). There was no doubting the club had talent and a manager who, to say the least, was different.

Stan Mortensen was warm and friendly with an incredible sense of humour. A Blackpool and England great, an old-fashioned centre-forward who will always be remembered for the 1953 FA Cup Final. Blackpool came from 3-1 behind to win 4-3 against Bolton Wanderers. The match became known as the 'Matthews Final' – Sir Stanley turned on the magic that day – but it was Stan who scored a hat-trick. A hero to all Blackpool supporters and a very popular figure.

During the Second World War, Stan was a wireless operator air gunner. In April 1943, barely out of his teens, he survived a plane crash that killed two of his colleagues. His injuries deemed him unfit for further operational duties. A career in football seemed equally unlikely, not least due to the metal plate inserted in his head to aid his recovery. How he went on to have such a career is beyond me: nearly 300 goals in almost 500 appearances for Blackpool, Hull City, Southport and Bath City; 25 caps for England, 23 international goals. Many of his goals were headers, too, with that heavy old ball. Perhaps the metal plate helped!

Before managing Blackpool, Stan was a boy about town. He liked a flutter, and his pals in the Blackpool nightspots always supported him. He was never short of employment when it was needed. He once had a summer job helping a pal who owned slot machines in venues around the town, including the railway station. After the last train had departed on a Saturday evening, Stan's job was to empty all the machines. His collection equipment was ten dustbins on wheels. 'I filled every one of these dustbins with pennies,' he told us. 'Full to the brim! And that was just the station! Imagine all the other machines on the seafront, all being filled by holidaymakers! There were no regulations, so we were making bloody fortunes!'

Before training, Stan would appear in the changing rooms, often looking like he'd slept in his raincoat, and within five minutes would have the place rocking with laughter. He'd then disappear for the day. He had a wonderful personality, full of humour and humility that appealed to everybody. Bloomfield Road was a happy home when Stan was there. On matchdays he'd come in, tell more stories, get the team together, then let them go. But it couldn't last.

Stan was an example of what you could get out of players through personality, through his modesty and wit. He didn't take charge of the training, letting Wilf Dixon get on with that. Wilf did so with gusto and enthusiasm; he was a strict disciplinarian who demanded hard work and dedication (he went on to become Harry Catterick's right-hand man at Everton). One of his specialities was track work. It was a return to my Preston days, where track work was part of the curriculum. At Liverpool I never ran round the Anfield track once, so I found this new regime deeply unsatisfying. Wilf's challenging routines, many against the clock, were totally alien to how I'd worked for the previous seven years. Entire mornings passed without even seeing a football, a whistle signalling when to start and stop dictating the scene. I wondered what I'd let myself in for. Jimmy, who could run, said, 'Don't worry, it's only once a week.' I wondered whether I'd survive.

The new season was underway, we'd moved into our new home in Preston, the kids were in the local schools and all was good. It was yet another new challenge, enjoyable, but unfortunately we fell just short. A good season saw us finish third in the Second Division, just one point separating the top three teams. Ipswich Town were crowned champions, and we only missed out on promotion through goal difference (only two teams were promoted), to Queens Park Rangers. To be so close was a bitter disappointment. Not being able to visit Anfield again (at least not yet) was a big personal miss.

* * *

Having come so close to promotion, the following season's dip in form was probably inevitable, and we eventually finished eighth, and with no significant cup run to speak of, it proved to be a bit of a 'nothing season' really. Unfortunately, Stan paid the price and was sacked.

He was replaced by Les Shannon, who was assisted by Jimmy Meadows. Jimmy was a good coach who advised me to adjust my game. At 32 I could no longer be the box-to-box player I always had been. My football brain was still developing but the legs were heading in the opposite direction. Jimmy suggested I sit deeper and pass the ball more than run with it (or indeed, without it). It was sound advice, but unfortunately, I wasn't listening properly. I wasn't being arrogant but, subconsciously, it was something I didn't want to hear. Also, in the back of my mind I was already thinking beyond my playing days. I'd found it considerably harder to maintain a high level of performance and knew my playing days were numbered. One positive, however, was that I'd already completed my coaching courses and was now fully qualified as an FA coach. I always knew that once the boots had been hung up, I'd want to stay in the game, and I couldn't do that without qualifications.

I'd started the process when I was still at Preston; the idea of coaching obviously appealed to me even then. There was a preliminary course, followed by top-ups, although playing full-time meant qualification would obviously take a while. I completed my courses during my final season at Anfield, following a final intensive two-week assessment at Lilleshall (a much happier outcome this time in stark contrast to my last visit there in 1966). Again, I wasn't alone at Lilleshall: this time another team-mate, Ian St John, was alongside me.

Every student was assigned to a group of around 20 individuals from all walks of life, all at different levels and with different abilities. Each day you had to prepare a session then execute it in front of the assessors. One day the Saint was conducting a shooting session with his group, which included two pros who had played at a reasonable level, while the rest were amateurs. And herein lay the problem: as a professional footballer we were always working much more than the amateurs, as some of them could barely kick the bloody thing! Consequently, many sessions didn't work. The Saint, being the Saint, had no patience for this. He couldn't understand for the life of him why people were on this course when they simply couldn't play. Some couldn't cross, others couldn't shoot, but it was the Saint who was being judged. Enveloped by frustration, he gathered all the balls together and stood next to a hedge running alongside the pitch. One by one, in front of his group, he threw each ball in the air and volleyed every single one over the hedge and out of sight, each time with a different insult: 'You're f***ing useless!' 'Have you ever seen a football before?' 'You can't even kick the f***ing thing!' And then he walked off. Coaching, it seemed, wasn't for him.

Our results weren't divulged immediately (although the Saint didn't need telling), but a month or so later we each received a letter. Thankfully, I'd passed. Unsurprisingly, the Saint hadn't, although in his defence, many great players have struggled to make that leap: Bobbys Charlton and Moore, to name just two, although in fairness to them, playing football came so naturally to them that they simply couldn't understand why others couldn't do the same. The Saint was in the same boat.

Back at Liverpool, Shanks asked the Saint how he'd fared. You can imagine the Saint's reply. And Shanks agreed with him because he didn't like Lilleshall either. He'd visited once with Bob and Joe, supposedly for two days, but they only lasted a morning; he'd seen enough, so went home. The Saint did move into management for a spell, but TV punditry eventually led to his own show; well, half his – the phenomenally successful *Saint and Greavsie* alongside Jimmy Greaves. And what a duo they were! Their on-screen chemistry was undeniable; had they ever got together on the pitch there would have been a goal or two in that partnership, I'm sure!

* * *

In the summer of 1969 I received tentative approaches from a couple of First Division clubs looking for a coach to work with their youth teams, but neither offer excited me; the adrenaline rush required to motivate the brain in times of major decisions was simply not there. This is no disrespect to those two clubs but, having spent most of my playing days in the First Division, the thought of joining a rival club to Liverpool (Preston were no longer a First Division club) was an uneasy one, and not how I wanted to approach my next job.

Arthur Horrocks, who my dad knew well, was a successful Lancashire businessman operating in the travel industry. He was the chairman of Wigan Athletic, then playing non-league football in the Northern Premier League. Arthur had thrown quite a bit of money at the club and was desperate to reach the Football League. When we met, I was immediately impressed with his Shankly-esque enthusiasm, energy and love for the club. As the conversation progressed, he gradually introduced the word 'we', as if I was already on board. The role was player-manager, a full-time position.

The job really appealed to me. Here was the opportunity to accept the challenge on my own terms, to do things my way and try to build a team and club to be proud of. What an education it would be! I didn't view the move as a step down; it was a level of responsibility I wanted at the right time. Having done my badges, I thought I'd move into coaching, never once thinking management would come first, yet somehow it didn't feel alien to me. It was quite a bit of pressure to put on myself, but I didn't ask anyone's advice on the decision. Once again, I felt I was in the right place at the right time. I accepted.

Derek Temple, a good Everton winger back in the day, was also looking for a new challenge. He had chances to play in the Second or Third Division but never fancied it either, so I took him with me to Wigan. Neither of us had any hang-ups about what we'd done previously. Having been a Liverpool and England player in the not-too-distant past, many may have thought non-league football would have eaten me alive; I'd get clattered every week and wouldn't last five minutes. It wasn't like that at all and turned out to be as pleasant a period as any of my entire career.

A deserted football ground at nine o'clock on a Monday morning isn't the usual welcome a new signing expects. I was meeting Mr Horrocks at 10am so was on my toes. I slipped through a small side gate and took in my first-ever view of Springfield Park. A covered terrace stood opposite the main stand, which housed the dressing rooms, directors' box and offices. But what hit me immediately was the size of the surrounding area; the vast areas behind each goal meant lots of potential for development. It wasn't the sort of place where you could build a hostile environment, but it *did* feel like a football club, even if it was a little run down and needing some TLC.

Mr Horrocks arrived, bang on time (I'd always remember that). A tour of the premises ensued and concluded with an introduction to Bill, the groundsman, the only other full-time employee. After a single conversation, I immediately knew: if Bill was an example of the type of person who the club and Mr Horrocks liked to associate with, I was already on firm ground. Bill was a wonderful man who could turn his hand to any challenge – and there were many – without assistance and without complaint. We became very close.

I knew immediately a routine was required. Players would train Tuesday and Thursday evenings, 6.30 to 8.30, and many travelled nearly an hour to the ground, which had to be considered. My time with them would be a priority. Non-matchdays were devoted to how I thought the club should function, so I regularly reminded myself of the brief: it was my job, no one else's. Besides which, there was only me and Bill at the ground, so it was clear where the responsibility lay when there was no hot water for the showers! (Echoes of my boiler-stoking days at Preston with my dad.)

Because changes hadn't been made at the end of the previous season, the administration department (also part-time) had drifted into uncertainty and lethargy. This was only for a couple of months over summer, but decay and indifference need no assistance to grow; they must be identified and dealt with. Direction, optimism and leadership all had to be part of the clarion call. This was my responsibility.

Bill, with all he had to do, was a good barometer of where the club was at. I once found him out on the pitch repainting the lines, on his hands and knees, with a brush! I said, 'We've got to do something about this!' We went to buy a machine that paints the lines as you walk it up and down, but having not paid for previous acquisitions, the club had no credit. I paid for it myself, and thought, *Christ, if we can't afford to buy this, how the hell are we going to buy a player?* It really was the other end of the spectrum, and I quickly learned the importance of people like Bill. Heroes. Underrated, paid a pittance, but bloody heroes.

During pre-season we set up a friendly: local, but away from home. We were all at the ground waiting for the bus. We waited. And waited. No bus. Kenny Banks (who had played for Wigan during the '50s and assisted my predecessor Ian MacNeill) rang the local firm and discovered nobody had booked one! That was when I realised: I should have done it! It was another eye-opener. I could no longer assume buses would turn up, showers would be hot, the laundry would be done, or there would be pies for the lads after a match. I had to learn all these things all over again. It harked back to the days with my dad, but much of that had long slipped my mind. These things I'd never thought about as a player were now down to me.

We had a part-time secretary who took care of wages and other administration issues, and who *needed* to know what *I* was doing. I had to learn the art of communication. Sometimes, with so much in your head, it's easy to forget to tell somebody something important. There weren't too many people I had to relate to, but I had to be clear with those who needed to be in the loop. And it was a two-way street: they had to know and understand what was in my head. I learned to understand the roles and responsibilities of those who never got a mention: the groundsman, the laundry and office staff, those who are vital to the running of a football club, and never more so than when the club is part time.

I was grateful for the insight and the education I was receiving. It was one of the most enriching periods of my life. The lack of funds and the part-time set-up weren't difficulties, but challenges that I wanted, accepted and embraced, as did Derek. The training facilities weren't great, nor was the kit, the showers were poor, and so on – but this was non-league, what did we expect? We accepted it for what it was and turned those issues in our favour. It worked, too. I didn't know there was going to be no hot water, for example, but the players realised that from the look on my face when I found out! They recognised I was in the same boat as them; we were all in it together. And that was beneficial to us all.

It was a fantastic time. We'd get four or five thousand at Springfield Park, terrific for a non-league club, even more so considering the Wigan rugby league team was the big noise in town, streets ahead of us in terms of local interest. Football came a distant second in Wigan. Nevertheless, some of our attendances were better than those of several Fourth Division teams, so there was a definite degree of credibility about the club. That only increased when we won the Northern Premier League in 1971, but we'd already made a mark that season.

On 2 January we travelled to Maine Road, home of the FA Cup holders Manchester City. (They'd go on to win the League Cup and European Cup Winners' Cup, so it's fair to say they were a half-decent team!) Under the stewardship of Joe Mercer and Malcom Allison, City had a team packed with superstars: Joe Corrigan, Franny Lee, Colin Bell, Tony Book, Mike Summerbee – the list goes on. Their defence of the famous old trophy began against my 'little' non-league outfit. For us, a third-round tie, away from home, against the holders – there could hardly be a bigger challenge. This electrified the Wigan public, and as it was a big payday for us, everyone at the club was buzzing too.

We gave an excellent account of ourselves, giving them a bloody good game. They beat us, but only just, thanks to a solitary Colin Bell goal. Our performance earned rave reviews, not just in Manchester but nationwide. There were more than 46,000 there that day, and very few of my lads had played in front of such a crowd; that, how well we played, and the numerous plaudits we received from City players, management and the national media, meant it was as good a loss as you could ever hope for.

I've mentioned the quality of the opposition, but it would be wrong of me not to mention those heroes who played the game of their lives for Wigan on that memorable day. Playing against superstars can sometimes bring out that bit extra; it seemed to do so for our boys, and I suspect for many Wigan supporters those lads are household names. Fans of a certain age will be able to reel off the starting 11, I'm sure, but for the record: Dennis Reeves, Alan Turner, Billy Sutherland, Gordon Milne, Doug Coutts, Ian Gillibrand, Derek Temple, Bobby Todd, Geoff Davies, Jim Fleming, Graham Oates; Ian Ledgard (sub).

That day will live forever with Wigan Athletic fans. It was the biggest story of my time there and I believe a major factor in my appointment as the England U-18 manager (which in turn led me to Coventry City a year later). I was very fortunate, as we were part-time, Mr Horrocks kindly allowed me to fill the Wigan and England roles with his full blessing. It was good publicity for Wigan too, still desperately striving for Football League recognition.

A few months later we won the Northern Premier League but there was no automatic promotion, nor was there automatic relegation from the Football League's Fourth Division. Up until 1986, the bottom four clubs of the Fourth Division had to reapply to maintain their league status. Non-league clubs could also apply for a place, hoping to make the leap and replace one of the four. But the league clubs tended to stick together, usually voting to maintain the status quo.

Boston United were our biggest competitors. (Jim Smith was at the helm, another player-manager; that's when I first met Jim, the start of a lifelong friendship.) They used to spend quite a bit of money lobbying for votes. Wigan lobbied too, but not to the same extent. They once sent every Fourth Division club a box containing a pen and pencil: 'Best wishes from Wigan Athletic.' Nicely presented, too! But despite such grand gestures, the club would be lucky to receive a single vote. Promotion never happened during my time there, and it wasn't until 1978 that Wigan became a Football League club.

I owe my subsequent career to Wigan Athletic. Part-time we may have been, but such status provided a greater education than I ever expected, one I never would have received elsewhere at a higher level, and it humbled me. This was football at its purest. The groundsman, Bill, represented what football was all about; to put it bluntly, if he didn't turn up, we were knackered. I was incredibly fortunate and to this day remain grateful for that fortune. Those days at Wigan were invaluable and when I left I was far better equipped than when I arrived. I have so much to thank them for.

The following year I tasted international success, leading the England U-18 squad to the European Championship title in Barcelona, a squad including names such as Trevor Francis, Phil Thompson, Kevin Beattie and John Gidman. My managerial profile was boosted considerably, my name now beginning to be whispered in higher places.

Chapter 12

IN 1972 Coventry City, then of the First Division, were looking to replicate Manchester City's two-pronged management structure of Joe Mercer and Malcolm Allison. Joe had left Maine Road, however, and Coventry wanted him and me to form a new partnership: Joe as general manager, me as team manager. With no league experience it would be a huge leap for me, so employing a senior partner made sense. I'd already met Arthur Waite, the Crystal Palace chairman. Edith and I visited Selhurst Park, had lunch with Arthur and his wife, and were impressed. But now the Coventry offer had come in. Here was I, a non-league coach, no league experience, with two First Division clubs chasing me. What to do?

I decided to approach Shanks – who else? – for advice. He was on holiday at the Norbreck Hydro in Blackpool, our old haunt from my Liverpool days. Shanks invited me to Blackpool. After 20 minutes in reception, I was summoned to his room, and it was quite the sight. It was still early but Shanks was in his pyjamas and had Vaseline all over his face. It was something he'd always used – old-school moisturiser! Desperately trying not to look shocked I stepped inside the room but no more than a couple of yards.

As ever, Shanks cut straight to the chase, although much more quietly than I was used to: 'What is it then?' It felt like a role reversal. More than a decade earlier Shanks had come to my house with his sales pitch, trying to sign me for Liverpool. This wasn't quite the same but there was a definite whiff of familiarity.

'I've been offered this job, Boss,' I said, before explaining the intended set-up regarding Joe and myself.

Shanks paused for thought, before asking, 'Well, do they want Milne, or do they want Mercer?'

I said, 'Well, there will be both of us involved, and—'

He cut me off mid-sentence: 'I'll say it again, son. Do they want Milne, or do they want Mercer?'

'They want Milne,' I said.

'Well, take it then. Now, I'll have to go, and so will you, because Nessie's sleeping in there and I don't want her disturbed.' I was ushered into the corridor and the door closed behind me. Short and sweet; par for the course. (This exchange was symptomatic of my entire relationship with Shanks; just look how my Liverpool career had come to an end!) Looking back, I'm not sure what I was expecting. Maybe a cup of tea and a chat at least. But no. 'Well, take it then.' It turned out to be good advice.

I've often thought about such moments. Did I act too quickly? Did I give it enough thought? Should I have tried Arsenal? Did I leave Liverpool too soon? But I've never been out of work, going back to when I was a kid. There has always been a sense of continuity. I left Liverpool without too much thought and went to Blackpool. Then to Wigan, to Coventry, to Leicester, and to Beşiktaş. Most importantly, each move was my own decision. Throughout my career there were so many ifs and never any guarantees – are there ever? Heading into the unknown meant regrets were futile, so I never regretted anything. And all my decisions were exactly that – mine. And you can't ask for much more than that.

* * *

It was in the car park of the Malt Shovel pub on the outskirts of Coventry where Joe Mercer and I first met Mr Derek Robbins, the chairman and owner of Coventry City, and the vice-chairman Sir Jack Scamp. They were sitting in the back of Derek's Rolls-Royce, parked in the corner away from any other vehicles (although there weren't many at 10.30 in the morning). It wasn't quite as sinister as it sounds – the windows weren't blacked out – but there was an air of cloak and dagger about it.

I'd not heard anything official from Coventry; everything had come via Joe, from Eddie Plumley, the secretary (who became a big pal of mine, and still is) and Derek, who wanted to meet at the Malt Shovel. Derek was tough to deal with. As the main man, if he shouted loud enough, it got done, but if you stuck up for yourself, he respected you.

Sir Jack was really nice, highly intelligent, and the perfect foil for Derek. Years later, during my management tenure he said, 'Gordon, you know I'm chairman at Leamington Spa? Well, at Leamington, at the end of each season we bring in five or six new players. The fans demand it. But if we can't change the players, we change the manager.' He gave a little chuckle before disappearing. 'The fans demand it,' made me chuckle to myself; if Leamington got 500 at a match they were doing well! It made me think though: *He's sending me a message here*, as by then I'd been there seven or eight years and was maybe going a bit stale. He was telling me to pull my finger out.

On that day in the car park Derek was delighted Joe and I had agreed on a working relationship, one he felt would be beneficial to all concerned. Coventry had a reputation for being progressive and forward-thinking, so we too were happy knowing we'd have the board's full support. After 20 minutes it was handshakes all round and Joe and I were on our way.

The summer allowed me to get organised, plan pre-season, get to know the staff and learn how the club functioned. The first order of business was finding an assistant. Joe recommended Tommy Casey, a Northern Irishman who had worked in the First Division with Everton. As a player he'd chalked up 400-odd matches during the '50s and '60s, most notably for Newcastle United. Tommy was hard-working and enthusiastic, with a typical flavour of Irish humour (which always helps); no-nonsense, he could also handle top players and look after himself.

Tommy, Joe and I were stationed at the Leofric hotel in the centre of Coventry, 20 minutes from the training ground. Ryton was a first-class facility with three full-sized pitches separated by high grassy banks, great vantage points from which to watch training and games and one that sheltered the pitches from annoying winds. With a fantastic canteen too, Ryton was as good as anything in the First Division.

Pre-season was soon under way, warm, with blue skies for the Sky Blues and a great training area. Our first 11 vs 11 was a chance to take stock. Bert Edwards, the youth team manager, knew all the players and had been instructed to try to pick two balanced teams to make the game competitive. Tommy and I perched on top of the bank and with a single blow of Bert's whistle, away we went. Fifteen minutes later I told Bert to blow again. I couldn't stand it any longer. This had to stop. Players were going through the motions, fannying about, with the odd one or two even smiling at each other. The whole atmosphere stank. If this was an indication of what this group was all about it was little wonder the previous manager lost his job. I told everyone to gather in the gym. This was a test … for me. The club had several experienced players who had been around the block and who had strong opinions. I knew what they were thinking: *Where's this guy come from – non-league? What's he ever done? What's he all about?* Their messages were loud, clear and deliberate.

I was being tested, so I knew my message back to them had to be as loud and as clear as theirs was to me: 'If you're going to f**k me about, it'll be very easy for me to f**k you about.' That might not be word for word, but it's close. I tried to keep my eyes on the big hitters, three or four of the senior players, as I felt that would have more impact. I explained where I was coming from and what I was all about, then told them we'd try again that afternoon at four, before turning and walking out; short but not sweet. I knew a four o'clock session wouldn't go down well as it meant we wouldn't finish until around half past five, buggering up any afternoon plans and commitments such as picking up the kids from school and so on. I knew this might upset them, but I also knew it might upset their wives and sometimes that can have a bigger effect than a bollocking and a fine. I'd made my point and was satisfied with how I'd done it.

We kicked off again at four, and for 30 minutes it was like watching 22 different players. There was no messing about, no laughing, no joking. If anything, it was the opposite – they kicked lumps out of each other. I didn't want that either, but it was still preferable to what I'd seen that morning. As far as I was concerned, my message had been received and understood. I'd made a statement.

I believe the transformation was down to my playing days, albeit indirectly. Earlier I'd said to them, 'I've played this game, so has Tommy. We've both been in this game a lot longer than all of you. And all you're doing is arsing about; you're taking the piss, and it's not acceptable.' A key line was, 'I've been where you've been.' Everything I said to them, and the way I said it, came from a player's point of view rather than a manager's. What also helped was the way I spoke. I didn't want to be effing and blinding all the time but in this case I've no doubt a bit of industrial language helped. Tommy felt the same, although he was more aggressive than me. If he'd had a machine gun, he'd have shot half of them.

* * *

Our first pre-season friendly was against Bristol City at Ashton Gate. Alan Dicks, who I knew well, was the manager (we'd meet again in more serious circumstances a few seasons later). They were well supported, so we were assured of a decent crowd and a good pitch too, perfect conditions for our first outing.

We were relaxing in a private lounge at the hotel, watching TV. In my head I'd already written the script of what I wanted to say. Suddenly Joe burst out, 'Lads! I'd just like to wish you all good luck for the coming season. Gordon, Tommy and I are all looking forward to working with you, and I personally believe we have the talent here to do well.' Joe was soon in full flight. The only problem was, he got everyone's bloody name wrong! 'The talent in this room is worthy of success, especially with players like Billy Carr,' his name was Willie, 'our captain, Ray Barry,' real name Roy, 'and our goalkeeper. You need a top, experienced goalkeeper, that's vital, and we have one in Bill ...' Here, Joe managed to get Bill's first name right but whatever surname he mumbled sounded nothing like Glazier, as it should have! 'We have the talent here to succeed. No question!'

The room remained quiet as we listened intently, but I could see some of the players shaking, straining every sinew to remain straight-faced. And the rest of the room? Likewise! And this was Joe Mercer, remember. Prior to this moment, they'd all been frightened to death of him! But now, in the first team talk, he had all the players looking at one another, trying not to die laughing, and I couldn't help them as I was struggling myself. Something had to give.

It did. Joe moved on from naming the players and said, 'Anything to add, Gordon? Tommy?' Tommy immediately replied, 'Just one thing, Mr Mercer: thank you for getting my f**king name right!' The whole room exploded!

Sometimes, desperately trying not to laugh can be more difficult than trying not to cry. Here, albeit unintentionally, Joe had the whole room laughing together. It was perfect preparation. A buzzing, buoyant group boarded the bus, all raring to go thanks to Joe Mercer. It was a pity it was only a friendly. That day established the recognition in all our eyes of Joe's warmth, knowledge, experience and humility. The lads were all happy he was on board. And I was happier than all of them.

* * *

With five matches remaining of the 1972/73 season, Derby County came to Highfield Road. I sat up in the directors' box, a rarity for me – and a bloody mistake! Phil Mead, one of the directors, was alongside me. He was the only one, mind; nobody else showed up. Perhaps the rest of the board were anticipating a bit of negativity, given the circumstances. We were midway through a run of losing nine of the final ten league matches. Behind the directors' box was a walkway for the supporters; if you were sitting on the back row, your head was at the fans' knee height as they passed behind you. There were three or four rows of seats, and across thc front row was a ledge about eight inches deep running the width of the box.

With around 15 minutes remaining we were losing 1-0 and the natives were restless, trooping out already, effing and blinding. Suddenly, something hit me on the back of the head, then something else, then something hit Phil. Our own fans were throwing their season tickets at us. Calm as you like, Phil picked them up one by one and piled them neatly on the ledge. I remember thinking, *These lads are more accurate than our bloody strikers!* Phil soon had a dozen or so tickets stacked in front of him.

'What are you going to do with them?' I asked.

Phil replied, 'Gordon, we've got names and addresses of all these people. And I'll guarantee you, no matter how pissed off they are now, 75 per cent of them will renew their tickets next season.'

Whether they did or not, I don't know. But Phil's handling of the situation was another example of what I could learn from different people. He didn't get flustered or angry, he didn't stand up and storm off, there was no (melo)drama from him at all. He took the sting out of the situation with tremendous dignity. It was a lesson, from a senior board member, in how to behave and handle yourself in a moment of stress.

That public gangway behind the directors' box meant you'd hear plenty: lots of advice (some good, some not); insults and compliments (the former considerably outweighing the latter); and plenty of classic football humour. I always remember 'The Irishman', fondly, in fact, despite him being far from complimentary. When we were losing, he'd *always* appear towards the end of a match and would politely say, 'Mr Milne. I know I've mentioned this before, but I don't mind repeating myself. If you go, I will gladly move your f**king furniture out of your house for you – free of charge.' Despite his message, he made me smile. My lads at home would bring him up as often as they could: 'Dad, you've lost again but look on the bright side: free furniture removal!' It didn't make me feel any better, but I had to laugh. It was football in a nutshell: light-hearted in one way, but at the same time deadly serious.

* * *

When Tommy left the club, I brought in Ron Wylie. Ron had been a top player for Aston Villa and Birmingham City, beginning at Notts County in 1950, having left Scotland as a fresh-faced 17-year-old; a massive step in those days, but in the heartlands of Glasgow they bred them tough. Ron was dedicated and determined to succeed and in 1958 he joined Aston Villa, where none other than Joe Mercer took him under his wing. I remember playing against Ron, who referred to me as a 'f**king nuisance' (I took it as a compliment, although I'm not sure it was meant that way). Ron and I had a great working relationship but, more importantly, we shared a friendship that continued all our lives.

Ron was completely different to me, which was perfect. He didn't want to be a manager, he just wanted to be a coach; he wanted the responsibility of working with the players. Players get bored quite easily, but Ron would always keep it fresh and interesting. And if they did get bored, he wouldn't give a toss! He could handle all aspects. Back then, most managers were the main voice, if you like. I liked to be out on the grass as well, but with Ron next to me I could relax in terms of not thinking too far ahead about what to do in training tomorrow, and the next day, and so on. Ron took care of so much of that, was very good at what he did and just got on with it. The combination worked, and our relationship took a lot of weight off my shoulders.

Ron was also fitter than me! I thought I had an engine, but he'd leave me behind all the time. We were both still fit enough to join the five-a-sides at the end of training, which we both loved. He'd be on one team, I'd be on the other, and we handled ourselves quite well. For 15 minutes or so we'd have a nice little runaround and still play some decent football. I suppose we did it for our own egos as much as anything – 'we've still got it' – and were both in reasonable condition, but at the same time I think there was a quiet respect from the players. When we played alongside them, Ron and I were recognised as ex-players rather than as management. It harked back nicely to my days at Melwood, watching Shanks and co. playing five-a-sides every day. I like to think Ron and I shared the same levels of enthusiasm.

* * *

Liverpool visiting Highfield Road was always special. They'd ask to use our training facility at Ryton for a pre-match loosener on the morning of the match, and we always obliged. As a courtesy I'd ask whether they wanted to wait until our lads had finished, but Liverpool never bothered about things like that, they were never interested in privacy. They were here to work, and to them there was nothing to hide. In their minds, everyone knew how they'd play. Ian Rush and Kenny Dalglish will be up front, Terry McDermott in midfield, Phil Neal at full-back. No surprises. Such a mindset echoed Shanks in the early '60s. Prior to kick-off, Shanks would say, 'Bob, I can't believe it. There are six clubs watching us here today. Six!' Another method of motivation? Almost certainly. 'I can't understand why they send these scouts – everybody knows how we play, the same way every week!' It was a philosophy Shanks summed up perfectly when a reporter once asked after midweek training, 'Any chance you could tip me off, Bill? What's the team for Saturday?' The reply: 'Of course I can, son. It's the same as last year.'

One day at Ryton, during five-a-side time, I wandered over to have a word with Bob Paisley. 'Hello Bob, how are you?'

A friendly, characteristically mumbled greeting was returned. After five or ten minutes of small talk I was about to leave when Bob suddenly gestured towards the Liverpool lads and, without taking his eyes off them, said quietly, 'Listen, son, this is the job for you.'

I wasn't sure I'd heard him correctly. 'Sorry, Bob? What was that?'

Bob gestured towards the players again. 'They're going to need a manager.'

This time I definitely heard him. But I didn't understand him. This made no sense whatsoever. It was late August 1973, only the second fixture of the new season. Liverpool had won their eighth league title only four months earlier, a title followed swiftly by their first European trophy, the UEFA Cup. Bill Shankly was their irrepressible, irresistible and surely irreplaceable manager, with no intention of going anywhere – unless Bob knew otherwise? Perhaps he did, as the following July the football world reeled at the news of Shankly's resignation, leaving Liverpool just two months after guiding the club to their second FA Cup triumph, defeating Newcastle United 3-0 at Wembley. If Shankly had been planning to leave, very few would have known about it, although if Shanks were to confide in anybody, it would almost certainly have been Bob, his most trusted lieutenant. What's more, neither would ever betray the other's confidence, and they both knew it.

'What are you talking about, Bob? You're joking, aren't you?'

'No, they're going to need someone.'

Aside from my questioning, I was speechless. I found it so hard to believe. I didn't know what to say, so didn't say anything. It wasn't in my nature to think, *I've got to push this*, so I didn't push it either. And nor did Bob. That was him in a nutshell: a man of very few words. He may have spoken to the board about me, he may not; to this day I simply don't know. I've always been of the thought that if you try to imagine what's gone on, you're usually a million miles away from the truth. Sometimes, whatever the truth is, or was, you never know, and again, sometimes it's better not to know. What I do know for sure is there were no more conversations between myself and Bob. Typical Bob, typical Liverpool. And – dare I say it – typical Milne? Normality resumed and the season rolled on. Coventry City was my priority. I pretty much forgot about everything Bob had said. It was almost as if, having appeared out of nowhere, the subject disappeared just as quickly.

After a long season came to an end I received a phone call from the Liverpool secretary Peter Robinson, asking if I'd meet him, along with the chairman John Smith, at an airport hotel in Manchester. As it was now close season I felt comfortable accepting his invitation (I'd never have dreamed of speaking to another club during a campaign). This was so far removed from a training pitch chat with Bob, both in time and type. The club had now surprised me twice, 11 months apart. Typical Liverpool again? Perhaps. They had a way of working that, while not exactly secret, was certainly not squarely in the public eye. Now, however, it was somewhat surreal. This would be an actual interview. There seemed to be genuine interest from them in me perhaps becoming their manager. Naturally, I felt enormous excitement, and enormous pride too, which I didn't fully recognise at the time. It was my first meeting with John so I'm sure nerves played their part. I can't remember what I did or didn't say; I can't remember how the interview went, other than John, a very meticulous man, was quite clinical and somewhat forensic in his interrogation. I did get the impression, though, that he wasn't overly impressed. The one thing I know for sure, however, is that I should have said, 'I'll walk up the M6 in my bare feet to manage Liverpool.' But I didn't. I still don't know whether they were interviewing anyone else at that time (although there's every chance they were). They could have been weighing me up just in case Bob, their obvious preference, wouldn't accept the job. Either way, it wasn't long before he was appointed.

My initial surprise at Bob's suggestion was accentuated simply because I already thought Bob himself was the natural fit. Based upon my years as a player working with him, I knew he'd slot in easily and with the minimum of fuss – which he did. The club always allowed the players to play; Bob would continue that. He was a great reader of the game, a shrewd tactician and had everything in place already. And even though he worked differently to Shanks, he'd never start doing things outside his character or that made him uncomfortable. He'd never upset the applecart.

Bob's biggest issue was his self-imposed pressure. He worried about whether he could handle it. Did he really want to take on what the job entailed? Would he have been happy working under somebody else? Would that somebody be happy working with him? Had the forward-thinking Paisley actually been sounding me out, knowing what lay ahead? It's well documented how reluctant he was to take up the reins; he *had* to be persuaded. The club may even have said, 'Bob, in six months' time, if you don't fancy it, don't worry. You'll be at this club for the rest of your life anyway, and we'll find someone else to manage.' Knowing Bob, and knowing the club, I'm sure they'd have given him options.

Ultimately, the club was delighted when Bob accepted the challenge. Stability – paramount in their thinking – would be maintained. And, as they say, the rest is history, played out at the highest level. It was arguably the best decision the club (and Bob) ever made. There was no disruption, the transition seamless. The machine simply changed gear, moving forward with purpose and momentum, with Bob firmly in the driving seat.

Nothing would have given Bob more pleasure than knowing he'd managed to continue and enhance the work of his great friend. The foundations he and Shanks laid so carefully, with such vision – all eyes pointing to the sky – were the beginning of all those incredible years to follow. And for one of Shankly's first signings, as a member of that first, wonderful, trailblazing team of the magical swinging 60s, that closeness to Bob during those early years remains a lifetime memory, never to be forgotten. It was an honour to be invited to the table. I feel fully qualified to put my hand on my heart and say: that was the true beginning of the Shankly/Paisley Anfield era, an era that would see Liverpool Football Club go on to achieve so much.

And who would have believed at that time when Bob took the reins, he'd not only continue the cycle of success – a huge challenge in itself – but would take the club to another level, eclipsing all that had gone before?

Chapter 13

SUNDAYS IN the Shankly household followed a pattern. Bill rose first before delivering a cuppa to his wife Nessie in bed. When she came downstairs, the scene that greeted her was a barometer of how the previous day had panned out. As Nessie told it: 'If the newspapers were spread all over the floor, Liverpool had won. He'd open each paper, seeking out the relevant pages. He'd only read what mattered to him; the other pages would be dismissively discarded. But if the papers were all still folded on the table, things clearly hadn't gone well. He just wouldn't read them.'

The media has long had a topsy-turvy relationship with football managers, both parties eyeing each other with an element of trust alongside a degree of suspicion, both parties trying to use the other for their own benefit. And as managers, we all had our own methods.

In Turkey, not knowing the language, I couldn't read the papers, but when I saw the letters MIL in print I'd immediately think, *That's my name there!* And I'd try to work out what they'd written. It's human nature: when you see your own name emblazoned across the pages, the chances are it's not good news. And you want to know.

In Istanbul, every day I'd have 30-odd reporters around me but no idea whether a particular journalist had given me a right going-over the day before. And because I had no idea, I'd never know whether said reporter was standing a foot away from me on the Monday morning. I had a great translator, Ali, who protected me. 'Ali, what's this saying here?' Ali would glance at the paper I was waving under his nose, before dismissing it: 'That? That's nothing, Gordon.' Bless him. Alongside his tactful diplomacy, my inability to read the papers meant I was protecting myself. I suppose the lesson is that there are things you can control, so long as you don't expose yourself. For me, that meant not reading about myself.

It was all about dealing with outside pressures and in that regard I have a great deal to thank Joe Mercer for. He used to say, 'Always remember football's a game of opinion. Everybody has one, but you can't worry about them.' So true. He'd go on, 'When those f***ing directors talk about this, that and whatever … well, their companies have an AGM once a bloody year! We sit in front of our shareholders [supporters] once a week – sometimes twice!' How right he was.

I was extremely aware of Joe's contribution. At its most basic level, I was looking after players, Joe was looking after directors, which was vital. Joe kept any moans or complaints away from me. After matches we'd sometimes go into the boardroom and if we'd just been beaten 3-0, the chairman and the board, three or four whiskies to the good, would be feeling brave and want their pound of flesh: 'Why did you do this, Gordon? Why didn't you do that?' Joe took all that away from me.

However, other pressures did fall under the remit of a manager. At Leicester City I had five lads living in Birmingham who travelled to training together in the same car. Stevie Lynex was one of them and one day came to see me, after more money.

'Boss, you know we're all coming over in the car every day. It's so far, it's a pain in the a**e, it's costing us money.'

'Why don't you move closer?' I replied. 'It'll save you money, and hassle.' He was obviously not happy, but if I gave him an extra fiver a week (and that's all he wanted, by the way, a fiver!) I'd have had to give the same to the other lads in the car. And after that, the rest of the squad would all have been at my door. I said, 'Stevie, it's not the right time, we're halfway through the season. We'll talk again when the season's done, but for now, you'll have to get on with it.'

Stevie said nothing. He looked me in the eye, got up, walked out, and slammed the door behind him. Two seconds later, the door opened. He poked his head back into my office, looked at me and shouted, 'YOU F***ING C**T!' He slammed the door again and buggered off.

Now I had a problem. The following morning, I was trying to wind them up for Saturday's match – not easy after the altercation with Stevie. I could picture the five of them in the car, and once one of them says he's been in to see me, the rest are soon saying, 'F**k it, I'm going to see him too!' I wouldn't be surprised if it was a plot from the very start: 'Stevie, you go in first, see how you get on. If you get a result, we'll all go in!' To his credit, though, Stevie didn't kick up a fuss, he just got on with it. A great pro.

Such situations highlighted one of a manager's biggest off-field responsibilities back then: we controlled the wages. Today, a request like Stevie's goes straight upstairs, a change for the better in my view. There's no need for managers and players to fall out over finances, thanks to that man in the middle. The title of that man's role varies today (chief executive would do it) but the role itself – a senior position requiring knowledge and experience of life in the fast lane, an understanding of the bread and butter of the game, and enough wisdom and nous to marry that with commercial life – is invaluable to a manager *and* the club. For me, at Coventry, that was Joe. He was the buffer between myself and whoever was gunning for me and he knew exactly how to play that position, taking the sting out of any situation; the perfect cushion between the manager and the board and, when required, between the manager and the media. The importance of the buffer is hugely undervalued and rarely receives the attention it warrants.

As a manager (or a buffer), 'playing the game' (with directors, supporters or the media) has always required certain levels of tact and diplomacy – and a thick skin. Bobby Robson was once asked, 'Bobby, is it true you need the skin of a rhinoceros to be a football manager?' Bobby replied, 'No, no, no. You need the skin of six rhinoceroses.' And that's never changed. In 1959 Aston Villa were relegated. Joe was their manager, and it was his second relegation in three years. Shortly afterwards he received a telegram – at home. In those days telegrams were usually only sent to congratulate or commiserate. This was neither. 'Congratulations Joe STOP You've done it again STOP'. The sarcasm was hardly subtle; the spite was all too clear. The sender was anonymous. (Nowadays such attacks are a dime-a-dozen on social media, but the intentions are the same.) A thick skin offered some sort of shield and was essential to a manager's defence system. Joe had that thick skin; without it, he'd never have become the great player and manager he did. Let's not forget he went on to lead Manchester City to Second and First Division titles, alongside successes in the League Cup, FA Cup and European Cup Winners' Cup.

Alongside Joe throughout those Manchester City years was that great character Malcolm Allison – 'Big Mal', a terrific coach, one of the best of his generation, and the combination worked. Joe was the senior man, stability and solidarity. Malcolm was cavalier, eccentric, big cigar, big hat, a bit of a noise on the London scene. Everybody loved him. Malcolm was much more hands-on than Joe, out on the pitch with the players, picking the team, leaving Joe to handle the board. It just worked – at least until it didn't! But when it did break down it led to Joe and I having a similar set-up at Coventry City. And again, it worked. (Joe also impressed as caretaker manager of England, winning the 1974 British Home Championship, and was in the frame to become permanent manager, possibly with me assisting him. In fact, I applied for the post myself, but instead Don Revie was handed the blazer.) Joe was extremely likeable, and very funny, but you needed more than that. He'd experienced the downside of the game but had the thick skin required to handle it.

Bobby was made of the same stuff. In 1990 he informed the FA he'd step down as England manager after that summer's World Cup. When this became public knowledge the press went after him, going so far as to call him a 'traitor'. Bloody ridiculous! I remember one headline a year or two earlier, in huge print in the *Daily Mirror*: 'GO! IN THE NAME OF GOD, GO!' Soon afterwards, following England's draw with Saudi Arabia, the *Mirror* adapted its own headline: 'GO! IN THE NAME OF ALLAH, GO!' Bloody disgraceful. Totally disrespectful, and in more ways than one. It still boils my blood today. But it never bothered Bobby, he just shrugged it off. His ultimate response was to take England to a missed penalty away from a World Cup Final. Not bad for a traitor, that!

Following the World Cup, Bobby went to PSV Eindhoven in the Netherlands. I was managing Beşiktaş at the time and went to watch PSV ahead of a European Cup tie. Having a drink afterwards, I noticed the back of Bobby's suit was in a right state. 'Bobby, what's all this on your back?' Very matter-of-factly, with no emotion either way, he replied, 'Oh, that's just the fans spitting at me.' He was talking about his own fans too! At PSV the players' tunnel was very tight, covered only by a light wire mesh. The fans were practically on top of the tunnel and the dugouts, so had easy access to the managers. Bobby just shrugged it off. To him it was completely incidental, just part of the job. He was successful at PSV too, winning a couple of league titles but, as ever, during a lean spell, the mood quickly changed.

Jimmy Hill was another I learned from. He too suffered at the hands of the media and the public, although in a slightly different way, as for many years he was a member of the media himself, hosting the iconic BBC show *Match of the Day*. And he took more stick during those years than at any other time. But rather than be cowed by it he went the opposite way: he embraced it, turning it to his advantage. He was extremely clued up as to how it all worked, how to 'play the game'. 'Every week, my fan mail is fantastic. They can't get the bags through the door, they're so full. But 95 per cent of them are criticism and complaints. Gordon, that's why I stay in the job.' He knew the interest lay not so much in the programme itself but, in Jimmy's own words, 'in what this prat was going to say next'. It was a classic example of 'playing the game' and reinforced my determination to improve in that area.

Fortunately, I was learning from some of the best. Joe, Bobby and Jimmy were masters.

Shanks was never overly patient with the press, although they did like him. But when asked a difficult question, he wouldn't shirk it. He might have been sarcastic, humorous or extremely dismissive; he might have been all three at the same time. In short, when he wanted, he could, and would, be awkward with them, even abrasive. Alex Ferguson was the same, as was Kenny Dalglish, Tommy Doc too. They were all quick-witted, but they'd bite. In such circumstances the Doc would often reply with something funny, immediately making a mockery of the situation and embarrassing whoever asked the question. (Of course, the Doc was the king of the one-liner, which always helped. Of his spell managing Rotherham he said, 'I was brought in to get this team out of the Second Division, and I did – I took them into the Third.') It didn't work for everybody. Some would simply say, 'F*** off,' and feel better for it; others would never dream of doing so. What this proves though, is that there are no rules set in stone, no definitive right or wrong. Every manager handles things differently – in their own way.

If further proof were needed, look no further than those two great knights, Sir Alex Ferguson and Sir Alf Ramsey: polar opposites, yet one was the most successful manager for godness knows how long, and the other won the World Cup! Alf was cool, calm and considered, methodical, precise, always on an even keel. Alex was ... well, not, almost as well known for his 'hairdryer' treatment as his management prowess! When it came to emotions the pair were at opposite ends of the spectrum. Their management styles differed wildly, yet they became as successful as anybody could wish to be, steering their teams to victory while driving in different lanes. For any young manager perhaps thinking, *I should do it this way, but definitely not that way*, Alex and Alf proved the error in such thinking. And neither of them did too badly, did they?

Chapter 14

AT COVENTRY, staying afloat financially was a massive challenge. Avoiding relegation wasn't our sole aim – if we ever stated as much the supporters would have rightly gone potty – but it was obviously key. However, we had to balance the books. Not having the biggest fanbase, we couldn't rely upon cash flooding in from our supporters. The only way to succeed was to produce good young players and sell them on for a profit. This led to a pattern emerging: every other year we'd sell one or two of our better kids. Unintentionally, Coventry began to harvest a reputation as an ideal place for young players to receive a good grounding and, more importantly, opportunity, enabling them to enhance their careers. Significantly, we also became known for selling to 'bigger' clubs. The fans didn't like it too much, understandably, and I wasn't too keen either, but it was what we had to do. We weren't well off but wisely remained vigilant; it didn't matter at what level we were working, only that we could afford it. Thankfully, we reached a point where the bank was supporting rather than chasing us.

The wonderful Bert Edwards oversaw the youth set-up. Bert had a good eye for a player and was responsible for recruiting these kids and bringing them on. We always had three or four youngsters in the team, so the kids coming to us – and perhaps more importantly, their parents – knew they'd get half a chance at the very least. The likes of Liverpool and Arsenal were more attractive propositions but at such clubs there was no guarantee of actual game time. With us, it was different. The players and parents recognised that, and recognised Bert's qualities and how much he cared. That was crucial; it meant they trusted him.

It was another lesson for me: how important it was to have someone like Bert at my side, an expert who I trusted and relied upon. Kids would come for a weekend to play and train, and mum and dad would come too. They'd meet Bert and he'd win them over immediately. He was like a father figure. We had good facilities too, which obviously helped. Add it all up and we pretty much had a supply chain of young talent.

A few names you may have heard of: Dennis Mortimer, Gary Gillespie, Ian Wallace, Danny Thomas, Mark Hateley, Steve Whitton, Les Sealey, Mick Ferguson, Garry Thompson ... just a few to pass through Coventry City on their way to bigger and better things. Larry Lloyd and Tommy Hutchison too, although they were seasoned professionals when I brought them in. Initially, many of these lads didn't set the world on fire – only natural, they were still teenagers – and the board may well have been thinking, *What have we got here?* But, with time and patience, they'd (hopefully) have been thinking differently.

Dennis Mortimer is a prime example. He was only a kid, already at Coventry when I arrived. Bloody good player and a great lad, he and I got on well. He went on to play 200-odd times for us before another 400 or so for Aston Villa, one of which was of course their famous European Cup win in 1982. Dennis was the captain, and that night he lifted the famous old trophy. For Coventry, losing someone like Dennis typified the reality of our financial situation; we never really had a choice, but we always did our best for them all.

Centre-half Gary Gillespie was another success. He was 17 and had only played a handful of matches for Falkirk when I signed him. Six years later, after nearly 200 appearances for us, he signed for Liverpool (another healthy profit), where he became a key player under Kenny Dalglish as Liverpool won trophies galore. In the 1987/88 season Gary played nearly every match for what many still think is the finest Liverpool team ever assembled. Not bad for a kid we signed for peanuts!

Tony Hateley was a contemporary of mine (he joined Liverpool just after I left the club). By the time I joined Coventry he was overseeing his son Mark's career and was keen for Mark to join us. Mark was a teenager, but Tony knew we'd give Mark a chance. He spent five years with us before spells at Portsmouth, AC Milan, Monaco and Rangers. Another of our success stories, Mark was capped 32 times by England.

Some, like Les Sealey, were brought in from further afield. Sadly no longer with us, Les was a typical cockney, full of confidence and with plenty to say for himself, who we got in as a kid for nothing before selling him for six figures. Les was a better goalkeeper than many gave him credit for, me included! Sir Alex Ferguson saw what we didn't, famously picking him for an FA Cup Final replay, which Manchester United won. Les kept a clean sheet that night.

Little Danny Thomas was another. He joined Coventry as a ten-year-old; we later sold him to Spurs for a quarter of a million pounds. He was one whose parents I spent a lot of time with as I was very keen on him (plenty of other clubs also wanted him too). Danny was capped by England before injuries sadly cut his career short.

At 25 – no longer a kid – Larry Lloyd, who I signed from Liverpool, is another notable name on the list. I was surprised to get him as he was doing well under Shanks, but Bob took over and seemed to prefer Phil Thompson. Larry was well established, with more than 200 appearances behind him, but wasn't the type to hang around if he thought he wasn't going to be involved. We were delighted, however, although at a quarter of a million pounds – a club record transfer fee – he wasn't cheap. We tried to recoup some of the costs by selling Mick McGuire and Jimmy Holmes to Tottenham, but when the Spurs manager Bill Nicholson resigned, both moves fell through. Consequently, we found ourselves financially in the red for some time after that.

Larry was a good lad but could be difficult. He wasn't a 'big-time Charlie', but his character suited the big time, if that makes sense. I struggled to get the best out of him though, and a couple of years later Brian Clough came after him. In those days transfers were sorted by the two managers. Cloughie and I agreed a fee. I informed the board and hoped for their approval. I spoke to Larry, and he wanted to go. That day after training, Larry headed to Nottingham's City Ground. Two o'clock rolled around … silence. Three o'clock … still nothing. Four o'clock … all quiet. By this point my chairman was demanding to know what was happening. We all wanted the move to go through as the club needed the cash! At around quarter to six I was in my office, still having heard nothing. I dialled Cloughie's number. It rang and rang … no answer. I waited 20 minutes before trying again. This time I was successful.

'Brian, it's Gordon here, just wondering what's going on with Larry. Has the deal been done?'

I'll never forget Cloughie's reply: 'He's like that f**king monkey who puts his hand in the jar, grabs all the f**king sweets, then gets his hand stuck!' I thought *Christ!* I assumed Larry must have tried to screw him for a few quid, and immediately thought the deal had gone sour. There was a long pause before Cloughie continued: 'Anyway … he signed.' And he put the phone down! It was good news, I suppose, but the lack of communication, alongside the delaying tactics and accompanying intrigue could – and did – cause mistrust in a delicate situation.

For Larry it was a great move. He struck up a formidable central defensive partnership with Kenny Burns, marshalled by the legendary keeper Peter Shilton behind them. Larry went on to win the First Division, two League Cups and two European Cups. (Forest were the only team to win the European Cup with two centre-halves who couldn't run, but they headed and kicked everything – and everyone!) Coincidentally, Larry later stepped into my shoes, becoming manager of Wigan Athletic, then moving to Notts County where, following his first match in charge, a reporter remarked that nine of his 11 players had been booked that day. He asked for Larry's thoughts. 'Well, I'll have to question the commitment of the other two.'

Years later, our striker Mick Ferguson was wanted by Forest. Mick and I arrived at the City Ground and sat down to wait. And we waited. And waited some more. We'd arrived late morning and, after countless cups of tea, even more biscuits and with patience rapidly running out, were still there late afternoon; neither sight nor sound of Cloughie. Peter Taylor turned up around four o'clock. He was apologetic but remained calm: 'Sorry gents, I didn't realise you were here. Brian's out playing squash.'

I thought it was bulls**t – it was so obviously some sort of tactic and, to my mind, a dodgy one.

We'd had enough. Mick and I left. Here was a player Cloughie supposedly wanted, yet on the day he never came near the place and, bizarrely, never pursued Mick again (which to me made Cloughie look worse). I couldn't understand the psychology but that's what it was: tactical and deliberate. I was furious, but what about Mick himself? He was about to sign for the European champions, but in the blink of an eye they no longer wanted him. It was a hammer blow for the lad.

We had a similar situation with Mick's strike partner Ian Wallace. Cloughie wanted him but once again the deal was on, then it was off, and so on. Coventry wanted a million pounds for Ian. Trevor Francis had recently become the first million-pound player when he left Birmingham City for Nottingham Forest; this was now the climate surrounding the game, and Coventry, like everyone, were looking to capitalise. Cloughie offered no more than £800,000. The Coventry board stood firm. Cloughie had been awkward – deliberately so – and not for the first time. At the end of the season the transfer still hadn't occurred. I told Cloughie I was off on my holidays for a fortnight and we'd talk on my return. He agreed.

A couple of days later I was in Marbella when Jimmy Hill got in touch. Cloughie had been nagging him to get the Wallace deal done. I told Jimmy that Brian had agreed to leave it until I got back. Jimmy was brilliant: 'Gordon, leave it to me. If he doesn't pay £1m, he won't get him. In fact, because of his behaviour, it'll now be a million and one … £1.1m.' Jimmy had been a manager, was sympathetic to my cause and was showing me loyalty and support. What's more, he had the stature and personality to operate that way; he had the clout to carry it off. The deal eventually went through for around £1.25m. The disappointment for me was that Cloughie had gone behind my back. I'd never have done that to a fellow manager. I accept that he was doing his job for Nottingham Forest, but it didn't endear him to me, I can say that much.

Strangely, there were other occasions when Brian seemed anonymous. It was difficult enough to believe he'd behave in such a way, never mind work out why. They'd come to Highfield Road, play the match (usually beat us), and go home. We'd never see him. I felt it was a conscious effort to avoid us. We wouldn't even bump into him outside the dressing rooms or when we headed to and from the dugouts.

One afternoon, an hour before kick-off against Forest, Ron and I were having a drink in my office when there was a knock on the door. There in the corridor, looking rather timid and sheepish – not like him at all – was Peter Taylor.

'Peter, come on in, have a drink with us.'

For some reason, Peter was reluctant: 'No, no, no, I won't, no thanks lads, if you don't mind. But is it possible to have a little whisky for Brian?'

'Tell him to come and join us!'

'No, no, I won't Gordon, he's not too keen on coming in.' It was like we had the bloody plague! 'If you could just give me a little whisky for him that would be great.' Bloody hell! Ron poured the whisky, handed it to Peter, and off Peter went. There was nothing wrong with them not joining us, but the way they went about it was certainly strange. It was as if Cloughie wished to avoid any sort of social interaction with us, and Peter himself could be a bit tricky too. With Cloughie (and Peter), nothing was ever certain. Many of his players spoke in later years of how unpredictable he was. They couldn't read his next move, but it kept them on their toes.

I realise I'm painting a certain picture of Cloughie here, but I'm not just throwing poisoned darts at him; these are my experiences. Three times I'd had dealings with him; three times I felt I'd been messed about. But I must also stress that, despite my misgivings, to this day I still tip my hat to him for what he achieved. I have enormous respect for him in that regard, and you have to remember he did it with both Derby County *and* Nottingham Forest and, most importantly, playing great football. Both teams were a credit to their clubs and their cities.

All that said, there was another side to Brian. After one match against them I was in my office with Ron – again, no sign of Brian or Peter – when there was another knock on the door. This time it was Joe, one of the groundsmen: 'Can I borrow you for five minutes, chaps? I want to show you something.' Immediately I was thinking, *Bloody hell, what's happened now?* Joe led us to the visitors' dressing room, with me thinking the worst. Joe said, 'Look at this,' and opened the door. The dressing room was spotless, as if the cleaners had been in and given it the full treatment. No filthy bandages or discarded plasters, no tie-ups, no mud or dirty puddles; no mess at all, as if there hadn't even been a match. It was quite something. What had happened was Forest had brought three apprentices with them, and they'd been instructed to clean up. And they'd done a fantastic job. What was the thinking behind all this? I thought it was brilliant. The apprentices had been taught: this is what you have to do; this is how to behave. You can't fault that, but it was confusing. It contradicted the way Brian (and to a lesser extent Peter) tended to behave regarding other matters.

On another occasion I was watching a local news report on Cloughie receiving (yet) another Manager of the Month award, and his words startled me as much as the tidy dressing room had. 'This award shouldn't be coming to me,' he said. 'It should be going to that young man at Coventry City who's doing a wonderful job at that football club.' Was it genuine? Did he mean it? Or was he playing mind games? Who knows? It was a lovely thing to say but Brian and Peter were contradictory at the best of times. To me, at its most basic level, this was ultimately the way he liked to manage. With Cloughie, the only thing you could be sure of was that you couldn't be sure of anything. And that was how he liked it.

Chapter 15

IN 1976 Jimmy Hill and Prince Faisal of Saudi Arabia signed a contract worth £25m to establish, promote and develop a new football infrastructure in the oil-rich state. In essence, Jimmy became the head of football for the Saudis; this was his show.

Later that same summer, we were in Scotland playing a few friendlies when Jimmy called. He was coming up and wanted a 'working breakfast' with Ron and myself. (I had no idea what a 'working breakfast' was, having never even heard the term.) At the time there had been one or two thinly veiled warnings in the press that Ron and I were on borrowed time. These warnings were neither heavy duty, nor constant, but continued to float around the back pages every so often. Against the backdrop of the Saudi deal, rumours continued to swirl, so with Jimmy on his way, Ron and I naturally feared the worst.

We met at 7.30 in the morning. Jimmy got straight to the point: 'This Saudi project … the first thing to do is find a manager for the national team, so you two get your heads together and come up with a few names.' You can imagine our relief; the sausages went down easier after that. Jimmy then told us what the salary would be. I forget the exact number, but it was five times what we were earning! 'And it's tax free as well, of course.' That didn't exactly soften the blow!

Ron turned to Jimmy and said, 'Jimmy, look no further. You're looking at the two men who can do the job.'

A wry smile appeared on Jimmy's face. 'Ron, behave. You two are going nowhere.'

Our feelings were mixed. On one hand we felt slightly hard done by; none of the Saudi wealth would be coming our way. However, that paled into insignificance when compared to the relief washing over us. From thinking this could be the end, to then hear Jimmy say our positions were safe was the opposite end of the spectrum. Emotionally, it was a roller coaster of a breakfast, and you don't get many of them!

Another key player was John Camkin. John was on the Coventry board during the '60s and was instrumental in bringing Jimmy to the club (John later went on to set up the League Managers' Association (LMA) with Olaf Dixon, whom I became very close to years later during my time at the LMA). John was an established sportswriter, a commentator – a good one too, with a great voice – and a clever man who Jimmy obviously respected. John essentially became managing director of the Saudi project, Jimmy's right-hand man.

Dipping our toes in the Saudi sands, we helped Jimmy to find a manager, Bill McGarry, an old-school disciplinarian recently sacked by Wolves after eight years with them, but as for the rest of it, we knew nothing. I never wanted to know more. I already had my hands full managing Coventry – hardly a part-time job – with more than enough responsibilities to keep me quiet. I was kept up to date with the goings-on as the steady flow of messages between the Middle East and the Midlands meant I'd frequently hear directors discussing the project. My biggest contribution to the programme was staging practice matches for the Saudi players, after which we'd all have dinner. The hierarchy would be on show, and senior management were presented with fancy watches (most definitely worth a few bob). It was glitzy and glamorous, the Saudis obviously trying to impress, and duly brought a bit of excitement to the club.

We went over to play a friendly. By then there were plenty of coaches, most of whom I knew, already out there. I didn't envy them though, as I quickly recognised their life wasn't for me. It was great money, but they were working on single-status contracts (meaning wives and partners couldn't join them) and living on a compound in what were basically Nissen huts. Furthermore, any misdemeanours would see their employers not hesitating in getting get rid of them, so it wasn't the most secure of positions. You couldn't get a drink – you had to smuggle it in – and the climate was obviously an issue too. The project was exciting, though, a step into the unknown, new, fresh and different. I'd never have imagined that 50 years or so in the future a World Cup would ever be played in that part of the world. And never mind a World Cup, what the bloody hell are you doing playing football over there in the first place? It's 130 degrees! But it was all part of the adventure. And, of course, there was money everywhere.

Jimmy, initially, did extremely well out of it, but it didn't last. The late '70s saw the programme begin to run its course. Jimmy began looking elsewhere and was drawn to the North American Soccer League (NASL), then reaching its peak. Franz Beckenbauer, Carlos Alberto and Pelé had all recently signed for the New York Cosmos and plenty more of football's biggest names wanted a piece of the action: Johan Cruyff, Gerd Müller, Eusébio, George Best, Bobby Moore, Alan Ball and Trevor Francis are just a few who made the move to the US.

Jimmy, being Jimmy, saw an opportunity: if the NASL was good enough for superstars like them, it was good enough for him. Unfortunately, he invested at precisely the wrong time. Much of the Saudi money was ploughed into the Detroit Express football franchise just as the US recession began to bite. Detroit was hit hard. Trying to stem the tide, Jimmy turned to the Washington Diplomats, but there was little difference in the outcome. I don't know how much Jimmy lost but, given the friction with the Coventry board, I suspect the club lost a fair bit too. It certainly wasn't all plain sailing.

The American adventure had its moments, though. I signed Steve Hunt from the New York Cosmos; a good left-winger, great left foot and a terrific crosser of the ball who had struggled at Villa before joining the Cosmos in 1977. Steve was reluctant to sign for us – with good reason. As he said himself, 'I'm playing with Beckenbauer and Pelé here!' Fair enough really!

We went out there with Coventry and were invited to a party in New York after a Cosmos game. I'll never forget it – it was like Hollywood! Beautiful weather, wine, champagne, models everywhere – incredible! Us English lads had never seen anything like it. The US was scratching to give the game a boost in its own country, and such shindigs were a big part of it all. However, many observers viewed the NASL as a Mickey Mouse version of the game, which is why they turned to the superstars in the first place. That too was seen as a gimmick, but nevertheless, with the showbiz, the razzamatazz, the cheerleaders and all that sort of stuff, it was a completely different world. It's little wonder that Jimmy was attracted to it, and I could see why. Sadly, though, it wasn't to be.

* * *

In 1977 I came as close to relegation as I ever would. Stoke City and Tottenham Hotspur occupied the bottom two places and the final day's fixtures would confirm who would join them in the Second Division the following season: Sunderland (who faced Everton), Bristol City or ourselves, all three on 34 points. And we'd meet Bristol City at Highfield Road. All to play for …

In my office prior to the match, I received a visit from the chairman Peter Robbins (Derek's son). This was most unusual. 'Gordon,' he said, 'as today's so important, what do you think about putting the lads on an extra few quid?' He was talking about the incentive of a win bonus, but it didn't sit right with me, it wasn't something we did. I also thought it would create extra pressure, which we obviously didn't need. I believed incentives should be written into contracts. I felt that suddenly telling the lads of an impromptu win bonus, right before this make-or-break match, would have been counterproductive. Some players might respond favourably (most would probably bite your hand off) without fully thinking about whether such an incentive actually does any good. To me that's a matter of opinion. My opinion was negative, and Ron agreed with me. The idea was shelved and the players knew nothing about it. Ultimately though, the issue added extra spice to the uniqueness of what was already an incredible occasion.

Alan Dicks was Bristol City's manager and already had a relationship with Jimmy, having coached alongside him at Coventry during the '60s. By the time I joined I knew Alan a little, and every time we spoke he knew more about the city than I did! He'd go on to manage in Bristol for an impressive 13 years. But that day in 1977 our relationships were just more ingredients to throw into the pot. They were good relationships but that only meant that with so much at stake I wished we'd been playing against somebody I disliked!

It was a 'winner takes all' job. Bristol brought 15,000 fans with them – our home advantage would be nullified – but traffic issues meant many were snarled up on the motorway so wouldn't arrive before kick-off, which was delayed by 15 minutes. Jimmy, now our managing director, took a lot of stick for this. Many assumed, wrongly, that he'd pulled a fast one, engineering a situation where we'd all know the Sunderland result before our own match had finished. That wasn't the case (although I wouldn't put it past him!). Jimmy was flying around all over the bloody place, winding up the fans, doing his PR thing, up in the stand, in the press box, on the Tannoy (he had a relationship from his old days with Sky Blues radio, the in-house entertainment). It wasn't Jimmy who delayed the kick-off but, like the rest of us, he could recognise the advantage in the situation. The delay ramped up the tension even more. I vividly remember the atmosphere in our dressing room and imagine Bristol City were feeling something similar across the corridor.

We took a 1-0 lead into the break thanks to Tommy Hutchison. Six minutes into the second half Tommy struck again. We were coasting. But a minute later Gerry Gow halved the deficit and with 11 minutes remaining Donnie Gillies levelled: 2-2. Bristol, with the momentum, now looked the more likely winners. Around this point the full-time whistle blew at Goodison Park. Everton had beaten Sunderland 2-0, meaning our current score of 2-2 would be good enough for both us and Bristol City to avoid relegation.

It was time to scramble. Both dugouts desperately tried to get the message to the players, which proved more difficult than you'd think. Terry Yorath was our captain, his former Leeds team-mate Norman Hunter his opposite number, both extraordinarily competitive and neither had it in him to play a friendly, nor did the rest of them. Everyone was still going for it, tackles were flying in. I'm thinking, *Christ, what if someone gets sent off here?* No matter how hard we tried to get the message to them, the noise and atmosphere made it nigh-on impossible. I eventually got hold of our full-back, Bobby McDonald, and told him to tell Terry, then get Terry to spread the word. Alan Dicks went through a similar process trying to get word to Norman! It probably only lasted five minutes, but it seemed like five years.

The news was announced over the Tannoy (and I'm sure Jimmy *was* behind that), although given the noise I don't think many fans heard it, and as a player you could just as easily remain unaware. Often this sort of thing is just more noise – it's not specific. So, given the circumstances that day – the atmosphere, the fervour, the occasion – it was understandable that it took so long for the players to register what was going on. Once they did, thankfully, the last five minutes or so became a knockabout. Our striker Mick Ferguson was even told by a Bristol voice to stay in his own half! By the skin of our teeth, we were safe (there was even a suggestion that had the *Titanic* been painted sky blue it wouldn't have gone down) and so were Bristol City. I'd imagine, however, that Sunderland wouldn't have been too happy had they seen those last five minutes.

Avoiding relegation isn't the greatest of achievements (but I know three clubs who would have gladly swapped places with us). The best part was after full time, of course, with everyone having a drink together – more through relief than anything else. Looking back at the tension and the pressure, I think we deserved a drink!

The following days brought the unsurprising news of Sunderland objections, and how they were preparing to appeal against the outcome, but it never happened. In all honesty, the noise wasn't massive and both us and Bristol City were soon exonerated of any wrongdoing. I can confidently and categorically state that nothing untoward took place. Jimmy didn't put the kick-off back, but the rumblings in the media remained and, of course, Sunderland and their supporters weren't best pleased, which I fully understand. However, as the only grounds for appeal was the kick-off time, and that had been decided by outside forces, there was never a case against us.

* * *

In June 1981 I became Coventry City's director of football, working directly with the new manager Dave Sexton. Dave was a great bloke, highly respected, and a top coach – a deep thinker, quiet, but a lovely man. His dad was a boxer and Dave himself had fought as a young amateur, so he had a streak in him, but he had a cheeky sense of cockney humour, too. You could have a laugh with Dave, but at the same time you'd think twice before taking him on.

One afternoon I received a call from the secretary, Eddie Plumley. The chairman wanted to speak to Dave, but no one could find him. He'd disappeared after training. I didn't have a clue where he was and nor did anyone else. I remember thinking, *I've got to be careful here, this is a new role for me and it's not my job to be checking up on the manager, where he goes and what he does in his free time.*

The next morning, I thought, *I've got to address this.* I had to tread carefully, so tried to keep it casual: 'Hello Dave, you alright? Was trying to get hold of you yesterday but no luck. Everything okay?'

'Oh yeah, fine,' he said.

'Where were you?'

'I was in Leamington,' he said. 'There's a brilliant little book shop. I was in there all afternoon!' I certainly wasn't expecting that, although wasn't surprised. Dave was an avid reader – history, world wars, who knows what else (some of the stuff he read was up in the clouds for me) – so I could easily picture him browsing away an afternoon. He kept very good diaries and journals of tactics and training sessions, stuffed full of different ideas and sessions (two against two, three against four, and so on), some of which he gave to me when I went to Turkey. I've still got them. Dave was ahead of his time in a way. I'd never experienced anybody as thorough as him regarding planning and preparation. He was meticulous, yet it was so easy to follow. Sometimes people give you written sessions, drills or tactics and you could be looking at algebra! But Dave's stuff was always so clear. He was a student, Dave, and not just of football.

When it came to the football, though, he only wanted to coach, be out on the training pitch with the players – nothing else. He kept it simple: do his work, then disappear. That was his makeup. He was so easy to work with, there was never any friction between us – just a great deal of mutual respect. He got on with his stuff, I tried to get on with mine. He'd never overly concern himself with the powers that be, was never disrespectful towards them, just preferred to remain at arm's length. He didn't really know the directors that well anyway.

Besides, he believed it was my responsibility to take that heat off him, and he was right.

From the outside, the two positions working together did just that – they worked. Unfortunately, from the inside, the position I occupied wasn't working for me. The truth is, I wasn't ready for that role. I was too young. The finest example of how the role should have been occupied was Joe Mercer at Manchester City, and then again at Coventry. Joe was ready. He was older, although not by much (but I do believe the role requires a little more seniority), old enough to have left it all out there on the pitch and to now be easing off, old enough to want to avoid the day-to-day grind at the sharp end. I, meanwhile, missed all that stuff, including the pressure. The director of football position wasn't what I'd expected. I had to develop a different personality and face up to different responsibilities – and I wasn't ready for that. Moving away from the bread and butter of the training ground was very difficult. I missed the buzz.

Leaving Coventry was very difficult, especially as the club had been so good to me. I'd been there for a decade and had I stayed I could see myself inevitably (although unintentionally) treading on others' toes. I desperately didn't want that to happen. Turning up at training, watching a session, coffee with the staff – none of that would have been the right thing to do. I'd joined Coventry all those years ago with the best of intentions and all the right feelings, and I left in similar vein. Thankfully, it was my own decision. I shook hands with the chairman, who fully understood, and moved on. And – again, thankfully – the mutual respect remained intact. I'd had a go, but I wasn't ready.

Chapter 16

BARELY TWO months later, the popular Leicester City manager Jock Wallace surprised everyone, unexpectedly announcing he was leaving, returning to Scotland to manage Motherwell. I liked big Jock. He and his loyal assistant Ian McFarlane were regular visitors to Highfield Road. Both were Scots, as was Ron, who would always invite them to have a drink in the office. There would be a knock on my door like someone had hit it with a sledgehammer before Jock and Ian appeared, both well over six feet tall, wearing big expensive overcoats, Ian with his trademark big flat cap (like an old Scottish football fan from the '30s) and both with an air of menace about them. To the untrained eye it may have looked like the KGB were in town! (They reminded me of the two army officials who blocked all the light in my bedroom when I was struck down with glandular fever all those years ago.)

Jock and Ian were always welcome. Three Scots and I (although admittedly I have more than a hint of a Scottish background) sharing a drink, talking football, moaning then laughing about shared problems. That was what football was all about, and I cherished such moments. They always wished us all the best, and their sincerity was never in doubt. I'd shake Jock's hand on his way out and always feel as if I'd broken three fingers. And in a funny way it was motivational too: both Ron and I would head to the dressing room on a high, and the boys would soon be revved up. Whether that was thanks to our visitors or the large whiskies, I'm not sure. I'd like to think a bit of both.

Jock's sudden departure left Leicester in a bit of a hole, but rather than sit around feeling sorry for themselves, they acted quickly. The following day the Leicester City manager's job was advertised in all the national newspapers. The position was now vacant and the club was interested in interviewing applicants as soon as possible. I must give credit to the board here; they had to act quickly to minimise the negative mood in the city, and they did just that.

I hadn't yet caught my breath since leaving Coventry but as I knew Alan Bennett, the Leicester secretary, it wasn't difficult for me to throw my cap into the ring. Without discussing my intentions with anyone, not even my wife, I called Alan and told him I was interested in putting my name forward for an interview. Less than a week later, the chairman, Terry Shipman, invited me to a meeting at a Leicestershire hotel with three other board members in attendance. In my youth my father had continually preached that I should never be late for any appointment so I arrived at the country hotel in good time, although due to all the media speculation I suspected I wouldn't be the only candidate there that day. This was confirmed later when entering the interrogation chamber, which was obviously expecting to accommodate more than one victim that day. The pressure was on.

The competition was fierce; the Leicester City job was a very attractive proposition. I felt the interview went okay but in such a situation uncertainty prevails and remains with you. But following a nervous 24 hours, a phone call from the chairman confirmed that the board had unanimously agreed to offer me the job. I was proud and delighted to be given the opportunity to manage another special club so quickly. Once again, I seemed to have been in the right place at the right time. I was back in football management.

The seismic shock of big Jock's departure was still resonating throughout the city when pre-season began, with supporters still trying to work out Jock's thinking, but after a single season at Motherwell Jock returned to his beloved Glasgow Rangers. When that happened, for many, his leaving Leicester finally made sense: in effect, Motherwell appeared to have been a stepping stone on his way back to Rangers.

Jock was always going to be a hard act to follow, having left at the height of his popularity after four years in the job. But it was his decision, and his alone. I remember big Jack Charlton, after leaving Middlesbrough, saying that five years of working with the same players and staff was enough. My take on it is that after five or six years in charge (if you're lucky) change is inevitable. In truth it happens daily: owners, players, management and staff change, even the supporters change. Nothing stands still in our daily lives, and football is no different. Should you find yourself in a position to influence change, which may or may not be in your best interests, careful and serious consideration is required. That old and trusted saying, which has stood the test of time, immediately comes to mind: be careful what you wish for.

For more than ten years, on reaching the end of my drive I turned right and headed west, 13 miles to Ryton on pleasant rural roads with time to think. Now I turned left and headed east. Similar rural roads and, would you believe, around 13 miles to a different training ground, Belvoir Drive, Leicestershire. I remember Bobby Robson, then enjoying success with Ipswich and being regularly courted by the big clubs, saying, 'D'you know, Gordon, I drive from my house to the training ground and not pass a single traffic light.' That simple pleasure meant so much to Bobby, and undoubtedly influenced his decision-making on many occasions when rejecting offers from the big boys. It proved – and I realised – how important it was to welfare and performance to be settled in a comfortable environment. I used to drive to Ryton and there were no traffic lights on my route either. I found that drive extremely helpful; vital thinking time and, especially after a bad day at the office, a chance to cool off. Bobby painted the picture of rural life beautifully, and he got it dead right.

Gerry Summers joined me as my number two. A good competitive midfield player in his time, he came with 12 years of managerial experience gained at Gillingham and Oxford United. He now wanted to concentrate on coaching, and I was glad to have him on board. Was I following a pattern here? My right arm at Coventry, Ron Wylie, had been an aggressive midfielder who could play a bit too, was in great physical condition and a top coach who knew how to handle players. Now, in Gerry, I had another aggressive midfielder at my side with similar qualities. Gerry had played more than 250 times for Sheffield United and, like Ron, was still in great physical condition, and a top coach too. They both loved their jobs and set the highest standards, which players and staff respected. Gerry wouldn't suffer fools, and could handle directors as well, unlike most coaches who preferred not to get involved. But he was most comfortable out on the grass, working with players. Like Ron and Tommy Casey before him, if he were a player, you'd have him in your team. I was set up and ready to go. Having someone like Gerry alongside me – someone to set standards that the players had to respect – was more important than I initially realised.

Before I arrived, big Jock used to have the players running up and down sandhills, effing and blinding at them, the regimental sergeant major type, a throwback to his National Service, more motivator than coach. Fans and directors loved that style of management, but it wasn't the way I worked. Change was coming. Nothing stands still.

* * *

Later in my career I got to know Jupp Derwall, the famous former coach of West Germany. He'd just finished managing Galatasaray when I began at Beşiktaş. Over a cup of strong Turkish coffee, I once asked him what he thought were the essential qualities necessary to become a top player. He didn't hesitate, and was adamant: 'Three things: ability, of course; character; and if you're talking *special* players, intelligence.' He viewed the latter as the most important, but he was talking about emotional intelligence – common sense, really – which surprised and interested me most. Most people think ability and character are enough but there have been plenty who possessed both who never made the most of themselves. Paul Gascoigne comes to mind, as does George Best. Jupp was talking about being clever enough to handle and maximise what you've got, and was emphatic: 'Two out of three isn't enough.' It was something that stuck with me, and I realised I'd experienced what he was talking about.

Our first pre-season encounters were against Northampton Town – two matches, our first team and reserves facing their equivalents at our training ground. The players were nowhere near full fitness, but I was eager to see what I'd inherited and how they approached the contests. Thankfully, there were no similarities to what I'd experienced more than ten years earlier in my baptism of fire at Coventry. This group gave it a go.

In my experience, senior players are no lovers of 11 vs 11 practice matches, particularly during pre-season when it's roasting hot. Remembering such occasions as a player, the search for fitness, touch and timing can create frustration and anger; not getting it all together generally means an untidy outcome, uneasy on the eye. As a coach, you're in tune with this, but as a new coach, the quicker you identify the players' characteristics, the better, regardless of the circumstances. So, what were my observations? Without going too deep, two or three who had been first-class servants for the club were looking their age; many were in second gear (understandable, given it was still pre-season); one or two had been at the club too long; and there were two or three interesting reserve prospects. Perhaps that was the norm everywhere?

Alan Young was a big, powerful centre-forward, a fans' favourite who that day was leading the first XI. I was casually drifting between the two matches when a young lad galloping about and enjoying himself in the second team caught my eye. At half-time I made a few changes to both teams, one of which was swapping this youngster with Youngie. This kid had only been at the club five minutes but continued to enjoy himself, banging in a second-half hat-trick.

The following day he was my priority. He'd just signed from non-league Alvechurch and had been studying at university while playing part-time, so was brand new to full-time professional football. It quickly became obvious he was unsure whether he had what was needed to make it at this level. Based upon that one practice session, however, it was also obvious we had to convince him that he was more than capable. As it turned out, he did this himself on a daily basis. His strength and fitness improved, and with that came confidence. He was 6ft 3in tall, mobile, had a good first touch and good game appreciation. He could only get better, too, if he was prepared to work and listen, which he was. When he put the No. 9 shirt on for the first match of the season, he'd only experienced one month as a professional, jumping from non-league football straight into a very competitive Second Division, a major leap. What he achieved in that short period was amazing really. Alan Smith had arrived; it was now up to him. And the rest is history.

Another young player who caught the eye, not only because of his pace and enthusiasm but also because he possessed that same intelligence, was a young striker called Gary Lineker; still only 22, a local boy who loved the club. He'd just experienced his first full season, scoring 19 goals in 47 appearances (not bad for starters). The potential was obvious, but as a youngster, never operating in second gear, so eager was he to turn and run at and beyond defenders that his first touch would sometimes let him down. But once he'd mastered the art of getting the first step right when facing his own goal, his game took on a different dimension. Now on the half-turn and facing his preferred way, he could and terrorise the opposition. His electric pace and intelligent running off the ball meant he was always looking to receive the early pass, always creating fear in the opposition. Gary was a midfielder's dream, particularly one who played with his head up, who could see a pass and execute it. Thankfully, we had one or two of those.

I didn't know the true qualities of Gary and Alan on day one, of course, but could see the potential and knew that with a bit of work we could have something very good on our hands. Both were willing to learn and had the nous to understand what was required to improve. Gary was totally focused and fully aware of his potential. He also had the self-belief to bring his dreams to fruition; whatever the challenge, he possessed that steely determination to succeed and was already setting a great example for his new partner. Alan was an intelligent boy himself, and the two complemented one another perfectly, not just on a matchday, but in training too, as their confidence and mutual respect grew. Jupp Derwall would have liked these two boys. They were another example of one of those combinations that had played such a huge part in my playing career.

What Gary and Smudger went on to achieve is well documented and I consider myself fortunate to have had three special years working with them. History proves that both possessed all the qualities required to be top professionals: talent, drive, resilience, intelligence. They were a great example to the game, but their partnership didn't take off by chance; they worked bloody hard at it, realising they had to, that hard work would improve them as individuals and as a partnership, and that each would benefit from, and improve, the other. Their first season together saw them share 35 goals, their last brought 44. Not too shabby at all.

Two players don't make a team, of course, but the signs were encouraging and the objective clear: return to the top flight, ASAP. However, the 1982/83 season didn't start well – personally or collectively. Welcome to the Second Division.

* * *

Football managers often make decisions based upon instinct, and operating that way, thankfully, tended to work for me. But not always. In 1980 Jim Melrose had been a big-money signing by Jock Wallace, a quarter of a million pounds, a club record at the time. Jim became a fans' favourite at Leicester, was a good lad, popular in the dressing room too, and prepared to compete with Lineker and Smith – all of which I should have considered when I decided to let him go.

Given our terrible start (just two wins in the first seven fixtures), I was soon under pressure – and didn't help myself. Tommy English had come through the Coventry ranks as a youngster, so I obviously knew him well – or thought I did. He was blessed with a natural ability to hit the target and score goals and showed as much regularly in training and in early matches. I felt I could maximise his potential, and my old pal at Coventry, Dave Sexton, thought the same about Jim Melrose. We agreed on a straight exchange, no money involved: Melrose to Coventry, English to Leicester – both happy? As it turned out, no. My decision to get rid of Jim was wrong – big time. He scored a hat-trick on his home debut for Coventry against Everton, but Tommy struggled with us and failed to live up to expectations, especially under the weight of the Leicester fans never really accepting him. It wasn't easy for Tommy, and I felt for him.

I couldn't have got off to a worse start: poor results, low attendances and trading a fans' favourite for a player who had never really got going. And with Jock having been so popular before me, it was little wonder that after a few short weeks I wasn't exactly flavour of the month. Furthermore, after only one season at Coventry, Celtic paid the Sky Blues £100,000 for Jim. All told, Leicester had originally paid £250,000 for him, received no financial gain when he left, and had now missed out on £100,000 from Celtic. It was a triple whammy. Ultimately, Jim's career never quite hit the heights it could have, but that doesn't vindicate my decision to exchange him. I should have hung on to him longer, but his subsequent achievements suggested I was correct in my initial thinking.

What to learn from this? Despite the Jim/Tommy deal not working out I still believe you should stick to your instincts; they're part of your DNA and will never leave you. You don't have to declare them to anyone either, until you're ready to do so – if even then. Don't speculate, for whatever reason – you're gambling, and the stakes are too high for that. Whatever decision you make, right or wrong, will declare itself – over time and free of charge. You can only hope you'll still be around to witness it.

* * *

We steadied the ship with four wins on the trot in October but then went six matches without a victory. It was a frustrating season, very bitty. And in the back of my mind I was still conscious of Jock's popularity, how the board supported him, how the players and the fans were behind him. I was feeling it. There was most definitely a job to do, and it was in my face daily. There was no escape, but at least I knew what was required. There was no mystery: win. And if we can't win, don't lose. Even then, though, that might not be enough.

By mid-February we were nowhere, but a 14-match unbeaten run took us to the last day of the season, Burnley at home. Queens Park Rangers and Wolves occupied the top two spots but incredibly, after what had felt for so long like a 'nothing season', alongside Fulham we were now chasing the final promotion spot.

How did we get here? Natural causes. There was no secret, it was all down to hard work. As a coach, six months into a new job you're still in your infancy in terms of working with players and directors and getting the fans on-side. But everyone wants instant coffee, don't they? Fans and directors want something good straight away, but it rarely works like that. The players and I had begun to develop an understanding, we were improving as a unit and growing in confidence. The likes of Gary and Alan were learning how to play with each other, Stevie Lynex on the wing too, and suddenly we had momentum, so important in football.

All season we felt we'd gone about things in the right way, but for six months the results weren't there, and there were no quick fixes. We were never ultra-attacking, but we'd have a go, and subsequently would be caught out, not tidy enough at the back. But with the likes of Lynex, Smith and Lineker, playing negatively would never have worked and, had we done so, names such as those wouldn't have hung around too long. We had to play to our strengths. A flying winger like Stevie was one of them so we had to get as much out of him as possible. In turn, he'd bring the best out of Lineker and Smith. Ian Wilson, and in later years Gerry Daly and Gary McAllister, were of the same mindset as Stevie: playing with their heads up, always looking forward. Players who could see an early pass and deliver it were encouraged to do so.

I also asked players their preferred positions. It seems obvious, but I didn't want anyone playing somewhere they didn't want to be. Gary, in his early days, was often played wide. He was quick and he hadn't yet established himself through the middle, so there was a logic to it. As a kid he wouldn't have worried, as at least he was in the team, but at the end of the day all players have their favourite positions. Fortunately, we had them in the right slots, although it didn't work immediately and, when we were struggling, the dreaded 'R-word' popped into my head on several occasions. I tried to block it out; relegation to the Third Division would have been disastrous, so players of this calibre had to be encouraged and given the best possible ammunition to do what they did best. It proved a successful policy: in three seasons Smith, Lynex and Lineker scored more than 150 goals between them. It's important to remember too that these players hadn't yet developed any sort of reputation. Now, of course, Gary and Alan are well known for their television work, but with Stevie, because he hasn't pushed on in the public eye, you might well ask, 'Who's he?' However, that season as they were all just starting out, 'Who's Gary Lineker?' was as valid a question as 'Who's Stevie Lynex?'

Gradually we emerged from the doldrums. As results improved so did the crowds – essential. That 'here we go again' mood of a bad run can be extremely damaging and, once it takes root, is very difficult to dig out. The longer our unbeaten run continued, the greater the atmosphere became. There was now belief rather than hope, so much so that, with promotion on the line, the final match against Burnley would draw a crowd of nearly 30,000 – three times what we'd been getting earlier in the season! That can happen on big days, but it did indicate Leicester's potential. If we could produce a good team, the support was there.

Five matches previously we'd visited Fulham who, under Malcolm Macdonald, were well in the hunt for promotion. We were still lagging behind, so nobody took us seriously as promotion candidates, least of all Malcolm, who, never short of confidence, had plenty to say beforehand: 'There's only one team playing proper football – that's us,' and plenty more besides. He had less to say after we beat them 1-0, mind! Ian Wilson didn't score many, but right in front of our own fans he rifled in a beauty from 25 yards. I wasn't impressed by Malcolm's conduct, making us out to be second-class citizens, so that win was especially sweet, not least for the fans. We had a hell of a crowd at Craven Cottage that day, filling the whole terrace behind the goal. I always remember walking off the pitch, past our supporters and thinking, *We can do this*.

The players thought the same. We never dreamed we'd be in such a position but on the final day, with promotion up for grabs, we believed. Burnley were bottom of the league, staring relegation in the face, but with a match in hand their destiny was in their own hands – they'd be fighting for their lives. Our task was straightforward enough: win and we were up. It was all set to be a cracker – full house, great atmosphere, the away team down in the dumps (yet still fighting), the home team going for glory. But how often do favourites fall by the wayside? We were aiming for 15 matches undefeated, yet even that might still not be enough. We'd put ourselves in a great position, but if we blew it now ... it didn't bear thinking about.

I arrived early, and the fans were already there in their droves. I'd not seen anything like it all season. As I pushed through the throng, I said to one chap, 'This is bloody great, isn't it?'

'I don't know, mate,' he replied. 'I've never been here before.' Brilliant! He didn't know who I was, but that didn't matter. The occasion brings people in, and this was certainly an occasion ... make or break. We huffed and puffed and finished 0-0. It was now out of our hands. A Fulham win at Derby and we'd miss out on promotion.

Derby themselves weren't safe from relegation so Fulham had a battle on their hands. When Derby took the lead with 20 minutes remaining, the match descended into chaos as fans spilled on to the pitch and continued to do so for the next quarter of an hour. Ray Chadwick, the referee, eventually blew for full time, or so everyone thought; he actually blew for an offside decision, but with fans swarming all over the pitch, the teams returned to the dressing rooms. Chadwick informed both sets of players and management there were 78 seconds remaining but, given the scenes outside, there was no chance of the match restarting. It meant we were promoted, and Fulham missed out. Naturally, Malcolm was furious, and I sympathised. I was quoted as saying, 'If I was in Malcolm's position, I'd have had the referee by the throat and made sure there was another game.'

Somebody brought the champagne into our dressing room, and we were off, time to celebrate. We were back in the big time! Or were we? About 20 minutes later we put the champagne down. Fulham were appealing and wanted the match to be replayed. Their appeal would be heard two days later, on the Monday. Our celebrations fizzled out quickly.

We were in limbo, but it was out of our hands. I met with the chairman Terry Shipman. 'Terry, whatever happens with this appeal, there's nothing we can do. If we go up, we go up; if we don't, we don't. The lads have done all they can so we're all going to bugger off to Majorca for five days.' Terry, bless him, said, 'No problem.' So 24 hours later we were on the beach, still none the wiser. The following day Fulham's appeal was heard. Two days after that their appeal was rejected. The result stood and our promotion was confirmed! The saga meant we'd missed our deserved drink-up on the Saturday, so we had it now instead – on the Wednesday, Thursday and Friday!

It was amazing, really, uncanny echoes of 1977, when my Coventry City team avoided relegation with Bristol City thanks to that 2-2 draw that suited us both (that day there was talk of Sunderland appealing but thankfully that never came to pass). It had been a nervy few days, and I felt for Fulham, but we hadn't done anything wrong.

Having come through some testing times, I'd led Leicester City back into the big time at the first time of asking. I'd also learned a great deal, most importantly the value of patience. As a young coach struggling for results, it's difficult to gain any credibility; you feel as if you're just getting shot at, but I was fortunate enough to have ten years' experience under my belt, so was equipped to handle the rough start at Filbert Street. And, crucially, I was mature enough to continue to believe in what we were doing.

* * *

We were back at the top table after a couple of seasons in the wilderness. To clubs of Leicester's standing and expectation that was the perception of the Second Division: a wilderness. The reality, though, was quite different: it was more like a jungle! It was a bloody tough league, with bigger clubs than ours desperately thirsting for the same recognition, all trying to restore credibility and status. 'Take no prisoners' was a fair indication of the mindset of us all, and the minimum requirement if you were to have any joy. And so it proved.

There were many similarities with the challenges I'd faced at Coventry: a limited budget; searching for consistency in performance; the desire to be taken seriously in the pecking order, which in turn would (hopefully) attract serious players to the club; ultimately, all (hopefully, again) leading to successful First Division football.

At the start of every season at Coventry the national press had consistently viewed us as likely candidates for relegation – hardly encouraging. Thankfully it never happened, although there were plenty of bigger clubs who did suffer that fate during those years: Manchester United (Denis Law famously back-heeled his former team into the Second Division while playing for Manchester City), Chelsea, Tottenham Hotspur and Newcastle United, to name but a few. Now, with Leicester, I was back where I wanted to be. The challenges hadn't changed: win as many matches as possible, play attractive football, give young players a chance, balance the books. This was certainly nothing new to me; I knew what was required. Knowledge and experience thrive over time, allowing the brain to absorb the numerous different situations a manager faces. Today, time isn't a commodity that appears to be as important as it once was in the pursuit of success. But how do you define success in the first place? Each division has its own criteria, priorities and values. Take the Premier League, for example: for some, a top-six finish would be deemed a success, while for others, mid-table would qualify. But as a season begins, few clubs (if any) would ever dare make such a statement of intent for fear of a negative reaction from supporters and sponsors alike.

Survival was – for many, still is – the dreaded word, but why so important? Well, we all knew why: retaining top-flight status would mean dining at the top table, deservedly, every week, not to mention the financial rewards on offer; the country's finest players appearing on our own patch (and our own lads would now be, on merit, First Division player themselves); sharing another season in the world's most competitive, exciting league with our loyal supporters and friends; and the publicity such a position generates for the home town/city. What's not to like? Survival was hardly in the same bracket as striving for trophies, but it was important for us to look positively at what we did have, rather than look negatively at what we didn't.

My three seasons in the top flight with Leicester would be a constant struggle (finishing 15th, 15th and 19th), but we dug in and stayed there. Facing such difficulties, a coach is always looking for a glimmer of hope. I'd found one through hard-working players (many of whom were responsible for promotion in the first place), and another through the ability, progress and development of Gary Lineker, Alan Smith and Stevie Lynex, a trio to challenge the big boys, especially given their appreciation and knowledge of the game. It didn't hurt either that all three performed consistently well and scored goals (more than 150 between them) in a team struggling for recognition. This, alongside our mentality – constant positivity, trying to play on the front foot – proved to be our salvation.

* * *

Like most strikers, Gary Lineker was never a lover of talking tactics; he never had the patience. If you wanted a 10 vs 10 or 8 vs 8, he'd get bored. John McVay was our physio, a good lad, another Scot with a dry sense of humour. One miserable November morning John approached me: 'Gordon, Gary's not feeling too well, a wee bit of a sore throat. I think it would be best if he doesn't train today, we don't want to take any chances.' I agreed.

The following morning rolled around. 'How's Gary today, John?' 'Oh, much better, boss. He'll be okay to play tomorrow, don't worry about him.' This didn't happen often enough for me to say it became a pattern, but it did happen, and occasionally I'd bite my tongue. But, on the Saturday, he'd go out, score two goals and win the match.

And he wasn't the only one. Big Lawrie McMenemy told me about Mick Channon (who went on to become a successful racehorse trainer), who on more than one occasion at Southampton approached Lawrie with bad news. 'He came to me one Thursday saying, "Gaffer, the groin's not going to be too good this weekend. Just wanted to let you know early." It was bollocks, and we all knew it,' said Lawrie. 'There was a race meeting at Kempton on the Saturday, and Mick had a couple of horses running!' Lawrie went on: 'There are two options: you can start World War Three by saying, "I know what you're up to, and you're not going to the f***ing races!" or you can tell the press he's got a sore groin but should be available for the game next Wednesday – which was often what we did. Mick would go out on the Wednesday and score a hat-trick!'

It was all about man-management. I'm not sure it would work today, but it's a tricky one. To be clear, though, Gary wasn't like that; he'd never say he was injured if he wasn't. But if a player doesn't fancy training one day and tells you he wants to be right for the Saturday, what do you do? You find a way to get the best out of them, physically and mentally, and ensure they're fully tuned in for the next match.

* * *

I always enjoyed heading north of the border when scouting for new talent; hardly surprising, as many players recruited there proved worthy of the journey: Ian Wallace, Gary McAllister, Gary Gillespie, Colin Stein, Jim Brogan … all recruited on the advice of my chief scout John Rice. 'Come up and have a pie,' he'd say, 'I've something for you to look at.' After training I'd be on the four o'clock flight from Birmingham to Glasgow (from where there were several grounds within an hour-and-a-half's drive), and I'd be back for nine o'clock the following morning, ready for training with no one the wiser. Or so I thought.

Once or twice I bumped into that unique character Jimmy Sirrel, the Notts County manager, at the Glasgow Airport hotel, obviously on the same mission as me (a true Scot, Jimmy knew the territory). I first met him when a group of managers visited the World Cup finals in Germany in 1974: two weeks of continuous laughter listening to Jimmy's stories and his take on the game. Holding court one day, he mentioned a player, 'a continuous pain in the arse, always moaning, always asking, "Can I have a word, Boss?" And remember, the ones who are the biggest waste of your time are the ones who can't play.' The player in question eventually secured his meeting with the manager.

'Well, what is it I can help you with, son?' asked Jimmy.

'Well, Boss … I've not played many games, I don't know if I'm coming or going, and—'

'Let me stop you right there, son,' interrupted Jimmy. 'You're f***ing going!'

That was Jimmy – no nonsense. It might have been the same player involved when Jimmy opened a meeting with 'Now, before we start, son, is this going to be poison darts or peashooters?' This was Jimmy at his best, in an era long gone.

Prior to returning from one of our scouting missions, Jimmy and I were having breakfast in the hotel. Enjoying our sausage, egg and bacon, neither of us questioned the other on which match we'd attended the night before. We may have been to the same match, studying the same player, but that was never discussed. The priority was attacking the breakfast as time was tight. Jimmy was applying the HP sauce in vast quantities all over his eggs. 'After you please, Jim,' I said. He then gave the top of the bottle a good big lick before replacing the top and thrusting it towards me. He was from a big family, Jimmy.

It was a different era. Jimmy was old-school Scottish, like Shanks and the Doc, and successful too, taking Notts County from Fourth Division strugglers to the First Division. Before home matches he'd have a quick drink and a chat with his long-time chairman Jack Dunnett. After once failing to show up for this little ritual, Jimmy eventually appeared shortly before kick-off. After the match Jack caught up with him: 'Missed you earlier, Jimmy, everything alright?' 'Yes, sorry I was late, Mr Chairman. My wife passed away this morning.' Incredibly, this was true. His wife had indeed died that morning, yet Jimmy was apologising for being late. He wasn't being disloyal to his wife by still turning up. As he saw it, he had a responsibility to the club and a job to do. The Notts County fans knew that about Jimmy; that's why they loved him, and why he stayed so long. It's who he was, and who and what he represented mattered to him. And you couldn't help but love him for that.

* * *

When your league form isn't the best, a decent cup run can ease the pain. In 1985 we drew non-league Burton Albion away in the FA Cup third round, a local derby that caught the attention of fans and media alike. Burton's ground at the time didn't meet the FA's safety standards so the match was moved to the Baseball Ground, home of Derby County. This gave the tie even more spice, an opportunity for Burton to play at a big ground and for us to take a bigger travelling support (which we did). For a week the media was in full flow: local TV previewed the match every night and the national press did their bit too. Furthermore, both clubs shared a sponsor, the brewery Ind Coope (founded in Burton itself), who offered the extra incentive to the winners of a barrel of ale containing 288 pints!

It was my first meeting with Neil Warnock, Burton's manager, an interesting experience, especially having watched his TV interviews – you'd have thought we were the non-league club, and the result would be a classic cup shock! Even when he was young, Neil already had plenty to say. He stoked the coals, creating extra interest and a bit of needle, which in turn boosted the attendance that day to more than 30,000.

The result? A big win for Leicester, 6-1, but sadly marred by the behaviour of some mindless thugs with the sole intention of causing havoc – which they did, big time. The Burton goalkeeper Paul Evans was hit with all sorts of debris thrown from behind his goal – beer cans filled with sand, coins, blocks of wood torn from the seating – and required prolonged treatment. I fully understood the reactions from Neil Warnock and his bench. The atmosphere was nasty. At the time, English football was tainted by basic hooliganism (and not only football, but any events where crowds gathered). Ultimately, following the violence at the Heysel Stadium in May that year, English clubs were banned from European competition for five years. A disease was festering in our game, one that could destroy all our principles and way of life should it be allowed to continue. This was supposed to be the magic of the cup – a non-league club against a First Division team from down the road – but the magic was ruined, right in front of our eyes. Unsurprisingly, the FA ordered the match to be replayed 11 days later at a neutral ground, Highfield Road, behind closed doors. How sad.

Neil Warnock's predictions for the original tie were way off the mark, but the replay was much closer to what he'd envisaged, and much too close for my liking. On a cold, grey day in the ghostly atmosphere of an empty stadium, where the club's cat strolled down the touchline and pigeons settled on the terrace barriers, Paul Ramsey scored for us after just four minutes, and that was as good as it got. We limped to a 1-0 win. The reality was that hooliganism was seriously affecting our way of life.

At the end of the season Terry Shipman and I decided to treat ourselves to a trip to Brussels for the European Cup Final between Liverpool and Juventus. It should have been a nice little trip but instead became a nightmare that neither of us could ever foresee. When all the post-match inquiries were over, the tragedy, which saw the deaths of 39 Italian supporters, didn't speak well of English football fans, but sitting with Terry in the main stand an hour before kick-off, it was difficult to anticipate what was about to take place. There was the typical goading between rival fans, the usual uncomplimentary gestures, although it was noticeable the behaviour was becoming increasingly aggressive. This was the European Cup Final though, between two passionate clubs, so what did we expect? Sadly, this is what we *had* come to expect in England (without the fatalities though, thankfully); this was now normal. We were in the midst of hooliganism, north, south, east and west, and it was bloody horrible.

What was brewing in Brussels was similar to what we'd experienced against Burton four months earlier, albeit on a much bigger scale. It quickly became obvious things were getting out of hand. We could see the police were involved, and the serious change in the crowd's behaviour was frightening. It was difficult to say how I truly felt: helpless and fearful, but also saddened yet again by what was happening in front of my eyes at a football match. Tragically, worse was to come.

My next recollection is of Terry and I outside the stadium – leaving. Not conscious of time or place, we began, slowly, to walk. On reaching the far end of the main stand we came across a scene that will stay with me forever. Against a wall of damaged terracing lay bodies. People who had come to a football match to support their heroes now lay dead, six feet from where I was standing. Some were in their club's colours, others shabbily covered in whatever material had been found. And, as I stood there, the bodies kept arriving, supporters carrying dead or dying colleagues, in eerie silence, with blank, expressionless faces, numb, in shock.

We couldn't dwell at such a scene. Terry and I walked and walked, away from the stadium, through the wailing ambulances and police vehicles. If we'd wanted to talk, which we didn't, it would have been impossible. The silence had been replaced by the soundtrack of an emergency, and neither Terry nor I handled it well. On reaching our hotel we were amazed to learn the authorities had decided the match should go ahead for security reasons. My chairman and I finished half a bottle of brandy and went to our beds. Neither of us slept. We travelled home the following day, abandoning our plans for a longer stay. Terry wasn't much older than me. I wouldn't call him a father figure, he was more like a brother, somebody I was comfortable with and, in a strange way, what we experienced in Brussels brought us even closer. I don't think we talked about it ever again but there's no question that what we'd experienced never went away.

Of course, then came the accusations, recriminations, inquiries and opinions. On the flight home I'd never felt so low. Only days before, we'd all witnessed the horrific fire that engulfed Valley Parade in Bradford, which took 56 lives – innocent supporters who had gone to watch a football match and never returned – and injured hundreds more. No one could have prevented such a loss. The images of the main stand engulfed in flames were still fresh in the mind, and now this at Heysel. Where was football going? On that sad journey home, in my mind, only one way.

Chapter 17

IN FOOTBALL, as in life, change is constant. Collectively, my Leicester team wasn't generating much interest, but individually Gary and Alan were catching the big clubs' eyes, and it was only a matter of time before one (or more) of those clubs moved in.

In Gary's case it was Everton who, as league champions, were ahead of the pack. Given his statistics – in 1984/85 he was the First Division's joint-top scorer alongside Chelsea's Kerry Dixon – it was no surprise Gary was a target. I always thought had Leicester been a little more progressive at that time Gary wouldn't have left us when he did in the summer of 1985. He was never knocking on my door suggesting it was time to move on; no one wanted the club to succeed more than him. Gary was a local boy and proud of it, happy at home and at the club. He was always upbeat and liked a laugh and a joke, so much so that you wondered sometimes whether he took football seriously enough! That was probably why he scored so many goals: he was simply enjoying his football, and when that happens, players tend to be at their best.

Everton were managed by Howard Kendall, who I knew well and liked a lot. I had fond memories of Howard's Preston North End days when my father, as his manager, selected the 17-year-old for the 1964 FA Cup Final. Now, Howard and I began negotiations. Having confirmed Everton's bid was serious, I informed Gary. Media speculation meant it would have been naive to think this was the first he knew of Everton's approach, yet his reaction was typical: 'Okay, I'm happy to have a chat.' He was in no way carried away by the overtures of one of Europe's top teams.

Our valuation of Gary was around £1.2m (still a bargain in my view); Everton wanted to pay no more than £500,000. A stalemate ensued. There was nothing personal between Howard and me, nor any animosity between the clubs, but with neither prepared to budge, the fee would ultimately be decided by an FA tribunal.

Gary arrived at Lancaster Gate with Howard, where both clubs were represented by managers, chairmen and secretaries. But who would have the necessary qualifications to establish his true value? Former managers or players who understood the game? No. Scouts or coaches with specific expertise in identifying talent and potential? Not them either. No one 'in charge' that day had any such experience. I found the whole situation unsavoury. Here was a young, guaranteed goalscorer with electric pace, perfect temperament and whose best years were undoubtedly still ahead of him. Yet here were two good clubs bartering like market traders, in front of FA officials who didn't have a clue. (In fairness, it wasn't the FA's fault; they were only involved because we couldn't agree a fee between ourselves.) Consequently, the process was both predictable and inevitable: Howard knocked Gary down, I built him up. Their take was, 'He's still young, hasn't yet proved himself consistently,' even though he had, 'so we're taking a punt here. It's a risk.' (I couldn't blame them; in their shoes, we'd have done the same.) Our standpoint was, of course, the polar opposite: 'He's scored for fun these last couple of years and will only get better; he's already played for England, and he'll play a lot more for them. He'll be world-class, no doubt about it.' History, of course, proves we were right.

The fee was eventually set at £800,000, unsatisfactory for both clubs, although I thought it was worse for us. We were promised another £200,000 if Gary were to leave Everton within the next two years. I remember saying, 'That's very kind, but there's not a cat in hell's chance of that happening!' Gary was moving to a top club and would be challenging regularly for trophies – why would he leave them so soon?

Of course, Gary did brilliantly for Everton. In his first (as it turned out, his only) season at Goodison Park he scored 40 goals in 57 matches, was the league's top scorer with 30 goals, Players' Player and Football Writers' Player of the Year, and Golden Boot winner at the 1986 World Cup in Mexico with six goals for England. All this, yet Everton agreed to sell him – work that one out! Gary began the next season at the Camp Nou as a Barcelona player; not bad for 'a bit of a risk'. Both Terry and I felt cheated.

I later discovered Gary travelled with Howard back to Liverpool and expressed his concern over Howard's earlier comments. Howard apologised, before reassuring him: 'Don't worry. I had to say all that to knock the fee down! We've got a bargain and are delighted you're joining us!' Then they went out to celebrate! Good luck to them. I wasn't pleased with the outcome, nor the process, but it was all part and parcel. And when Gary did leave Everton a year later, he joined arguably the biggest club in the world. Barcelona paid £2.2m so we got a few extra quid, and Everton more than doubled their money. I suppose it turned out alright for all of us, but to this day I still feel short-changed!

* * *

Gary's departure meant a big chunk of our goalscoring potential had to be replaced, as did a big personality – not easy. A significant signing for the club that summer was Ally Mauchlen, a tenacious, hard-working midfielder from Motherwell who, like many clubs, were struggling financially. I knew their manager Tommy McLean quite well, and a fee for Ally was quickly agreed. I was pleased, but my interest in Motherwell didn't end there.

One cold winter's evening back at Motherwell's home, Fir Park, as I enjoyed those wonderful scotch pies, I watched a teenager by the name of Gary McAllister. He stood out a mile, gliding across the pitch, comfortable on either foot. He took a corner right in front of where we were standing. It was a wet night, the pitch heavy and the ball too. He gently positioned it with one foot, before striking the perfect delivery with the other. One old-stager standing nearby, with his cloth cap and steaming Bovril, commented, 'He'll be a braw player, that boy. Mark my words.' Being from Scottish stock myself, I knew exactly what he meant – and how right he was.

Having already agreed the Ally fee (£150,000) and knowing Tommy McLean was aware of Gary's potential too, I gambled. Given Motherwell's financial situation, I thought they'd struggle to refuse if I doubled my offer to include Gary in the deal. To Tommy's dismay his board accepted. I was delighted. In Ally I'd recruited a mature player who would deliver straight away, and who would guide his young team-mate, allowing him to grow, develop and overcome the difficulties of being away from home as a 19-year-old. Ally did this brilliantly. He was a sergeant major type, not cocky, but confident, and took on that big brother role naturally. Mauchlen and McAllister might have sounded like a stage double act but were worth every penny of Leicester's investment. Ally went on to work for the club in hospitality with the same enthusiasm he devoted to his playing career.

Despite his youth, Gary was incredibly mature; such was his demeanour in training you might forget just how young he was. He could just play and was always going to make it. I saw in him similarities with Trevor Francis when Trevor first came through; undoubted talent, confidence in his own ability and a level of maturity well suited to making his way in the game.

I was lucky. I'd lost one Gary but acquired another. Lineker and McAllister were two special players I had the privilege of knowing as young men. I only wish I'd seen them in the same team.

* * *

Football and fate: Gary Lineker had left but we'd see him again – as soon as we could! The next season's fixtures came out, and would you believe it – first up for us? Everton. The league champions travelled to Filbert Street but thankfully we kept Gary quiet and managed a 3-1 win. Alan Smith was on the scoresheet, as was a young lad who, by scoring twice, was hoping the fans would think, *Gary who?* That young lad was Mark Bright. Mark had had limited opportunities the previous season but with a good pre-season behind him he merited his selection that day. There was tremendous pressure on him, facing someone across the centre circle who he respected so much and who was a Leicester City legend. But that day he rose to the occasion.

He'd joined us from Port Vale as a 22-year-old in 1984. Coming from a broken home and raised by foster parents, he'd not had it easy, but possessed a hunger and desire to make something of his life. He was tough, and had to be: as the season progressed, he suffered periods of inconsistency, struggling to get among the goals. More alarmingly, though, a small section of the Leicester crowd piled in on Mark whenever they could – and not just for footballing reasons. It was the first time I ever experienced significant ill feeling towards a player. Brighty took an horrendous amount of stick, especially over a misplaced pass or a squandered chance and, sadly, it was all down to the colour of his skin. He never complained, though. He was happy to be in the First Division, more than happy to work hard, and popular in the dressing room; a great lad, Mark, who, through his own determination, bravery and the support of his team-mates and staff, learned how to weather the storm, a storm that occasionally subsided but was always rumbling on the Filbert Street horizon.

Ron Noades was the chairman/owner of Crystal Palace, a shrewd operator and a likeable wheeler-dealer. During that season, whenever Mark was playing for our reserves, Ron was a regular at Filbert Street and made it quite clear his sole interest was this young centre-forward who we'd paid too much for, and who couldn't get into our first team – at least, that was Ron's patter! Ron eventually got his man, and Brighty blossomed. He created a wonderful partnership with Ian Wright, terrorising the best defences in the country with energy, skill and aggression – no one fancied facing those two. I was delighted for him. He's now regarded as a Palace legend, and rightly so.

Mark had been at Selhurst Park for about a year when one day I thought I'd check in on him. My call went directly to answerphone and in his cheery voice the message went something like: 'That's right, it's Mark Bright! Sorry I can't take your call; please leave your message and I will get back to you – if I want to.' I didn't bother. Brighty was fine.

His previous partner Alan Smith was still with us, but in the spring of 1987 Arsenal came knocking. George Graham was the manager, and a fee of £800,000 was agreed. After the deal was done we sat down for a drink and I said, 'George, I don't think you know what you're getting here. He's raw, just starting out really. There's so much more to come from him. You'll get him at his peak.' Alan turned out to be a magnificent signing. He could score goals and win matches on his own, but he could also bring others into play (it's why he and Lineker worked so well). He could lead the line, too. Only the top boys could do all that, and Alan was one of them. I was lucky to have him as long as I did.

Alan was loaned back to us for the reminder of the season but even he couldn't help stave off relegation. However, he's fondly remembered by the supporters and remains a popular figure at the club. At Leicester City there will always be a warm welcome for Smudger.

* * *

Having won promotion to the First Division in my first season at Leicester, I was conscious that three years later, as far as any critical supporter could see, we were going nowhere. We'd ended the season with a closing run full of tension and pressure (like most of the campaign, in fairness), most evident in the mood of our supporters. Home matches, which should have been advantageous, became a nightmare. The players were nervous, scared of making the slightest mistake. It was a toxic atmosphere that helped nobody. This was my responsibility, though; this was happening because of the performance, or lack of it, and that was down to me.

So where was I now, after four years in charge? Was it time for change? And what made me ask myself that question? Obviously, the current mood played a part – I knew most of our supporters would be glad to see the back of me, but that comes with the territory; selling good players was also a factor that put severe pressure on the squad. I had to ask myself: was I still up for the fight? And if not, would I be running away?

Or were other matters influencing my thoughts? In short, yes. I'd always felt that one day I'd like to experience the challenge of coaching abroad. Hooliganism was rife and seeping into everyday society; a year earlier we'd suffered the twin tragedies of Bradford and Heysel, the penalty for which – English clubs banned from European competition for five years – shook English football to its roots.

All these thoughts weighed heavily upon me, and I could see what lay ahead: retaining our credibility and status would become increasingly difficult. The stars were aligning, with all the signs pointing me towards the exit door. I still felt a certain degree of pride at the job I'd done. We weren't skint and were still in the First Division; not what I'd inherited, but now an attractive proposition for someone else to come in and have a go. Leicester City needed freshening up.

I felt it was the right time to move on, not least because I'd known for a while there were several directors pushing for me to go. There were accusations of me (potentially) abandoning ship; that was never the case. I believed I'd been doing the right things, and if I was failing, it wasn't for the lack of trying. Terry and Alan Bennett, the secretary, both wanted me to stay, and had always been so supportive. Equally, I wanted to be there for them; as they were heading towards another period of change, I had no intention of abandoning them. So, as I didn't want to continue as manager, we agreed I'd move upstairs – but only for one season. I hadn't enjoyed being a director of football at Coventry so knew I wouldn't particularly enjoy the role at Leicester.

Identifying the next Leicester City manager was top of the agenda. A year earlier we'd travelled to the Isle of Man to play a friendly against Wigan Athletic, then doing well under Bryan Hamilton. After about 30 minutes of a competitive encounter the ball was floated up the wing towards the halfway line, dropping right in front of Terry and me, sitting together on a long wooden school bench. As the ball hung tantalisingly in the air, a six-foot-plus Wigan defender appeared from nowhere, dispatched the ball into the distance and clattered into Terry, knocking him off his seat. The player apologised before sprinting back towards the action. Terry dusted himself down, regained his composure, and said, 'I like him.' The player was Steve Walsh, and a year later Terry was instrumental in bringing him to Leicester (Walshy went on to become a Foxes legend, making more than 500 appearances). Terry also brought in Wigan's manager that day, Bryan Hamilton. I liked Bryan too; he was bubbly and positive. He'd been a good player, done a good job at Wigan and had a completely different personality to me. When you do make a change, I think that's important. There's no point swapping carbon copies of key personnel. Bryan was younger than me too, which I also thought would help.

We all tried to make the transition as smooth as possible. Bryan fully understood the thinking behind it all and was happy and raring to go. There was optimism in the air, the mood at the training ground was good – 'a fresh approach on the horizon', said the local press – and the fans seemed encouraged.

You can learn so much from experienced people if you're prepared to observe, listen and be patient. An old friend once said to me, 'In our company we don't have problems – that word is banned. We have situations.' It was an approach I took on board. As a director of football, it was essential to distinguish between the two. If that can be done, and you can stay calm and focused during difficult days, by no means have you cracked it, but you'll be heading in the right direction. We'd chosen Bryan – that was the situation. It was up to him to do his job but was just as important that we *let* him do his job, thereby not creating a problem – sorry, situation. He picked the team, decided the tactics, motivated the players. Our job was to marry all our roles together with as little upheaval as possible, all in the best interests of the football club.

Sometimes, however, things just don't work out. Bryan didn't get the breaks, and Leicester City were relegated in 1987. It was always going to be a challenging season, one that affected all of us in authority. When the dust settled, shaking hands with Terry and Alan for the last time was an emotional moment. Together, we'd experienced the joy of promotion and the perks that go with that, but now we were parting company with the club heading in the wrong direction. It felt as if we'd achieved nothing together. But for all parties it was time to move on.

At the same time, as I mentioned, the idea of working abroad had been at the back of my mind and, without question, the tragic events in Bradford and Brussels, along with the continuing declining standards of behaviour in our domestic game, encouraged my mind to wander. I had experienced 17 years of management – a lifetime really – and 14 of those had been in the top tier. I understood the pressures and demands of the job, but knew I was ready for change. Time to talk Turkey perhaps …

Chapter 18

THE SUMMER holiday was on the horizon. I intended to have a good long one and take stock. When you're working at the coalface that's never an option, so for the first time in 17 years an extended time with the family was just what the doctor ordered.

However, barely a week into the break I received a call from my old pal Bobby Robson, in camp with the England squad, inviting me to spend the day at Lilleshall. As England manager, with his own pressures and responsibilities, he still found time for a fellow manager, one just out of work, to offer valuable time and counsel during his own hectic schedule. A class act, Bobby. I accepted, and thoroughly enjoyed watching Bobby in full flight with his squad, not to mention the time we spent chatting away in those beautiful surroundings. The afternoon flew by.

Bobby quickly read the situation regarding my attitude to change and the possibility – should it arise – of working abroad. In fairness, with all the s**t flying in Bobby's direction as England manager, I think the idea was lurking at the back of his mind too. (Three years later Bobby did indeed move abroad, beginning and ending at PSV Eindhoven, and including four years in Portugal, two at Sporting Lisbon, two at Porto, and a single season at the mighty Barcelona. Not a bad CV, that.) Don Howe, another who I'd known and respected for a long time, was Bobby's assistant, a first-class coach and student of the game. Don was in Istanbul, assisting Beşiktaş on a temporary basis (they were looking for a new manager) and would return to Lilleshall the following day. Bobby suggested I talk to him: 'He's been offered the manager's job at Beşiktaş, but he won't take it; he's happy with England.' Don had a good relationship with the Beşiktaş president and had actually managed Galatasaray for a year during the '70s. He'd kept an eye on Turkish football ever since.

The drive home passed in a flash. I'd accepted Bobby's invitation to return, but what was I thinking? I was looking forward to a long family break – football-free – yet barely a week had passed and already I was considering jumping back on the carousel, one I'd happily only just jumped off! Where was my mind? The only conclusion I could reach was that it was already abroad. I fancied it.

So back to Lilleshall I went. Sitting on footballs in the sunshine, overlooking manicured pitches, surrounded by mature trees and greenery, and in total privacy. Talking openly and honestly with two friends offering their advice and guidance with enthusiasm and sincerity (a hallmark of both men). I realised it couldn't get much better than this. Don was in full flight, which was always inspiring: 'Turkey is football daft, Gordon, and Istanbul is a fantastic city. BJK [Beşiktaş] always get big crowds, the president is a top man, and there are some decent players too. The only downside is the training facilities, which aren't great.' This didn't dampen Don's enthusiasm, however; his football brain looked deeper. He'd been there, witnessed the workings, met the people and the players, and fully understood what lay ahead. Even Bobby was impressed by Don's presentation.

Later, exiting the Lilleshall courtyard, I realised I hadn't seen another soul. Some of the best players in the country had been in the vicinity and I'd not come across one of them. That's what a private audience with the England manager and his assistant gets you. My head was spinning, but in a positive way. Imagination, if you allow it, can run away from reality and complicate fact. But in my head, the facts were crystal clear: Beşiktaş, one of Istanbul's big three clubs, were looking for a new coach. Was I interested? After the day with Bobby and Don, the answer had to be yes. I was prepared to talk.

That night at home, as I readied myself for bed, the telephone rang. A gentleman named Hurol Bilal introduced himself in perfect English. He represented the president of Beşiktaş – the Başkan – and asked if I'd travel, with Edith, to Istanbul the following day to discuss joining them as coach. It was very matter of fact, no fancy talk. The annual salary would be £100,000 plus bonuses; they'd provide flights home for the family and free housing. Standing in my pyjamas, trying to stay focused, I couldn't help but feel they were somehow ahead of the game. I later found out they were. As events unfolded it became clear that people had been talking; they'd done their homework. Hurol was firing all this at me as if I was ready to accept. If first impressions are important, this one certainly registered. The following morning Edith and I were on a plane to Turkey.

What was I going to do? I still wasn't sure. I'd done my homework too, was well-briefed and advised, and had received a verbal commitment from the club. I was offered three times the basic salary I'd been earning at Leicester, not including bonuses, and after tax. The opportunity to work abroad for the first time in my career – isn't that what I wanted? Or was I only pretending? This was a big club, one of Turkey's biggest. Furthermore, English clubs were still banned from European football (and would be for another three years), while Turkish clubs weren't. Beşiktaş had the potential to play in Europe every season. Even before the second gin and tonic over Munich, Edith knew where my thoughts were heading. There was excitement in the air, although apprehension too. Would the people feel right? Would I feel right for them? Would there be the abundance of bulls**t that often flies around at times like this? Would there be the genuine gut feeling that one can generate on such occasions?

Later that day, entering the Istanbul Hilton for the first time, I was venturing into the unknown. Mr Bilal informed me that we'd shortly meet the president, Süleyman Seba, on the Asian side of the Bosporus. While Edith rested at the hotel, in Europe, I was in a car heading to Asia. In highly congested and undisciplined traffic, the journey seemed to take forever. We eventually arrived outside a large office block in the business district of Kadikoy. Into the lift and out again on whatever floor, by this point I'd hardly said a word, or seen anyone; it felt very cloak and dagger. An impressive, and imposing, wooden door opened into a large office-type room with several easy chairs dotted about, and small tables laden with small glasses of Turkish tea, and an abundance of ashtrays (everyone in Turkey seemed to smoke then). Venetian blinds covered the windows, which were plentiful but closed. The air was thick with smoke but thankfully the room was air-conditioned. As I peered through the smog, I felt somewhat intimidated. The atmosphere was daunting, really, as if I was going for an interview for bloody MI5! It wasn't what I'd anticipated but it really set the scene, one I'll never forget. There were no more than a dozen people in the room, but those present were obviously big hitters, the ones that mattered.

Protocol was observed and strictly adhered to. Firstly, my introduction to the president Süleyman Seba who, despite his standing, appeared to be the lowest-profile man in the room (I'd hardly noticed him). Following a simple, warm handshake, he looked me straight in the eye, smiled and said, 'Hoşgeldiniz,' (welcome). I immediately felt he knew more about me than I knew about him (how true that turned out to be). I did know he didn't speak English and, as I didn't speak Turkish, I saw interesting times ahead. Further introductions followed: board members and influential friends, many speaking perfect English. One of those was Şenes Erzik, a member of UEFA and a senior member of the Turkish Football Federation, whose presence again gave me the impression that all this had come together thanks to a great deal of thought, effort and judgement, all of which made me feel more comfortable.

Without wishing to state the obvious, all of this was foreign to me, but I soon realised that many in the room, particularly the president, believed this was a fait accompli; in their eyes, the deal had been done. But I hadn't signed anything; I hadn't even seen anything *to* sign. I hadn't agreed to anything, and aside from what Hurol had told me on the telephone, nothing had been discussed. By around 6pm we were returning to the hotel. My feet hadn't touched the ground since we landed. I'd been over to Asia, was now heading back to Europe, rushing to the hotel to shower, change, then head straight out for dinner; I felt like a rag doll! I quickly told Edith what had gone on (although there wasn't much to tell) before Hurol took us out to be wined and dined.

During dinner he informed me that the Beşiktaş team were off to a training camp the next morning and asked if I'd join them! I hadn't said anything, either way, about my acceptance (or otherwise) of the offer, but here I was being asked to a training camp! In my head, I was pretty sure I'd take the job, but there was certainly nothing in writing, not yet. Time alone was needed.

After dinner on a lovely warm evening, Edith and I shared a nightcap on the hotel terrace, overlooking the İnönü Stadium, home of Beşiktaş, with the Dolmabahçe Palace and the glittering waters of the Bosporus as a backdrop. In the silence, the view was magical. To me – I thought this immediately and still think it now – it was one of the most beautiful settings in the world for a football stadium, and it got to me romantically. Now, I accept it's not a time for romance when you're trying to sort yourself out with a football contract, even less so on foreign shores, as you need to be on the ball and know what you're bloody doing. But I simply couldn't help myself.

These days the ground is known as Vodafone Park and is all-singing, all-dancing, all mod cons, as you'd expect. Back then though, it was nothing of the sort and needed more than a good lick of paint (similarities with the Anfield I'd first walked into all those years ago). But the setting, the history within the city, even the fact that the stadium had the look of a colosseum, all contributed to the magic. Vodafone Park was a total rebuild, but on the same site as the İnönü Stadium, and by keeping some of the original structure intact, that sense of magic and history still lingers – at least it does for me.

* * *

Two days later I did indeed head to the training camp, having flown home to pick up my kit before returning to Istanbul where

I was met by two smartly dressed gentlemen: Ali Emec, an ex-employee of Pan American Airways, well-educated, fluent in English and French; and Bahattin Baydar, a former player and long-serving member of the club. Bahattin's English wasn't up to Ali's standard but more than good enough for me. Bahattin took the wheel, another three hours of travelling ahead. Our destination was the rural setting of Bartın, a small town on the edge of the Black Sea.

We arrived around two o'clock the following morning. The players would be ready to leave for training at 9.30am so I requested a 7am wake-up call, but didn't need it as the adrenaline was flowing, the mind was playing games. Bahattin, knocking on my door at precisely seven o'clock, clean-shaven and immaculately turned out in his training gear, was a welcome and impressive sight. The players would be ready to have breakfast at 8.15, and he asked for my instructions. At that moment I became immediately aware that the notions of authority, responsibility and expectation, all revolving around me, had already taken wing. I was ready to fly. 'Tell the lads breakfast as normal and we'll have a chat at the training ground at ten o'clock.' Simple and straightforward, my first words of wisdom to my new family.

Two long wooden tables among the fruit trees of the hotel garden were both fully occupied, the players' faces full of anticipation, although I suspect they were more desperate to get stuck into breakfast than they were to hear from me. Nevertheless, I gave it a whirl: 'Günaydın!' I shouted, with a wave of the hand, and sat down quickly with the staff. Ali complimented my first attempt at the language (good morning); a successful introduction, I thought. Twenty-five minutes later the players suddenly rose from the table in unison and disappeared. Bahattin looked at me and smiled. 'Everything under control,' he said. I later learned that when the players were ready to leave, they waited for the captain's say-so; they'd look towards him, he'd survey the situation, say yes – 'evet' – and they'd all stand, then leave. I liked that.

We soon arrived at our training ground for the next seven days, an area the size of two football pitches, which had obviously been used previously by the locals and amateur teams. The surface was neither great nor green, but in the middle of nowhere there were no distractions – a bonus. I introduced myself to the players, explaining how much I was looking forward to working with and getting to know them. Without further warning, I shouted, 'Let's go!' and ran off towards the open ground (I was still in reasonable nick so could comfortably do a few circuits without embarrassment). Soon, I was happily leading a group of strangers, all gabbling away joyfully. The usual stretching followed, some body work, running drills, and so on. The morning passed quickly. I was thinking on my feet, determining how many players we had, which staff were in attendance and what everyone's role was. I'd had no time to discuss any of this, so didn't know anything.

The afternoon heat meant the session wouldn't start until 5.30pm, so after lunch it was down to the nitty gritty with Bahattin and Ali. We had 30 players, including two goalkeepers; a goalkeeping coach, Necme (an old team-mate of Bahattin's, which was a further help); Nejati, the physio and masseur; two hard-working kit men performing the thankless task of kitting out the lads, twice a day, with very limited facilities – two miracle men, really; a dozen or so footballs, mostly in poor condition; no more than 20 bibs, and limited markers and cones. Improvisation would be essential. But it wasn't what we didn't have that registered with me, rather what we did have: conscientious, hard-working staff, going about their jobs honestly and doing their best.

We were in the middle of nowhere, and the hotel was by no means five-star, but it was good enough and all we needed. Likewise, the training facilities were basic but sufficient. The setting was lovely, the food outstanding (morale is always higher when bellies are full) and the weather was superb. It wasn't quite the Boys' Brigade, but it wasn't far off, all in camp together, getting to know each other, working hard, but fun too. Given some of the facilities there was plenty of opportunity to complain, but no one did. The way everyone responded was special. Ali and Bahattin, in particular, who would become very close friends, looked after me, especially with the language. I was the odd one out but whatever I asked of them, they did; I was in good hands. In no way would they interfere with what I was trying to do, which remained the case throughout our years together. Everyone trained and worked with commitment and sincerity. My first impressions were good ones and over time would only be enhanced.

One morning I discovered Bahattin in the garden, hanging by his arms from an apple tree. He'd already showered, shaved and was his usual immaculate self. 'Good morning, Gordon. Two more minutes.' He eventually dropped to the ground. 'Stretches the whole body, Gordon. No stress, no pressure, no pushing or pulling. Just stretching the body and easing the joints.' He was right, too. Little things like that stick in your mind. Like the morning when I found myself face to face with a live sheep tied to an apple tree in the garden. A friend of a committee member was visiting the lads – they all knew him so there was no problem. He'd wanted to bring them a treat, so he did – a sheep! This sheep was to be our dinner later in the week (although to this day I'm still not sure what the chef's plans were). The next morning, the sheep was gone. It hadn't been cooked, though, it had been nicked! The poor lad who brought it had to go out and buy another!

We got into a routine. Train in the morning, lunch, afternoon nap (for the players), late-afternoon training, back to the hotel for dinner. After that it was coffee in the orchard and, with nowhere else to go, we were all there together: two or three players over here, another few over there, and so forth. It was a family-like environment and helped enormously in getting to know one another, which we did much quicker than we would have had we not gone away. That camp meant a lot. It was, to all intents and purposes, a week of conditioning with the odd kickabout, but to me it was much more, and vital to what lay ahead.

After seven days we waved goodbye to the loyal staff and left country life behind. I felt more comfortable, in a good frame of mind. Istanbul – 13 million people, a big chunk of those being fanatical Beşiktaş supporters – was waiting in expectation three hours down the road. The real work was about to begin.

* * *

At ten o'clock the following morning it was chaos. Bahattin had collected me from the Hilton, and on arrival at the training ground we were swamped. My official welcome had drawn quite the crowd: TV crews, journalists, board members, the president and numerous supporters, all trying to gain entry to where the 'ceremony' would take place. Having eventually shaken countless hands, the press and TV wanted their pound of flesh. It was the start of a relationship that would survive the good and bad times ahead. Ali answered our first serious questions. Twenty minutes later we were well past the scheduled start time for training, but Bahattin and Necmi were ahead of the game and had the boys out on time.

Already in my training gear, I was ready to go. Ali and I were shepherded through the crowd, downstairs through various passageways and doors, finally emerging into daylight and a vast arena the size of two football pitches, faced on one side by an enormous concrete retaining wall reaching to the sky. On the other, was a huge concrete tribune maybe 20 rows deep running the length of the arena. Directly behind that was the always busy main road, heavy with traffic heading in both directions. The whole area was covered in a sandy grit-like substance, hard in some places, soft in others, with potholes all over the place. The goalposts were immovable, fixed fast into the ground. There were no nets and no pitch markings. Behind one of the goals was a big area where the boys were working with Bahattin and Necmi. As Ali and I arrived, one of the players shouted, 'Welcome to Fulya, Hoca!' (Welcome to Fulya, Teacher!) I'd thought about these first moments, wondering what my first impressions would be. As a result, prior to my arrival I'd drawn up some mental bullet points that I'd try to adhere to:

- Not reveal what I was thinking (although as some players had clearly picked up on my 'What the **** is this?!' expression, I'd obviously failed that one immediately)
- Not give the players any reason to make excuses
- Not make excuses for myself
- These are the facilities we've got: accept them

- Make this work in my favour
- Push the right buttons, in the right way, to find some grass

I felt such reminders were the right way of going about things. However, I was already being tested.

When I caught up with the players, I noticed security gates, not just unlocked, but not even closed. I watched the journalists and TV crews troop in as if they bloody owned the place, right where the lads were all working. Cameras were set up, filming began, the written press started asking questions. If that wasn't bad enough, a load of supporters joined them! It was a far cry from my early days at Leicester, when I'd be grilled by four or five guys with notebooks; there were certainly no television cameras then, and no press conferences in front of a hundred people or more.

You can imagine how I felt. Trying to get my head around what I'd seen and how to deal with it, it was obvious I'd be falling out with people very soon – most likely the following day! The media clearly believed they could do what they wanted, because no one stopped them. I was going to have to shut that down, and quickly, despite knowing it would put me in their bad books.

This was the reality; this was the environment in which the team had to work. That first morning there were people walking everywhere with an air of entitlement, as if saying, 'This is what we do.' Their numbers may have been boosted because there was a new trainer in town but, that notwithstanding, this behaviour was clearly the norm. I must stress though, at no time were the media aggressive or disrespectful (that would come later), but there was a total lack of control. The situation was simply not workable. I couldn't do anything about the state of the pitch, not yet, but I could do something about the press.

Media facilities were non-existent. There was no shelter at Fulya. If we trained in the rain, the press waited in the rain. The only refreshments available were supplied by the chi boys, young lads who appeared intermittently carrying trays laden with small cups of tea. If any of the journalists needed a pee, they had to use the bathroom in the changing rooms (never a pleasant experience). We shared changing facilities with the club's other teams (basketball was very popular), of all ages too, so the changing rooms were pretty much in constant use. They were managed, but used so much they remained basic, never looked after as well as they could have been. They were never really clean, and occasionally vermin were spotted running around. You wouldn't believe it, really; it was much worse than I anticipated. The club eventually arranged the use of a building that was at least close to being civilised where the players could change in comfort and get something to eat, but that was still a few months away.

The media were treated like second-class citizens. Consequently, they marshalled themselves, creating their own meeting places and deciding among themselves how they observed training. They did the same when it came to grabbing interviews. There was big competition among rival publications and TV companies, so I was fully aware that theirs were demanding jobs. I was also aware there was no official link – the club had no press officer – to aid communications between them and us. The closest we had were those who had been at the club for a long time and therefore known some of the journalists a long time. Bahattin was one, so initially became that link man. He had relationships with some of the senior hacks, and knew the rest too, so when they cried and moaned it was to him. He'd then come to me to mark my card.

I discussed how I wanted to work with the media with Bahattin and Ali. A raise of Bahattin's eyebrows – no words required – revealed his thoughts: *Good luck with that!* It was one of the many Turkish mannerisms I'd become accustomed to (like the shaking of one's head from left to right: very often it wasn't a 'no' – as it is in the UK – but in fact a 'no problem'). My plan was that at all future training sessions, while we went about our work, the media would be restricted to the far end of the training ground behind a fence, denying them access to the pitch. That first day there had been journalists three yards from me and the players, listening to our bloody conversations! I wasn't having that, so stuck them all at the far end, away from us. After training we'd walk through that area, giving them an opportunity to talk to us. I never refused, but remained conscious that it wasn't great for them. I wasn't flavour of the month, though, that's for sure, but it was the best we could do. In essence, we were all in the same boat; we all had to work in the same environment. It was a rude awakening for the press boys, but it was the beginning of a semblance of organisation and discipline, without which I couldn't have done my job (they used to credit me with that word, 'discipline', which I didn't particularly like, but I did understand their reasoning). I didn't need to be brain of Britain to come up with such a plan, as it was the only option because if you give the media an inch, they'll pinch a mile. It had to be done.

As my translator, Ali drew the short straw and began telling them what I did and didn't want. Ali had to take their s**t, but was a sensitive guy and hadn't been exposed to anything like this in his life, so when the s**t was flying around, he was uncomfortable. Working in camp had been a doddle compared to this. We eventually established that I'd talk to the press in the morning before training. I'd speak to them again after we'd finished, then after lunch would do a bit of television work while the newspaper boys would have access to the players. It was a start.

* * *

New skills had to be acquired, but I wasn't alone. Ali too had been thrown in at the deep end. The importance of a translator is paramount, and thankfully I got a good one. There are two essential objectives for any translator: accuracy, of course, and expression. If a message is delivered correctly, with the right feeling, happy days; if not, the consequences can be dire. Ali took to his new role like a duck to water. He had to be on my shoulder constantly – no easy task as I was always on the bloody move – although my use of widely recognised international football gestures (a feint here, a twist there) gave Ali a bit of respite from time to time. Much of what I said, I shouted, but Ali had to pick out the pertinent words, wait for me to pause – sometimes he'd let *me* know when to pause – then try to deliver my message accurately and effectively; not at all easy, and harder still when dealing with the media. But he was brilliant. He soon learned my mannerisms and knew when to come in and when to get out. It was even more impressive as he was an executive from the airline business and had never been involved in football in his life! Now, here he was, having to deal with me, the players and the press, with a variety of attitudes and egos. It was a massive learning curve, but learn he did, brilliantly.

Bahattin used to write everything down – and I mean, *everything*. He'd make notes during training and matches, about everything. A few years ago, he tried to give me one of his journals, but I refused and said he should offer it to the Beşiktaş museum. These are records of a time long gone and are unique; no one else was recording this stuff.

Bahattin and Ali were instrumental to my future success in Turkey. I was so lucky to have them alongside me, helping and protecting in equal measure. Whatever I achieved during my time over there, none of it would have been possible without them. They were completely different personalities but equally important, particularly in those early days, and remained so throughout my entire time in Turkey, occupying their roles extremely competently and totally professionally, day after day. Their daily input and contributions can't be overstated. The pair were simply invaluable.

* * *

If the training ground changing rooms weren't the best, the admin office wasn't much better. It was quite big, comfortably fitting Ali, Bahattin, Necmi, Nejati and me, and was where we'd change before and after training. Bahattin would sit at the only desk – he was always writing something, so it made sense. Upon the desk sat a big red telephone, and because the building was so huge the phone used to ring incredibly loud for the janitor to be able to hear it no matter where he was. That same janitor also kept canaries in half a dozen cages fixed to the office walls, which I quite liked as it happened. But whenever the phone rang, the canaries started singing! Once when it happened, Bahattin picked up the receiver and began yelling over the noise. In turn, the canaries turned up their own volume, prompting Bahattin to shout louder still. It was one of many moments when I found myself thinking, *If anyone could see this now!* I always tried to see the funny side of situations; on occasions like this, it wasn't difficult.

Meanwhile, I remained camped in the Hilton. Finding somewhere to live was becoming a headache. I didn't have my own car (although didn't fancy battling the Istanbul traffic anyway) so most nights I'd walk the couple of miles or so from the training ground back to the hotel. I did so for two reasons: one, I enjoyed it; and two, because I had time on my hands, time I needed to kill. It was also time to think, and there was always much to think about. I never really got bothered in the streets. As autumn rolled into winter and the nights grew longer, I could disappear in the gloom. I'd wear a big black training coat with the hood pulled right over my head. Occasionally I'd get nabbed by a supporter or two, but not often. There may have been times when I was spotted but didn't notice as I was so absorbed in my thoughts about what needed fixing and the challenges ahead. I was constantly conscious of the firefighting I faced but, at the same time, continually boosted by the players' attitude: 'Let's get on with it.'

In contrast to the players, who were good as gold, some of the board members would appear at training unannounced (at my request the president eventually put a stop to this). They'd have their own agendas too, and would talk to the journalists, only too happy to offer their own opinions and questions: 'What's going on at training?' 'What's he doing?' And so on. Some were obviously enthusiastic and interested, others less so, but that was nothing new. I wasn't particularly affected by it but, over time, you learn to look out for the warning signs.

Once the season had got going, we'd train in the morning and have lunch at the club – the food was always fantastic – before more work in the afternoon. I'd then head back to the hotel, straight past reception, into the lift, up to the room, have a shower, then order room service. That was my life. At eight o'clock the next morning, back in my tracksuit. I'd sometimes go down for breakfast but, if not, would head straight to the training ground. It wasn't like this every day – I was taken out on several occasions – but I'm aware it might sound as though I was living like a monk. Not quite true!

* * *

The lack of grass remained an issue, as did the immovable goalposts (concreted in), the lack of nets, and even the balls (old, scruffy, well past their sell-by date). Working on crossing and finishing on a windy day, I'd knock the ball wide, the winger would go after it before whipping it into the box; at least, that was the idea. But the ball would bobble all over the place, making it difficult to control. The centre-forwards would make their runs, but often the ball never arrived. And if a cross did come in, often the wind would play havoc with the sub-par footballs. The strikers' runs were futile.

I had to stop the session and go back to basics – the conditions demanded it. So, a simple touch of a static ball, a quality cross and two strikers on their toes. It was Boy Scout stuff, but it was the only practical way of tackling this environment. Everything had to be simplified; I didn't want to make life more difficult for any of us. As we grew, such basic work helped us tremendously. I often wonder how the hell we went on to do what we did, given such circumstances. 'Simplicity' would be the best answer.

During this period, Bahattin was incredibly important. He'd seek help through the club first but if that got us nowhere, as was usually the case, he always seemed to know somebody, who knew somebody else, who had a friend who could help. One such friend was a farmer who owned a huge, thick metal chain. One day somebody turned up with it and went to work. The chain was attached to the back of his tractor and off he went, dragging it up, down and around a small square area of the pitch. It worked surprisingly well, smoothing out much of the uneven ground and filling in the potholes. I was incredibly grateful, not least because no one seemed to be rewarded for this. It was all about knowing the right people – friends of friends, all Beşiktaş supporters – all happy to help. It was primitive, but it was 'needs must'. During one windy session Bahattin's face was covered in sand, his lips dry and cracked, his grey hair yellow as if he'd been stuck in the Sahara for a week. Obviously, mine was the same, but it didn't matter. We were making progress.

That said, because 11 vs 11 was neither practical nor rewarding, we worked with smaller groups in smaller areas. It was amazing what we could achieve when we put our minds to it, and although it appeared basic, because it was, it worked, and the lads embraced it without complaint. Working in smaller areas helped. There was already a great deal of technical ability on show, and the little exercises and drills began to deliver results and, consequently, a certain satisfaction. The lads were beginning to master the conditions. And if they could do it on this surface, they could surely do it on grass.

The search for a proper surface continued. We arranged a few pre-season matches but couldn't even use our own stadium for training. The pitch there wasn't the best anyway (the groundsman was more amateur than professional), but at least it was grass. Not for the want of trying, however, we couldn't gain access. The club didn't own the pitch, it belonged to the municipality and there were little director generals in charge who never gave us permission. We tried to find a smaller club with a grass pitch, but the lower league teams all played on soil. I soon worked out I'd have to learn what the team could and couldn't do, and how much progress they'd made, in the matches themselves (although if you think about it, that's nothing new, really). The short-term future would be a huge challenge and in Turkey, from day one, you have to win. Draws are no good, especially for a new coach.

It was always going to be a journey into the unknown, and very different from English football, of course. I wasn't daft enough to expect it to be the same and, after all, that's why I was here in the first place. I was in Turkey, at a Turkish club, with an entirely Turkish staff. Respect was paramount. I used to remind myself daily, 'Don't forget, I'm the outsider here.' After a loss or two, when the fans find fault in you, it's all too easy to find fault in them. But I couldn't do that. I was the foreigner. I never forgot that, and eventually it worked in my favour.

What also worked in my favour was my work ethic. Getting stuck into my new role before even seeing a contract had stood me in good stead, particularly with the president. He knew I'd begun without a deal being signed, nor even agreed. But once the first contract was out of the way, when things began to develop and we started to have a bit of success, when I was building some sort of reputation, that early commitment was acknowledged and, I believe, appreciated, valued and respected. It was all I needed.

* * *

The first six months of any new job can be difficult. A settled home life is essential. Unfortunately for me, hotel life was beginning to take its toll, and not just on me. Edith came out every so often for a few days, but I never saw my boys at all during that initial period. Like my early days at Liverpool, finding a home became imperative, so most afternoons were spent house hunting, which rapidly became a chore. After training we were always knackered, and poor Ali had to accompany me everywhere, so I was dragging him away from his family too. It didn't affect my day job, but it wasn't doing either of us any good.

Hotel living normally provides free time in abundance but for me in Istanbul, not so. I was either busy searching for accommodation or we were on the road, and in those days we didn't fly. We'd set off on a Friday and could be on a coach for nine or ten hours – each way. Free time was therefore limited. It wasn't the enemy but wasn't there to be abused either. Not that it was with me but, nevertheless, becoming conditioned to hotel life wasn't where I wanted to be. One afternoon we found a top-floor apartment that overlooked our stadium. This might be the one, I thought. Until the estate agent said, almost proudly, 'This apartment has hot water on Mondays, Wednesdays and Fridays.' I passed.

Istanbul has changed. Today, it's like Manhattan: luxury apartments and penthouses worth millions, so attracting coaches and players to the city isn't a problem. But it wasn't like that back then, as those places just didn't exist. My house hunting reached the point where even as we pulled up in front of a property, I'd already be shaking my head: 'No thanks.' This was getting to Ali, and to me. I imagine it was getting to the club too; they must have been thinking, 'What does this guy want?' They'd have been well within their rights to ask, too, as I'd been here, there and bloody everywhere! I'd even been across the water into Asia but that was a non-starter: the traffic on the bridge (there was only one back then) was at a permanent standstill, which meant I'd have to cross the water by ferry twice a day, 20 minutes each way. That doesn't sound so bad, and in fairness the houses over that way were very nice (if anything, they were too grand; I didn't need a palace) but heading across the water meant heading into Fenerbahçe territory. It's one thing to wander the streets hiding under a big coat, but travelling side by side with rivals' supporters, twice a day, every day, was something completely different. Unsurprisingly, I didn't fancy it!

We eventually found an apartment in a small, secure, gated complex in Ulus, quite close to the training ground, three or four miles from the city centre. The building only had two storeys, so was quiet. There was a shared swimming pool, and the apartment itself was modern, with two bedrooms, two bathrooms, kitchen and lounge – all Edith and I needed. It was a nice area, close to work, secure and private. We quickly sourced some furniture and began to lead a more normal life. Edith came and went, and the boys could now visit too, which they did. I was comfortable, with no complaints and raring to go.

Chapter 19

I LEFT my Hilton hideaway around the same time we moved into our new training facility. Both moves turned out to be transformative. Off the pitch I was settled and far more able to concentrate on the job in hand; on the pitch, the improved training ground gave everyone a lift.

The building we moved into had always been there, but unused. It was in a bit of a state, but my moaning and groaning must have got through to someone as time and money were spent on refurbishing the building, as well as some of the facilities around it. There was now a grass surface (at last!) the size of half a pitch, a groundsman's facility where he camped among his equipment and paraphernalia, and a whiff of chi always on the go – magic! Many a rainy afternoon was spent in there, often alongside several fortunate members of the media. This hut had been around for a while, and you knew it by its atmosphere – you could almost taste it.

The groundsman, Joskun, looked after this area with dedication. He was so proud the players could finally work on grass, making it easy for me to stress how important it was to protect and respect what we'd been given. 'This could be our secret weapon, if managed correctly.' This we did. Doggies, twisting and turning, small-sided games and similar drills were all confined to the soil, which had been prepared, raked and watered. This was accepted by the players, and it worked. After these warm-ups we'd move to the grass, whereupon you could sense their anticipation and enjoyment; extra motivation wasn't required. The whole area was fenced in, totally secure, with a bridge from the camp building down to the playing surface ensuring safe passage for all concerned, especially important when the natives got restless; supporters would still turn up to watch training, and there were always more in attendance following a bad result, all primed and ready to have a go.

The revamped camp building comprised twin bedrooms for the players, single rooms for staff, a large dining/lounge area, kitchen, laundry, changing rooms, and so on. I had my own office, as did the camp manager, who was responsible for the day-to-day running of the whole operation. For the first time I had that feeling of belonging, and a true sense of purpose. We had a home to be proud of, we had grass, we had management in-house. We were heading in the right direction.

I was like a kid with a new toy. We'd gone from one end of the spectrum – poverty – to the other – paradise. Having put up with the bare minimum for so long, now the lads would gladly come in for breakfast, work hard, then have a nice lunch together. Bonds were strengthened, organically, and the boys were happy to stay as long as they wanted. We'd all be there together on the eve of home matches, sharing dinner, conversation, laughs, even visitors – it was magic and, I believe, the turning point in terms of what we were about to achieve. If we'd had this facility from the very start, I don't think it would have had the same effect; it was the step from poor conditions into such an obvious improvement that gave everyone such a lift. It also proved the club had ambition, providing further motivation. They say a bit of adversity is good for bonding; I find escaping adversity works just as well.

It wasn't all sunshine and roses, however. The backdrop to all this was, if not quite worrying, certainly unsettling: three or four months after my arrival in the country my wages suddenly stopped coming in. I wasn't alone in this. Erhan Solu, who became a lifelong friend, was new to the board. He and his wife Ayka occasionally invited me for dinner and were great hosts. Their hospitality was first-class, and fortunately they spoke English extremely well, having previously lived in London. Visiting them was always a treat. Erhan, the perfect go-to man, became my direct link to the president. The three of us would often meet at Erhan's apartment, which suited the president's fondness for privacy. Ayka would prepare a little something then leave us to our meeting.

I'm sure Erhan was already aware of the issue regarding my wages. I wasn't overly worried about myself but more concerned that if the same was happening to the players, morale would plummet – in such circumstances, it inevitably does. Erhan told me not to worry: 'This happens all the time in Turkey, Gordon. It's the same at Galatasaray, it's the same at Fenerbahçe …' He was right, too. I eventually picked up some salary when I moved out of the hotel, but it had been six months or so with nothing coming in.

On the top floor of the Hilton there was a great restaurant, a super spot; lots of live music and a great atmosphere. But one afternoon when it was closed the president wanted to meet me there (I'd been having a bit of a moan). He liked his privacy and didn't want people making a fuss of him, which, when he was spotted, invariably happened as he was a popular guy, loved and respected by all, even opposition supporters. We sat in a private alcove, in a completely empty restaurant. It all felt rather clandestine. With his usual chi in front of him he addressed me. 'Gordon,' he said, 'I understand your concerns, but I don't want you to worry. These are difficult times, yes. Money is tight, but don't worry. I will get it to you soon as possible. Please trust me.' I accepted his words. As I said, I didn't need the money, but the issue remained a concern. I wondered whether I should push harder but our relationship was strong, with a great deal of mutual respect. I trusted him, and he knew that.

Not long before I left the Hilton I was instructed to go to the club where (some of) my wages were waiting for me. This had happened before. I'd once arrived on a similar premise only to be told, 'Sorry Gordon, there's nothing here,' and if proof were needed, the clerk opened the big black safe behind him. 'Look!' he said. 'Nothing!' He was right, too, and I left empty-handed. I was expecting something similar, but this time there was an envelope with my name on it. I slipped it into my briefcase and returned to the hotel. In my room I emptied the envelope's contents on to the bed and began to count. There was supposed to be US$20,000. There was only $15,000. I re-counted: $5,000 short again. I'd waited months for wages, knowing it would be less than the full amount, but it was short of even that! I was straight on the phone to Erhan.

Erhan had the difficult job of explaining the situation to the president the following day. The response was swift and short: 'He's got 15, what does he want?' It was how he ran the club. I knew he'd have staff and players crying to him too, which softened my attitude. This was common, and making ends meet was always difficult. When Jupp Derwall experienced similar at Galatasaray, he'd had enough and told them so. They were playing in Ankara. Jupp told the board he'd return to Istanbul after the match but then fly to Germany and wouldn't be coming back. Sat on the plane among the players and the public, Jupp was approached by the club's general secretary. 'There you are, Jupp,' he said, dropping a newspaper-wrapped bundle in Jupp's lap. Inside the newspaper was cash – lots of it. 'Here are your wages.' Jupp said he'd never been so embarrassed in his life. But his message to me was clear: I had to be willing to take stronger action.

Ali said the same. Both he and Bahattin knew of my situation, and one day Ali took me aside: 'Gordon, there's an old Turkish saying, which might be helpful to you.' He looked right into my eyes. 'It's simple, Gordon: if you don't scream, you don't get a suck of the tit.' How true. Unfortunately, that wasn't really my nature. Jupp was different, though. He knew that if he suddenly left the reigning champions, the press would go to town; it would come out that he'd not been paid, reflecting badly on the club and its hierarchy. They obviously wouldn't want that, which Jupp knew. So, Jupp screamed; Jupp got a suck of the tit. (He also advised me on my quest for a grass pitch: 'You have to tell them: no grass, no championship!' Good advice, as always, from Jupp.)

Despite all this, still in my favour was not having to discuss wages with the players. I was conscious of the situation, but it wasn't my responsibility. Besides, the players were used to it and took it for granted. If they could take it on the chin there was no need for me to make waves on their behalf. That's not to say they didn't care. I had a good relationship with the captain Riza Çalımbay so was aware of the players' concerns, but no matter how relaxed they might have been I still needed them in the right frame of mind, and if they weren't being paid it wasn't doing any of us any good. It wasn't a common occurrence, but it wasn't uncommon either. The fact was that there would be periods when, for whatever reason, the club struggled to pay wages on time.

To his credit, the president was concerned too. Once we were close enough to discuss such matters, that much was clear. These discussions were always very respectful. 'Thank you for your patience, Gordon, it's very much appreciated. Thank you for understanding what we're trying to do. I will pay you. You have my word.' He was saying, 'Stay with me.' And I did. I couldn't take it personally – no one could – and I didn't. Had certain board members been saying the same I wouldn't have accepted it, but because it came from the president, I accepted what he said and got on with it.

Six years later, when my time at Beşiktaş came to an end, I was owed three months' salary, but by then was used to how things worked and wasn't expecting the club to do anything about it; after all, it had been my decision to leave. A couple of days before I left the club for the last time, over a coffee by the Bosporus, Erhan informed me the president had paid the remaining three months of my contract in full. Yes, I was entitled to the money, but a 'thank you' would have been enough. To say I felt humble wouldn't do it justice. The president was doing far more than simply honouring a financial promise. Having written off any chance of receiving what I was owed, to then be paid in full, by him, filled me with more humility than ever before. And leaving a club amicably is so much better than leaving under a cloud. Leaving on good terms makes you think fondly of everything you've come through together.

Times have obviously changed but I wonder how different things are in Turkey today. Players are much stronger now, with more power over their own careers, but back then, for the most part, they accepted it – at least to a point. Depending on how long they went without payment, they could and would eventually get a bit noisy. Then, more often than not, something would happen to appease them. All of that was in the mix of Turkish football at that time, and it applied to managers too.

That first season was always going to be interesting. The league campaign developed into a two-horse race between us and Galatasaray. With six matches remaining we led by a single point but, unfortunately, we blinked first. Galatasaray took a maximum of 18 points from their last six matches, while we took just six, with one win, three draws and two defeats. Galatasaray were crowned champions on 90 points. We finished second, 12 points behind, but we were a lot closer to them than the final league table suggested. You might think finishing second wasn't a bad outcome for my first season but, come the final day, it emphasised what I'd known all along: first is first, second is nowhere. Unsurprisingly, the knives were out.

During this damp squib of a finale the stick was really flying. In those days the players didn't go out to warm up – probably for the best, as if things weren't going well the abuse would fly and it wouldn't be pleasant. One Saturday at home, with time on our hands before kick-off, I ventured down the tunnel with my captain Riza. There weren't many supporters in yet, but some who were had unfurled a long banner, written on which, in perfect English, was a clear message: 'Please go to your home Gordon.' Riza turned to me. 'Take no notice, Hoca. Take no notice,' he said, waving a dismissive arm in their direction. The captain's sensitive response was something I'd never forget. The fans were clearly unhappy, and rightly so, but that small gesture from the captain gave me a boost. The scenario still makes me think, though: if the fans had had their way, all the good things that were about to happen, wouldn't have – at least not to me.

I'd never have jumped ship, however, I'd have had to be pushed. I was going nowhere. I'd found somewhere to live, we'd improved the training facilities, and despite our season fizzling out, all the signs were positive. There were still a few on the board who would have been happy to see the back of me, but the president was more enthusiastic; he could see our improved workplace could lead to something better and was prepared to support me. I ended that first season disappointed, but extremely positive and optimistic about what was to come next.

I had to remember, though – and in fairness, I couldn't forget – that there were three massive clubs in Istanbul, so there was always pressure, even when you were winning. Sometimes it was nothing to do with the football at all, but there was always an edge, always a challenge coming from somewhere. At that time, in a city of 13 million plus, football daft from morning to night, what else would you expect?

* * *

One of my most memorable conversations with the president took place at Erhan's house early during my tenure. The president said, 'Gordon, we have the horse. All we need is the jockey.' I replied, 'Well, Başkan, in my evaluation, at the moment, this horse has only got three legs.' To be fair he saw the funny side, but I could see what he was saying: the backbone of the team that would become successful was already in place; they now needed

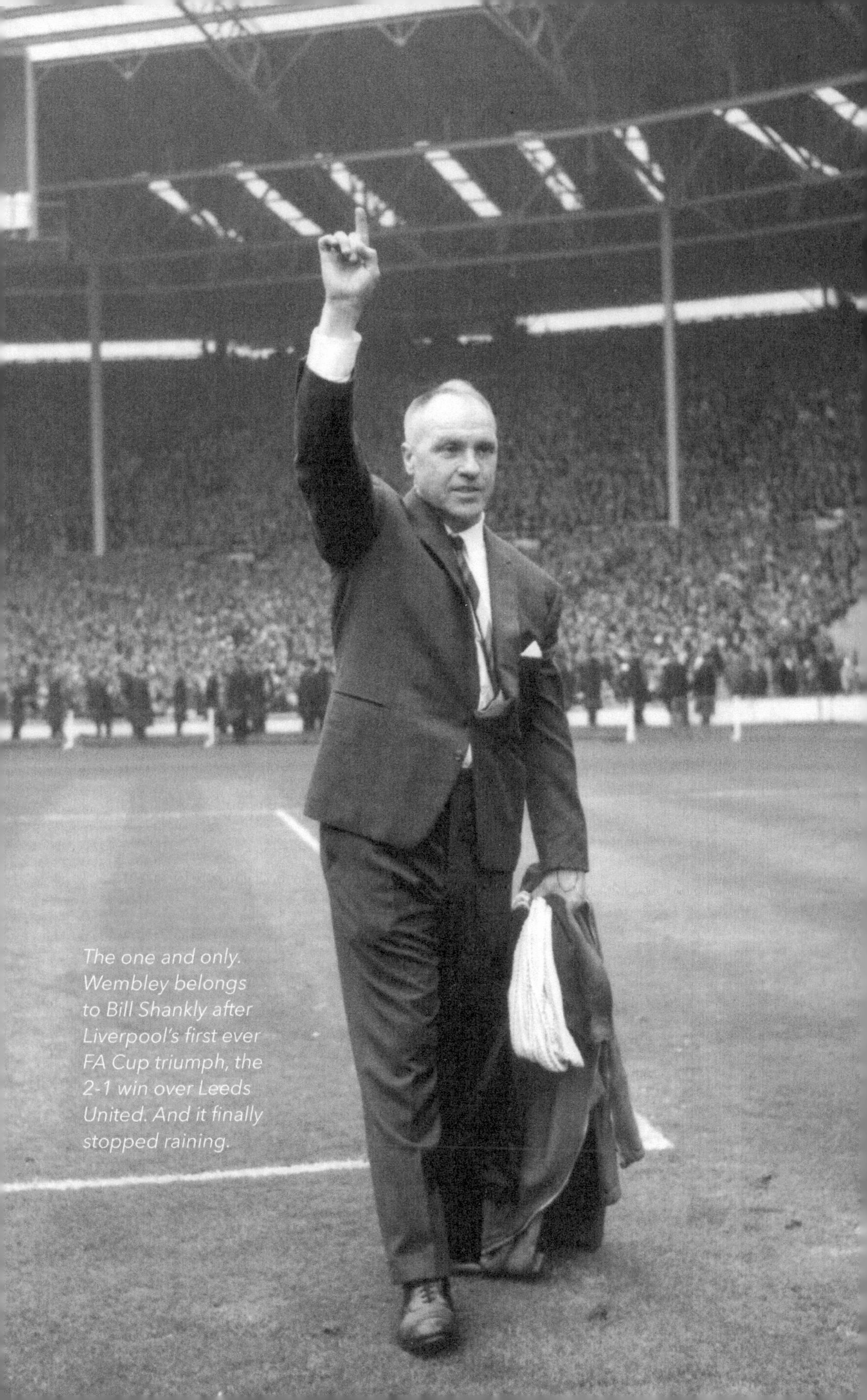

The one and only. Wembley belongs to Bill Shankly after Liverpool's first ever FA Cup triumph, the 2-1 win over Leeds United. And it finally stopped raining.

Big Ron re-enacts the famous coin-toss deciding moment v Cologne on our arrival back at Speke Airport, watched by myself, Ian Callaghan, Ronnie Moran, Roger Hunt, and Tommy Lawrence.

A unique moment if ever there was one. At the manager's suggestion, prior to the European cup semi-final first leg versus Inter Milan, Gerry Byrne and myself parade the FA Cup (won for the first time just three days earlier) around a packed Anfield. The gates were opened four and a half hours before kick-off; I never experienced an atmosphere like it, before or since. A masterstroke by Shanks? Perhaps ... we won 3-1.

The Liverpool Way. Shanks believed the kids had just as much of a right to be there as we did if not more …

The Battle of Britain: 1966 European Cup Winners' Cup semi-final second leg, Liverpool v Celtic. The Saint's challenge on Celtic keeper Ronnie Simpson epitomises the intensity of both teams in both fixtures. We lost 1-0 at Parkhead but a 2-0 win at home saw Liverpool reach their first ever European final 2-1.

So near, yet so far. At Glasgow's Hampden Park, Roger scores in the final against Borussia Dortmund but it wasn't enough; we never got going, and a poor performance saw us lose 2-1. It was a bitter disappointment.

Not a bad way to start my international career: 8 May 1963, Wembley Stadium, against the reigning world champions, the mighty Brazil. There were 20 other players on the pitch, I promise you! Here, I'm just hoping not to be nutmegged by the great Amarildo!

Lining up at the Maracanã to face the greatest - Pelé - and his pals, 30 May 1964. Back row L-R: myself, George Cohen, Maurice Norman, Tony Waiters, Ray Wilson, Bobby Moore. Front row L-R: Peter Thompson, Jimmy Greaves, Johnny Byrne, George Eastham, Bobby Charlton. We lost 5-1.

Lilleshall, June 1966, pre-World Cup: Roger (top left), Gerry, Cally, and myself, suited and getting booted for England training. Greavsie is inspecting the cut of the tracksuit trousers and next to him is Jonny the Stick! How he got past Alf I'll never know! This may have been my last session before not making the final squad.

The boys in blue. I may have just missed out on final squad selection, but to this day I remain incredibly proud to have been part of this gang. Heroes, every one of them.

The last line of defence – then me! I cover the goal line as Gordon Banks thwarts Scotland's Alan Gilzean in front of 134,000 supporters at Glasgow's Hampden Park. It was the biggest crowd I ever played in front of.

One bag of balls - that's all we had - but not a blade of grass in sight. The Besiktas training ground left a bit to be desired.

All in the same boat. The Besiktas lads deserve all the credit; despite the poor facilities they just got on with it, worked hard, and never complained. As did my trusty assistants Ali, Bahttin, Ali, and Nesme. I couldn't have survived without them.

THE FOOTBALL ASSOCIATION

LIMITED

Patron: HER MAJESTY THE QUEEN
President: H.R.H. THE DUKE OF KENT
Chairman: SIR ANDREW STEPHEN, M.B., Ch.B.

Secretary:
E. A. CROKER

Telegraphic Address:
FOOTBALL ASSOCIATION, LONDON, W2 3LW

16 LANCASTER GATE, LONDON, W2 3LW

Our Ref: EAC/KK.754 *Your Ref:* 30th July, 1974.

Strictly Private and Confidential

G. Milne Esq.,
Team Manager,
Coventry City F.C.,
Highfield Road Stadium,
Coventry.

Dear Gordon,

Now that the England Team Manager position is settled, I would just like to thank you for the interest you showed. It may be of some consolation to you that we have, in fact, gone for a relatively older man and I believe that Don will do a very good job for England.

I hope to have the opportunity of visiting Coventry early in the season, and will look forward to seeing you then.

Yours sincerely,

Ted Croker

Registered Office: 16 Lancaster Gate, London, W2 3LW
Incorporated in London Registration Number 77797

I was interviewed for the position of England manager, but it wasn't to be. Perhaps I dodged a bullet: Don Revie's tenure didn't work out too well, for him or the FA, and ended controversially. Courtesy of Gordon Milne guidance, organisation, management – whatever you want to call it.

The soil pitch restricted how we could work, so drills remained simple, straightforward and repetitive, but when we moved to the grass I saw a confident group with good technical abilities expressing themselves within the framework of simplicity and organisation – and all honed on the soil. I fully understood the optimism of the Başkan's 'missing jockey' statement. When Shanks first came to Liverpool, Chris Lawler, Tommy Smith, Ian Callaghan, Roger Hunt, Tommy Lawrence and Gerry Byrne were already in the stable – they'd grown up together, they'd travelled the same route and they could all bloody play, and we all know what happened there: the creation of a thoroughbred. Now, the Başkan recognised similar: these boys had grown up together, they understood and trusted one another (a big plus if they were going to make the horse a champion). So, could I achieve something similar with them? During that first season I established who I felt could deal with the challenge ahead, but they needed help. Hence my response: 'This horse has only got three legs.'

So it began. Phone calls to my pals ensued. Jim Smith was managing QPR. I told him I was looking for an English-style centre-forward who could put himself about a bit and lead the line (not too much to ask, really). Jim replied, 'I've got a lad here who doesn't know if he wants to be a professional footballer or a painter and decorator.' I can picture Jim with his feet up on his desk, smoking his cigar, with his afternoon brandy, finding humour in the situation as he always did. 'He's quick, good in the air and a great kid but he's on the fringe here. If you fancy taking him for a year it might do all of us a bit of good.' How right he was.

Les Ferdinand was on his way to the stars. None of us knew that then, but we all learned soon enough. He was indeed quick, and good in the air. He scored goals, could play and, as Jim had said so sincerely, was a great kid too. His cheerful personality, immediate acceptance of his new surroundings and his willingness to work immediately earned him the respect of team-mates and fans alike. He enjoyed the big crowds, being popular and respected, he responded big time to the challenge, and his confidence grew daily. He made a difference to everybody, not just because of his attitude but through his pace and power too; until Les we didn't have that type of player. He also had that winning smile, which followed him throughout his career. Everywhere he went he was a ray of sunshine. Les was on his way.

In 1987 we'd signed Bünyamin Süral from Malatyaspor. Malatya lies a thousand or so kilometres east of Istanbul, with a native dialect differing enormously from the Istanbul version. Somehow, Bünyamin and Les got pally, much to the amusement of the other boys, many of whom themselves couldn't understand Bünyamin, who couldn't speak English, never mind understand Les, who obviously couldn't speak any Turkish. 'What could they possibly be saying to each other?' But it's what Les did. Of his own accord he'd go to the laundry room just for a quick chat with the laundry team (a married couple and the wife's sister). Again, I don't know how he crossed the language barrier, but no matter, what was important was how such little gestures got around and were talked about. Les earned respect from the get-go. And then when the fans saw him play, they loved him too.

Les was only with us for one season but was hugely impressive, scoring 14 goals in 24 league matches. Jim had been right – well, half-right: the move had been good for Les, Beşiktaş and me, but Jim never saw the benefit himself as he was replaced at QPR by Trevor Francis. Trevor made it clear he wanted Les back at Loftus Road and, given the rave reviews of this talented young lad, who could blame him? The Başkan didn't want Les to go, and Les was happy to stay; he loved it and was a hero already. The Başkan would ask, 'Are you doing all you can to make him stay?' Unforgettably, he was so desperate to keep Les that he once asked of Erhan, 'Can Gordon talk to the Queen?' He meant it, too. That was the esteem in which Les was held. Funnily enough I didn't have a hotline to Buckingham Palace (nor any other of Her Majesty's residences) but his request wasn't as daft as it sounds: presidents of Turkish football clubs, particularly in Istanbul, were political figures as much as football ones, and regularly spoke to high-ranking government officials.

Les was the first player I brought in myself (before that, the committee was responsible). Jim was pleased too, especially as his own judgement of Les had been correct. Saying all this now, however, seems much easier having followed Les's career; it was quite different calling this when he was only 21 years old.

* * *

Second season syndrome: does it really exist? I'm not sure, but I do know my second season in Istanbul had to deliver an improvement on the first. As it turned out, 1988/89 was almost a carbon copy of the previous campaign, only this time we were vying with Fenerbahçe.

Our first league meeting in October, a 2-0 home win, took us to within three points of them (they were in top spot) and by new year we were leading, but in March a 2-1 defeat put Fenerbahçe two points ahead with ten matches remaining. Once again, we blinked first, with two draws and two defeats ultimately resigning us to a second runners-up spot in two years, this time ten points behind our (other) local rivals. Once again, finishing 14 points ahead of third-placed Galatasaray offered no consolation.

The stick was really flying, but my inability to read the newspapers, and not getting involved with television, helped considerably. And with the support of Ali and Bahattin (particularly Ali, who read everything that was written) I managed to retain, if not innocence, then a degree of ignorance – and ignorance is bliss sometimes, isn't it? Can you imagine how difficult it would be for an English coach in today's world to isolate themself from the media? Virtually impossible. I was fortunate in that I could remain professional enough to understand it but not get tangled up in it.

A good cup run, though, can keep the dogs at bay, and the Turkish Cup was our last hope of silverware. Curiously, we began that competition against our own second string, Beşiktaş II (reserve teams often featured in the early rounds), whom we defeated 9-1 over two legs. Three more two-legged rounds were successfully negotiated (4-1, 4-0 and 5-2), meaning just ten days after the league campaign ended, we faced a two-legged cup final against – who would have thought it – Fenerbahçe, the newly crowned champions. To give you an idea of where priorities lay back then, the first leg (away) drew a crowd of just over 6,000. Nevertheless, we were up for it and came away with a 1-0 win, courtesy of a stunning goal from Les Ferdinand. Receiving the ball with his back to goal, Les rode the first challenge, dissected two more and sent a fourth defender the wrong way before calmly slotting his finish beneath the onrushing goalkeeper (look it up on the internet, it really was a terrific goal). Four days later a 2-1 win (Ali Gültiken and Feyyaz Uçar with the goals) in front of our own fans – thankfully, nearly 17,000 that day – sealed victory. My first trophy in Turkey, and some sort of revenge over Fenerbahçe.

That Turkish Cup win was a life-saver for me. Having finished second in the league the previous season, with no cup run to speak of, then second once again (both second places behind our city rivals, remember), the knives were being sharpened, no question, and you could bet your last Turkish lira our rivals were watching with great interest too. But winning the cup gave me a bit of breathing space. On top of that, Les's impact can't be ignored: what he did, how he went about it and the sort of lad he was. Les gave the president enough ammunition to keep the natives relatively quiet, and because I'd brought him in it was a pat on the back for me too. And we all need one of those from time to time.

The cup win was also crucial for the players; they now knew they were capable of more. Football is about trophies, so no matter what else was going on, putting silverware in the cabinet said, 'Forget everything else – this is success.' It was as simple as that. Winning boosts confidence, and that cup win was part of the process of building what would eventually take care of itself. We already had the nucleus, which we'd shortly bolster with new signings, and knowing the president was (unlike some) totally behind us, was invaluable. He'd played for the club during the '40s and '50s, so saw the situation differently from other board members. There was something being built, he could see that, and the cup win, as well as a reward for all the hard work, was the foundation stone of what was to come.

By that point I'd signed a new two-year contract so was in the right frame of mind and only looking forward. Winning the cup probably did more for me within myself than it did for my credibility in the eyes of others, although I wasn't concerned about that. I was more excited about where the club was going, and the feeling was shared by the players, the president and myself; we might be on to something here.

The signing of Les had been a great success but come the summer of 1989 he'd gone and left a big hole to fill. There was more to consider, though. Even with Les, I'd been unhappy with the balance of the team. I had players on the right who could naturally and comfortably do their jobs, but the left was a different story. It was back to the phone again. I called David Pleat, who had recently succeeded Bryan Hamilton at my old club Leicester City. David was someone else I talked to a lot, and his football knowledge was encyclopaedic. Everybody knew the players in the top teams, but David knew every player in every division, even non-league. I told him I was looking for someone to play wide left, with a good left foot, a good crosser of the ball and, most importantly, fancied the challenge of playing in Turkey. I had to tread carefully as we didn't have much money, but David understood that. 'There's a lad at Bristol City,' he said. 'Alan Walsh. Not the youngest, he's 32, but how he's not played at a higher level I'll never know. He's six foot tall and has a magic left foot; can play it short, long, whip crosses in, and he's got a powerful shot on him too. The only downside is he lacks pace; if you want someone to run past people, he's not your man. That said, though, he'll not let you down.' Pleaty was right.

I also heard that Everton's Ian Wilson could be available. I'd managed Ian at Leicester, picking him regularly, so knew him well and was delighted when he joined us a month after Walshy. A good, aggressive midfielder, Ian had a great left foot and was extremely competitive; tough as teak, he'd willingly play through injury if he had to. A typical Scot and a first-class character. I rated him so highly I made him my assistant when I went to Japan, and he remained my number two when I returned to Turkey in the late '90s.

Walshy was laid-back, with a great sense of humour. One day at training, sat with the journalists (he'd been at the club a while by this point so knew how to 'play the game'), one of them said to him, 'Volsh …' – it was always Volsh and Vilson, as they didn't pronounce the 'W' too well – 'Volsh, you're 32, and you're slow!' Walshy replied, 'Yes, I'm 32 and I'm slow, but let me tell you something. When I was 22, I was also slow!' Blank looks all round. Walshy's British humour hadn't travelled so well. The supporters, though, quickly learned to appreciate him. In the last third he didn't need to beat his man; he only needed half a yard to whip it in. I always thought there were shades of Nottingham Forest's John Robertson about him. (Robbo never ran past anybody either, but he won the European Cup twice!)

Walshy was with me for two years, Ian only 18 months, but both were transformative for the team, playing key roles in the success that followed. They supplied that missing balance. My left-back Kadir Akbulut was strong and reliable, and now in front of him was Ian: experienced, aggressive, naturally left-footed. And ahead of him Walshy: tall, powerful, could put the ball on a sixpence with his magical left foot. A small triangle of players with such abilities, in an area of the pitch they were responsible for, and all with the right tools. They must have a chance, I thought.

The professionalism shown by Walshy and Wilson stood out like a beacon; two senior pros setting an example to all. They were motivational, and the entire squad fed off that. That left-sided trio didn't start every match but were great options – square pegs in square holes. Much of what proved successful in my early managerial work was positioning players where they were comfortable; sounds obvious, I know, but it worked. And by doing so, the language barrier was never really a barrier at all as what I was trying to do wasn't a foreign language to anyone. Someone on the right who was right-footed, two through the middle who wanted to play through the middle, left footers on the left. It almost became a mantra, one I preached all the time. The players gained confidence, knowing they'd have half a chance of playing where they wanted to play, and I took confidence from the way they worked. Furthermore, understudies replacing first-teamers already knew their roles, responsibilities and what was expected of them, because we *all* did it together every day in training. I wouldn't say we were developing a specific DNA (as is often talked about these days), it just seemed a sensible approach, one of consistency and repetition, leading to simplicity. As Shanks used to say, 'Why are all these bloody scouts here, Bob? We play the same way every bloody week!' Nothing in football is new.

It's also worth remembering that Ferdinand, Wilson and Walsh, each of whom had an immense effect on what was to come, never cost the club a penny (just as well, as we had no bloody money anyway). Les was a loan deal, the others were free transfers; considering what they contributed, individually and collectively, it was great business for the club not having to fork out anything other than their salaries. I wonder how differently a similar situation would play out today.

A year earlier my 'three-legged horse' quip was intended to be light-hearted but there was a truth behind it too: it was all about balance, and at that time we didn't have it. The British lads certainly helped to put us on the right road, but it was something the whole team bought into. As for me, I was hardly reinventing the wheel – I knew that – but the engine was now running more smoothly and we were heading in the right direction.

* * *

The bedrock of any team is its defence. The right to progress (and succeed) is based upon how well it defends its territory and how uncomfortable life is for the opposition. The mentality to never concede a goal, a corner, or lose a 50/50 challenge, becomes a must. During those early years my consistent back four of Recip Cetin, Gökhan Keskin, Ulvi Güveneroğlu and Kadir Akbulut provided the necessary stability, but top-quality Turkish goalkeepers proved harder to find. Eventually Metin Akçevre and Engin Ipekoglu staked their claims. But, as ever, goalscorers and creative players generated the most publicity.

Mehmet 'Şifo' Özdilek had joined us from Kahramanmaraşspor in eastern Turkey, in the summer of 1988. Şifo was signed by the committee (I didn't know him as Turkey isn't easy to get around on scouting missions). An all-round midfielder, he made nearly 400 appearances, scoring 100-plus goals, and went on to captain the club. Small in stature but big in heart, he had an unbending determination to succeed. Similar in stature to Paul Scholes, he had everything: left foot, right foot, could create and defend, and bring others into play; he could pass, put it through your legs, bend it into the top corner or put his foot through it; he'd get up and down the pitch, and was a great competitor. A great kid all round, a complete midfielder who the fans took to immediately. He was nicknamed Şifo due to his similarities to the Belgian playmaker Enzo Scifo and was referred to as Şifo as often as he was Mehmet.

Back in 1988 on a pre-season tour to Germany, the goalkeeping coach Alan Hodgkinson was with me (one of the best in the business, I'd used him before at Coventry). Şifo, in one of his first games for us, was having a blinder. Alan asked me, 'Who the f**king hell is this lad?' It's fair to say he was impressed. Şifo's progress was immediate, his effect similar to that of Les, a top-level player who fitted in seamlessly. When Walsh and Wilson later left, they were missed, but Şifo, magic in his own way, carried the torch. He was a fine addition to a strong group of like-minded individuals, all of whom complemented one another. Good players lift others, and if you're fortunate enough to have more than one or two with intelligence and ability, the chemistry created soon spreads. That core group – Şifo, Riza, and strikers Metin Tekin, Ali Gültiken and Feyyaz Uçar – all had the ability to play for Europe's 'bigger' clubs, no disrespect to Beşiktaş of course.

With three league matches remaining we were distracted by the Turkish Cup Final, having dispatched Rizespor, Boluspor and Fenerbahçe. Now we faced Trabzonspor. Two goals in six minutes from Feyyaz Uçar (68) and Şifo (74) delivered our first silverware of the season. Now the question was: could we do the double?

The answer was a resounding yes. We clinched our first league title in four years within days, five points ahead of Fenerbahçe. It was fully deserved. Our worst run had been early in the season, two losses and a draw, a run followed by a 10-0 win over Adana Demirspor, to this day the club's record win over a top-flight team. As ever, the derbies were crucial. If you couldn't win, you dared not lose! Thankfully we managed to win three (a 3-1 defeat of Fenerbahçe in our penultimate fixture was particularly satisfying) and draw one. It had taken three eventful seasons and lots of hard graft to win the championship, but we immediately felt we could do this again.

An hour before our final match I was standing in the tunnel gazing at a full stadium when my captain Riza joined me. He put his hand on my shoulder and said, 'Hoca, no problem. Next season – same again.' I felt a warm glow as I shook his hand. We'd not had the greatest start that season – the doom-mongers had been out in force – so this was a special moment. One of life's most pleasant feelings is remembering when you turned things around and achieved something, remembering a job well done.

Football, though, moves quickly and we were soon going again. Our status as league champions meant we were brimming with confidence and, as it turned out, with good reason. Riza's words – 'same again' – would prove prophetic.

A strong start (five wins and two draws) saw us top the table before dropping to second, then third following a run containing too many draws. However, and again crucially, once again we didn't lose to either Fenerbahçe or Galatasaray (a win and a draw against each). These matches were usually a good barometer of how the league might turn out, and so it proved. In February we returned to the top – and there we stayed. We lost just once all season, away at Gençlerbirliği, but it was only a blip. Five more wins confirmed our second successive league title, five points ahead of Galatasaray: won 20, drawn 9, lost 1. It was an incredible achievement, and I remember thinking, *How do you top that?*

We'd find out the following season. Momentum grows, confidence spreads and the effect is almost tangible. You never think of yourselves as invincible, of course, but are often portrayed as such by the opposition or media. Players can then be rendered arrogant, however wrong that may be. During the 1991/92 season we never thought ourselves invincible, ever, but our results proved we were heading in the right direction. We drew our opening match before winning the next eight; self-belief grew accordingly.

Our unbeaten streak created different perspectives for us and our opponents: while our confidence continued to grow, the oppo were (often) on the back foot. Such perspectives only increased the longer our run continued. At Christmas we were unbeaten in 15; by early March, still no defeats. But as the run continued, so the pressure built and that extra spice was added to every 'next' match. Would this be the one? Would our bubble burst? It was what every opponent wanted, to be the first to beat us. This heightened the intensity within us all as the countdown began to the next match. And every 'next' one was more crucial than the last.

In Istanbul, like Liverpool, families were often split in terms of who supported who. Even those who didn't go to matches had an allegiance one way or another. Fenerbahçe was the best-supported club in the city (and the country, actually), their rivalry with Galatasaray fiercer than their rivalry with us. Galatasaray were seen to represent the city's more sophisticated half, whereas Beşiktaş was the 'working-man's club'. Rivalries would shift, though, depending on the progress of each. Galatasaray fans would gladly support Fenerbahçe if it meant stopping us in our tracks, and vice-versa. That's natural, of course, but it increased the pressure, as nobody wanted us to go unbeaten all season. Few believed we could. It was up to us to prove them wrong.

The pressure was merely a by-product of our performances, but it was there, no question. There was no arrogance in the group though, and no matter who the opposition was we were always up for the fight. Of course, the derbies were the biggest matches but losing to a team lower down the league – or even worse, a team at the bottom – was a total disaster; you'd get more stick for that than anything else. Still undefeated, we had a bigger than usual target on our back, and remaining undefeated became almost as important as winning the league – almost, but not quite. As winter turned to spring, we were all conscious of the chat, but with ten matches to go none of that mattered. We hadn't lost (yet), but that didn't guarantee the league title. We had to remain focused.

With two fixtures remaining we stood five points ahead of Fenerbahçe, so victory in our penultimate match would clinch our third successive championship. That match was at home – against Galatasaray! As you'd expect, Fenerbahçe's supporters were right behind them, and it turned out to be one hell of a match. Galatasaray took a first-half lead, but we equalised almost immediately. Early in the second half we fell behind again, drew level again, then 60 seconds later trailed once more. Again we responded, equalising for a third time. With 25 minutes remaining, a red card for Galatasaray's Tugay Kerimoğlu (later of Blackburn Rovers fame) undoubtedly helped our cause, and in the 82nd minute Şifo gave us the lead for the first time. It remained 4-3. We'd defeated one of our greatest rivals in a thrilling encounter in front of our own supporters, but more importantly had clinched the league title once again – three in a row! With one match remaining we were untouchable – but could we be invincible? Could we finish the job in style?

An undefeated campaign had never been achieved, which only meant even more pressure at home against Sariyer (then some 35 points behind us). Nothing was more important than winning the league, but we now found ourselves in a completely different dimension. Aside from the BJK fans it seemed the entire country was supporting Sariyer – all wishing the thoroughbred would fall at the last fence. I suppose that's human nature in the life of fanatical football fans the world over. However, the Başkan's horse skipped over the last fence in style – well, an 87th-minute winner from Şenol Fidan and a final score of 1-0 was style enough for me! We'd made history. It was our third successive championship, and we'd been invincible.

Naturally, delight and pride were equally immense – especially for the jockey! I was as pleased for everyone else as I was for myself, and there was a little something extra in our achievement: in terms of prestige, resources and finances, Beşiktaş were always third in the pecking order in Istanbul, so this win against the odds was even more satisfying.

It was time for a well-earned family holiday and a period of reflection. Three consecutive championships, including a double, and a full season without losing a match. How could I temper expectations for the following season? How could I improve on that magical period? Would I become a victim of my own success now the bar had been set so high? Would familiarity creep in? Would attitudes change? As a seasoned campaigner I'd experienced the highs and the lows and understood the emotions created by both; they camp in your soul and live there forever. How you conduct yourself in the bad times, only you control. How you approach the better days? You hope to remain consistent. Fortunately, I had a president of similar mindset to me; we kept our feet firmly on the ground.

Stress and success affect people differently; the latter can sometimes be more dangerous. Time would soon tell as, unsurprisingly, the next season we were marked men. Motivation, for anyone, wasn't a problem, as we were going for four in a row, whereas the opposition wanted to bring us down a peg or three. We remained in the hunt right up to the final day, but Galatasaray clinched the title with an 8-0 defeat of MKE Ankaragücü, winning the league on goal difference only, eight goals ahead of us. Their triumph was swathed in speculation and rumour and incensed the BJK fans into a frenzy. Questions were asked over the Ankaragücü goalkeeper, Rade Zalad. He'd been at Beşiktaş during my early years, was a great lad, and in my mind there was no doubting his integrity. I don't believe for a minute that he'd been 'got at', although that's not to say something untoward didn't go on elsewhere behind the scenes. Nor did it stop the speculation or aggravation. Emotions were unsurprisingly running high; this was Istanbul, and two of the big boys were slugging it out for pride of place. I took a back seat, not getting involved in things I couldn't control.

In Turkey the passion for football is second to none. As coaches and managers we worked diligently to instil the principles of fair play, high standards and to show respect for our profession. In the heat of battle, passion sometimes takes control, but this is when the world is looking at you and your players to see whether you can handle it. Remembering my principles from days long gone, and sticking to them through thick and thin, I took great pride in how we won, but also in how we handled defeat, no matter how painful. I believed in setting standards, and we were duly rewarded, but also respected, for how we conducted ourselves. This cemented that belief and meant so much to us all.

The hangover kicked in the following season. Our first 15 matches brought only six victories. This was now my seventh season in Turkey, and after so long it was inevitable that gossip, speculation and opinions became more prevalent in my daily work. It wasn't all critical or negative; indeed, much of it was fair game. 'Where do Gordon Milne and BJK go from here?' was one valid headline. The mood was understandable. Speculation breeds uncertainty, which in turn creates confusion, and the mix is destabilising, gradually chipping away at any hard-earned credibility. I couldn't allow this to happen. It was time to leave Turkey.

Chapter 20

MY MOVE to Nagoya Grampus Eight in Japan originated through Jon Holmes, who I first met while in charge of Leicester City. Jon was representing Gary Lineker (the notion of football agents was in its infancy then), was sensible, intelligent and an avid Leicester City supporter. He was a shrewd operator, and thanks to him and Gary, I was truly well represented. Gary had moved to Grampus in 1992 and they were looking for a new coach. My history with Gary worked in my favour, and having handled his transfer from Tottenham, Jon had a good relationship with the Grampus hierarchy. In December 1993 Jon, myself and a Mr Nishigaki (a Grampus board member) met in London. Jon had already informed me of the deal (non-negotiable) terms, which in his view were fair. I respected his advice and accepted the terms but first required permission from Beşiktaş to break my contract halfway through the season.

Had I not been approached by Grampus would I have survived in Istanbul? If so, for how long? Was big Jack Charlton's philosophy – five years in the job is long enough – true after all? I'd done six and a half. On reflection, the timing of the move was both perfect and awful: perfect because I felt my time at Beşiktaş was coming to an end anyway (and others thought the same); awful because the offer came halfway through the season – never ideal. Neither the president nor I were too chuffed about this, but all things being equal, both sides parted company with dignity and mutual respect in February 1994. The sun was setting on the Bosporus and rising in Japan.

Few British coaches had ventured abroad. Frank O'Farrell, my old Preston team-mate and former Manchester United manager, had tried Iran. He once told me that success there brought no silverware; instead, he was presented with two white ponies! (I don't think he brought them home.) Despite such incentives, however, British managers abroad were still far from the norm. So, flying the flag once again, I approached the Far East with optimism.

Unlike my arrival in Istanbul, I was unwilling to face this challenge alone; it was imperative to have an assistant from the start, so I took Ian Wilson with me, and in January 1994 I entered the unknown once again. Grampus Eight was run by the Toyoda family, the owners of Toyota. Unsurprisingly, the club operated to the highest professional standards. My first meeting with the main man, Doctor Toyoda, was in his palatial office in Nagoya (my first experience of green tea, thankfully served only in small cups, which I struggled to finish); a brief encounter, politely executed as my official welcome to another world. I visited the training ground, which was more than acceptable and, in springtime, surrounded by rhododendron bushes, a magnificent sight. There was also a group of enthusiastic players with smiles on their faces – what more could I ask?

As always, it took time to identify players' strengths and weaknesses, but the enthusiasm and expectancy were immediately apparent. J-League rules allowed only three foreign players in a team at any one time. Grampus had four: three Brazilians, all good professionals, and Gary. If Gary was fit, he'd play, so one of the Brazilians would miss out. Such restrictions meant it was essential that players had the right temperament; for example, the Brazilians wouldn't be happy travelling halfway around the world to sit on the bench or, even worse, at home. As a former player, I know how I'd have felt; as a coach, such headaches are best avoided.

Our pre-season camp was in Okinawa in the tropical south – no problems getting a sweat on there – and all went well. We got to know the players and staff, and the admin was professionally handled and very well executed. On returning to Nagoya, however, a club official informed me that we'd signed two players from the former Yugoslavia: Dragiša Binić and Dragan Stojković. Said official was delighted to convey the news, although not too impressed when I didn't share his enthusiasm. I had good reason not to as we now had six foreign players. The headache had suddenly got worse.

The more mature (and I use that word loosely) one grows, the more time one has to look backwards, but being wise after the event doesn't always lead to fond memories; everything is easier with hindsight, isn't it? That day I should have acted. I should have requested a meeting to establish the club's thinking – but I didn't. Big mistake. This was exacerbated by the attitude and body language of the new recruits, as if they knew from day one that they weren't my choice; earning mutual respect would be a test. And all this before a ball was kicked in anger.

To be fair, on signing, they'd have assumed they'd be regulars in the team, but the regulations ensured such optimism would be severely challenged. Stojković in particular wouldn't have signed if he thought he wouldn't play. I understood that, but it didn't make the problem go away. He was a good international player, no mug. 'We're trying to support our new trainer,' could genuinely have been the club's message to the fans. Signing two experienced internationals – how could I disagree with that? But in principle I did. Six into three didn't go.

Would the Yugoslavs' attitude have differed if they were the only two foreigners, and therefore competing only against the Japanese players? Probably. Stojković's ability wasn't in question (Binić less so; he was signed from Cypriot club APOEL); he went on to play seven seasons for Grampus, eventually becoming manager and winning the league in 2010, although I don't want to give him too many pats on the back as he was a pain in the arse for me. In our first competitive match, with high expectations and the hierarchy in attendance, Mr Stojković got himself sent off early, showing no remorse for his actions or the problems he created for his team-mates. He was obviously sending a message via his demeanour and attitude, which I felt was deliberate: mentally, he wasn't in a good place with the coach, and not enjoying his football. Ian experienced similar in training, regularly speaking of a lack of respect and poor attitude. (Sometimes, if the coach doesn't find the formula, their assistant will, but not in this case.) The mood was uncomfortable and challenging and, given the regulations, discontent, somewhere, was inevitable. My intention was to seek the backbone of the team from the core of Japanese players (I'd done likewise with the Turks at BJK), still to me the most sensible approach. But time was short and we were soon into the matches so were experimenting on the hoof. Early results were poor, and to make matters worse Gary's injury didn't improve; sadly, as he'd have been undoubtedly injected what was required: goals, leadership and professionalism.

The Brazilian boys – defender Garçal, winger Elivélton, and Jorginho, a good, experienced midfielder and captain material – were no problem. Their translator understood football (as most Brazilians do) and spoke perfect English. We also inherited a young British boy as our interpreter: 6ft 3in tall, blonde, handsome, an academic with a university background who spoke fluent Japanese. Could this be an advantage? As it soon turned out, unfortunately not – he had no bloody clue about football. One day, travelling to training on the underground he was sat next to a group of young Japanese students who were, in his words, 'taking the piss'. He remained silent, apparently oblivious to the comments, until arriving at his station when, rising to his full height, he jabbed his finger into their startled faces, which suddenly drained of all colour. In fluent Japanese he gave them his full range of expletives before exiting the train just as the doors closed. He thought it was hilarious, but on hearing this the Brazilian translator's face turned ashen. We'd only been on board a short time but already were acutely aware of the required and correct manner of behaviour, so this didn't go down well. The British gang of four – two coaches, one player, one translator – not off to an encouraging start.

Another quirk of the J-League was the famous – or infamous – golden goal rule. A hard-earned draw was sometimes good for morale and could give a coach some breathing space. But in Japan there had to be a winner, so after 90 minutes it was next goal wins – and in my experience it was usually the opposition who scored it! I remember the Brazilian Toninho, playing for Shimizu S-Pulse, smashing the ball into the back of our net in overtime. He ran past our goal, waving his shirt in the air with his team-mates and staff in hot pursuit. For a brief second it didn't register with me; I must have been thinking there was another 15 minutes to play. Then I suddenly felt the cold sweat of reality, a knife in the ribs, and despondency all around. The golden goal rule: great if you win ...

During this period of struggle, I needed to speak with someone in authority … not easy. Lines of communication were different. In England a barney with your chairman would get things off your chest but in Japan club officials tended to avoid conflict. How could I reach the people that mattered? The protocol was to first speak to the club's representative closest to the team. He'd then discuss with his superior, who would do the same, and so on, further up the chain. It was organised, everybody knew where they stood, but the process didn't help me. I was in a hurry for answers but got nowhere.

It was uncomfortable for all concerned. Gary, more than most, understood my frustration so got involved. This wasn't easy for him. Despite his popularity he hadn't kicked a ball for months and questions were being asked. Nevertheless, he helped to set up a meeting. It lasted no more than ten minutes. Green tea was served once again and the club official listened politely and patiently to my concerns. As I anticipated a response, he paused. He rose gently to his feet, thanked me for coming, bowed courteously and left the room. From that moment, the writing was on the wall. No verbal exchange, no conflict, but the message was in the air: quiet, yet loud and clear – sayonara.

A little holiday was the cute (although bizarre) manner of announcing the party was over. As they informed me of my dismissal, the club also asked me to oversee their pre-season training camp in Australia. Why not? I'd never been to Australia before. I wanted Edith to join me and shortly afterwards a club representative spent the whole afternoon with her arranging the entire trip. As always with Grampus, the administration was first-class.

My time at the club had been short, but an experience that both Ian and I look back on fondly. Unfortunately, my track record in Japan was just not good enough: too many defeats, not enough victories. Simple really.

Japan was an eye-opener. The country is extremely structured, but I went there knowing it would take some getting used to. I admired the people and still do. Their politeness, respect, discipline and work ethic are simple concepts and should be cornerstones of all areas of society, not just the football world. That said, it was tricky to get to grips with, and proved to be quite a learning curve. I never look back at my career with regrets but there's a tinge of disappointment that I was unable to see out my contract. It's a fascinating place, with a fascinating way of life. There's so much to admire about Japan and its people and how they operate, so different to the Western way of working – but not necessarily within the vicious world of football!

* * *

In my absence, the UK game had moved on. My old pal Jim Smith had recently been appointed as the chief executive of the LMA. I vividly remember saying to Edith, 'I could've been interested in that job.' Was my mind drifting towards exiting the sharp end and looking elsewhere? After all, I'd been in the jungle nearly 25 years, much longer than my carefree playing days. Was it time for change?

John Camkin was one of the original visionaries of football administration and possessed the necessary skills to help establish the LMA, instigated by a conversation he'd shared with Graham Taylor, then managing England. Graham felt isolated from the club managers he knew so well and recognised this needed rectifying. Managers needed to talk more openly and honestly to each other and required some sort of body to enable that. For example, club managers hated players disappearing on international duty (it's no different today), and there was no relationship between Football League managers and the associations to calm such choppy waters. Graham pestered John, both recognised that managers needed a voice and a support system, and the LMA seed was sown. John was most ably supported by Olaf Dixon, who went on to become the lifetime assistant secretary, recognition for his dedication and hard work through thick and thin. It wasn't plain sailing, however. After only six months or so Jim decided (interestingly, considering what I too would decide a year later) that it wasn't for him, and duly returned to the cut and thrust of management with Derby County. He missed what you'd expect him to miss – the day-to-day involvement of running a football team – and when the Derby offer arrived, he found it impossible to refuse.

Just over a week later John invited me to his house in Leamington Spa for 'a chat'. I'd first met John during my Coventry days and was always impressed with his integrity, knowledge and genuine love for the game. He was disappointed Jim had moved on but not surprised. He stressed that he wanted stability and progress before asking whether I'd take on the challenge. I accepted. As I'd already been down the road they were now travelling, it was the perfect time to take on new responsibilities: representing the managers, their welfare, understanding their concerns. This was as close to the game as it was possible to be without the daily pressures of management – or so I thought; most club chairmen were still suspicious of change and wished to maintain their authority over managers, just as they did over the players. The chairmen still held most of the aces.

To move forward, recognition of the LMA was essential. We needed some clout, which we had in abundance with high-profile managers such as Alex Ferguson, Howard Wilkinson, Frank Clark, Sam Allardyce and Steve Coppell, all early custodians of the vision in which they truly believed. They were all still managing, with their own daily pressures, but simultaneously fighting for more recognition and status. Collectively, their voices were powerful but needed to be heard as one.

That was what we did have. What we didn't have was cash, commercial links or sponsorship, all vital to pursue the dream. Creating revenue streams and attracting companies looking for a link with the professional game was a priority. Without the support of mobile phones or the internet, these were pioneering days. John and Olaf already had lines of communication requiring constant attention, so I was immediately busy, one meeting after another. The initial interest was encouraging, especially as we were still operating in the word-of-mouth era. It developed so quickly that we decided to employ someone part-time to share the load. That someone was John Barnwell, who had recently left the managerial seat at Northampton Town. John was well respected, attacked his new role with gusto and wasn't shy of voicing his opinions when he had something to offer. It wasn't long before he was working practically full-time.

Progress was slow, however. John was enjoying his work, but I couldn't say that about myself. Long, boring meetings with non-football people tested my patience, even when the outcome was successful. I wasn't playing in the right position and gained little satisfaction; I was letting the side down. My responsibility was to every manager in the Football League, irrespective of what level, all of whom were in high-pressure jobs and doing their best. In return, they deserved the best from me.

My concentration had also been side-tracked by a phone call from Ali, my old translator in Istanbul. He'd been contacted by Bursaspor, wondering whether I'd be interested in returning to management in Turkey – and they wanted to know now. I immediately felt the blood pumping; excitement and apprehension rolled into one. I informed John and Olaf that I was prepared to meet with the Bursa president that week, but also, irrespective of the outcome, I was resigning from the LMA. It was the correct thing to do on three fronts: one, my respect for John and Olaf for their loyal support; two, I wasn't the man to take the organisation where it needed to go; and three, the man to do that job was already in place – John Barnwell.

It's strange, but unexpected opportunities often tend to be far more interesting than those meticulously sought or planned; the grass isn't always greener. Jim Smith thought the LMA job was what he wanted … it wasn't. I thought the same, Stevie Coppell too. It turned out to be a bigger job than we all first thought. The job demanded enthusiasm, energy, expertise and dedication. John, with the loyal support of Olaf, spent the next 12 years providing just that and more, patiently building the foundations of an organisation that has far outgrown the dreams of those early believers. Richard Bevan, ably supported throughout by Howard Wilkinson and his team, has taken the organisation into the 21st century in style. The LMA is now the envy of all football associations across the globe. I'm a fully paid-up member, and proud of it. I'm equally proud when remembering where it all began, and all the effort and hard graft of those who contributed so much to making a dream come true.

* * *

Initial telephone conversations with Bursa concerned the basics: salary, contract details, and so forth. The chairman was willing to travel to England for a chat and wanted me to return to Turkey with him to inspect the facilities and, if all went well, sign on the dotted line. A few days later, Ali, the chairman and three other board members arrived at my house, and following an hour or so of talks we were on our way to Birmingham Airport. We bypassed the regular departures point and headed to the area designated for private planes. *This is alright*, I thought. Settling in, I noticed the chairman was no longer among us. As we taxied down the runway, I noticed smoke coming from the cockpit. It wasn't as serious as it sounds, as most Turks seemed to smoke. The cockpit door was open, and one of the pilots was enjoying a cigarette. I suddenly realised it was, in fact, the chairman who was smoking in the cockpit – and he was flying the bloody plane, too!

The Bursa facilities were excellent: two or three good grass pitches surrounded by what they called *şeftali*, the peach trees for which Bursa is famous. Driving through these orchards was very picturesque, and very impressive. I met those I needed to meet, signed the contract and headed home. I was back in management. Three or four days later I returned to Turkey, accompanied once again by Ian Wilson. It was the beginning of a very enjoyable year. The people were very good to us, as was the chairman, who pretty much left me alone to get on with the job.

Ian and I quickly found agreeable accommodation not far from one another, soon hit our stride and were enjoying our work. There were weekly visits from various committee members, always enquiring whether we needed anything, always acting in the club's best interests. Our working conditions and the attitude of players and staff were encouraging. We were soon playing some good stuff, holding our own, and with a passionate home crowd our stadium wasn't an easy place to visit.

I've mentioned previously words of wisdom that stay with you throughout your career. At Liverpool, Bob Paisley continually preached how little it takes to knock the train off the tracks. He also stressed how you don't appreciate what you've got until it's taken away from you. It was his way of keeping us grounded and focused on our responsibilities. Unfortunately, the train that Ian and I were now on was knocked off the tracks all too easily, and only then did we appreciate what we'd had.

Things were going well but a phone call in early March changed everything – big time. There were going to be changes at my former club Beşiktaş, and would I be interested in returning as coach? My immediate answer should have been, 'No thank you, I'm enjoying life at Bursa.' But it wasn't. Ego took over and my brain ceased to function properly. I gave the caller the encouragement he was looking for. I should have put the phone down straight away. I didn't. Mistake number one.

I made the approach known to the Bursa board and informed them I was seriously considering accepting. From that moment, the writing was on the wall. Sure enough, the board requested a meeting. I had a very good relationship with them so felt there was nothing to fear. Ian and I weren't acting arrogantly and had no wish to disappoint anyone at the club. They were good people whom we liked, so we were as up-front with them as possible, just as they were with us. By now the gossip-mongers had sniffed a juicy one. This Beşiktaş business wasn't going to go away, so the board wanted to nip it in the bud. They understood my reaction to the offer, knowing full well how much I'd enjoyed my time there previously. They also recognised that I really fancied returning, and were prepared to offer us contract extensions and more money. We declined: 'Thanks very much, but no.' Mistake number two. And you don't get to make three and carry on.

I never got to the bottom of the original phone call. Süleyman Seba, for whom I had the greatest respect, was still the Beşiktaş president, so naturally our heads were turned. But the caller failed to mention that a new president was due to be elected. Had I known, would my reaction have been different? Would I have preferred to re-establish my previous relationship with my former Başkan, or would starting afresh with a new president have appealed more? I honestly don't know. Furthermore, whose camp was the caller in? In Turkey, with 20 or so bodies sitting on the same board, each member tended to have their own agenda.

As it turned out, none of the above mattered. Serdar Bilgili became the new president. I've met him several times and, for the record, have no problem with him whatsoever, but the bottom line is that he didn't fancy me, and the message soon came through that there was no way I was going to be offered the job. I couldn't blame him, either. He wanted a fresh start, to come in with a new broom, was young, had money and wanted to do his own thing. And that's exactly what he did. When the message reached us that the Beşiktaş job was never going to happen, Bursa, still understandably p***ed off with us, said, 'Well, you didn't do right by us so there's no way we can carry on.' I'd made a right balls-up. We intended to break a two-year contract, so didn't have a leg to stand on. We couldn't possibly expect them to want us to stay. Leaving was inevitable. At the end of the season, we shook hands and parted company. Our actions also meant we weren't entitled to any compensation, and there was no way we could challenge that either. It was no more than we deserved. We weren't proud of ourselves.

None of this was quickfire, however. On some occasions it was the hottest of topics; at other times the issue seemed to have gone away. But it never did. And eventually these things always come out, leading to relationships deteriorating. It was a shame. Ian and I, and our families, were happy in Bursa. We were working for good people in a city we enjoyed, had a good stadium and facilities, decent crowds. We couldn't ask for more, but had shot ourselves in the foot in Bursa, and missed out on Beşiktaş too. Bob Paisley was right: our train had well and truly come off the tracks, and it hadn't taken much at all. Ian and I now really did appreciate what we'd had at Bursa, but it was too late. The damage had been done.

I handled it badly and take full responsibility. I should have dismissed a return to Beşiktaş immediately – I didn't. I should have confided more in those I already knew at the club – I didn't do that either. And I also should have realised that by returning to Beşiktaş, in the grand scheme of things, I had nothing to gain – but I didn't. I got carried away, despite there never being an official offer on the table, which I even acknowledged but somehow pushed to the back of my mind. My heart ruled my head. I should have known better.

* * *

Reflecting on mistakes, bad decisions and what ifs does no good whatsoever (although neither does wallowing for too long on days in the sun). In football, emotions must quickly be confined to history. Sometimes lessons learned the hard way thicken the skin, and remaining on the carousel demands an extra layer every year. It's all experience, and it's how you use it – if you get the opportunity – that matters. And, once again, I found myself extremely fortunate as another opportunity appeared on the horizon.

The president of Trabzonspor, Mehmet Ali Yılmaz, was a successful Istanbul businessman. I was asked to meet him and had no hesitation. It was immediately obvious that this president was in sole control of all matters Trabzonspor, which he reinforced with an aggressive passion; nothing wrong with that, he was a local boy after all. He knew more about me than I knew about him and there was little room for small talk. The interview lasted no more than ten minutes. He'd obviously made up his mind to offer me the job (alongside Ian once again) and wasn't anticipating a rejection. I accepted. Ian and I soon found two apartments overlooking the Black Sea – perfect. The training facilities were good, but the culture here was very different to our previous Turkish experiences. It wasn't that we didn't feel welcome – we did – but were kept more at arm's length.

Trabzon lies on the Black Sea, close to Georgia and Russia. Its football team was renowned for having the most hostile fans in the country, which I knew well from previous visits. Win, lose or draw, we were always relieved to escape unscathed. Even boarding the coach was a nightmare, and driving to the airport we were a constant target for fans chucking whatever they could get their hands on. It was what they did. Welcome to Trabzon.

Trabzonspor always had good players. Many were local, who, interestingly, were reluctant to move on when Istanbul's big three were making advances. I'd previously tried to sign one or two, but they wouldn't leave Trabzon, as if their lives wouldn't have been worth living had they turned their backs on the town. A local boy considering playing elsewhere, especially in Istanbul, would be bordering on treason in the eyes of the fanatical Trabzon support. To say it was different there would be the understatement of the year. Trabzon was its own place, and unique. Our living conditions were good, but attractions were limited: one average hotel, no proper restaurants as such, and not much to occupy you socially.

Being so isolated, we flew everywhere. There was always a big contingent of committee members accompanying us. Away fixtures in more fashionable cities were opportunities for them to escape Trabzon and let their hair down (they all liked to gamble and enjoyed a night out). I recall one occasion heading through airport security when two board members took off their raincoats to pass through the metal detector. The security personnel pointed to the coats: 'Empty the pockets.' The committee members did just that – and both were carrying a gun! The guns were passed through the X-ray machine and picked up on the other side. Nothing to see here!

Trabzon had a bit of the Wild West about it. There was always something coming in (and usually something going out too). I remember a chap turning up at the training ground trying to shift a load of caviar! I'd never tasted caviar before (but when I did, I thought it was fantastic). The tins were small, because it's usually so expensive, but these ones would cost next to nothing. This was of no interest to the players; they were all accustomed to the regular visitors plying their trade, so ignored them. But the two strangers to the scene, Milne and Wilson, took full advantage of a good deal when they saw one! (Incidentally, I've never tasted caviar since.)

By and large the president left us alone, although one or two of his entourage appeared at training every day, not interfering but giving the impression of overseeing our every move. My feeling was that unless we produced and were winning, it wouldn't take much to ignite a bonfire, with me sitting on the top. Evidence of this came following a disastrous 3-0 home defeat to Galatasaray, with the fans venting their fury on the players and staff. Trying to reach the safety of the dressing room was difficult enough but worse was to come. On police advice we remained in our dressing room until further notice. We deliberately took our time, in shock at what we'd experienced. No one spoke or even moved. Listening to the continual abuse and aggression was unavoidable, coming as it was from outside the dressing room windows. And it wasn't going away.

It took more than three hours before the police managed to clear a safe exit path, and we boarded our bus to return to the training ground, 20 minutes away, in the same direction visiting teams would travel to the airport. We passed beneath a couple of bridges, the most likely spots to encounter hostility, as visiting teams knew all too well. But on this occasion it was the home team – us – that was bombarded with bottles, bricks and anything else that could be thrown, a terrifying experience, intensified further when recognising genuine fear in everyone's faces. After events of this nature, you reflect on the reasons why, and the answer can only be the team's performance. And that's solely the manager's responsibility.

What everyone was subject to on that sad day may have been brewing for some time, but I didn't see it coming. The consequences were mixed. The players were obviously shaken, but had no choice but to dig in, and to their credit they did just that, winning the next match, at home, 2-1 against Çanakkale. Meanwhile, some influential board members seized the opportunity they'd been waiting for, blaming the manager alone for the turmoil, one or two stating as much publicly. I wasn't surprised and *could* see that coming. As for the supporters: was that the mood in the tribune anyway? Were they always targeting me, and not the players?

The furore took time to settle. The players, obviously uncomfortable, could easily have crumbled and abandoned ship. I never once felt they let us down, however, although our final four matches – a draw and three defeats – may have suggested otherwise. Off the pitch too, the doubts were underlying; there was a funny feeling all along. Ali was always uneasy. Being Turkish he'd pick up gossip along the way, and the messages he received were simple enough. We weren't as comfortable as we'd been in the past, that was for sure.

When the club's final goodbye eventually reached us, I received a letter, as did Ian, which was far from complimentary. The powers that be may not have had the same grasp of English as previous employers, but phrases such as 'your disgraceful behaviour', 'poor tactics' and 'hopeless managing' left little room for doubt. They wanted rid of us, so such language, in their minds, was justified. They didn't want to fulfil our two-year contracts, hoping to avoid paying our salaries the following year. The president played dumb, but we knew it was his call; nothing happened without his say-so. We stuck to our guns, not leaving when they wanted us to. We hung on for a month or so, maybe six weeks, just to make the point that we wouldn't be easily shifted, but were on our own, dealing with difficult people. FIFA were our only source of support, but their lines of communication were painfully slow and bureaucratic (and there was no LMA to turn to). A private lawyer and eventual pressure from FIFA led to a conclusion. The club succumbed, and we eventually got paid.

My management in Turkey was coming to an end and, in a way, was bookended rather nicely. One of my first signings for Beşiktaş had been Les Ferdinand, one of my last, for Trabzonspor, was another English striker. When we first arrived in Trabzon the president knew about Les and wanted someone similar – who wouldn't? We eventually signed Kevin Campbell from Nottingham Forest. Kevin was a lovely lad. Paul Stretford was his agent and we all met in Nottingham. Dave 'Harry' Bassett was the manager, and an agreement was soon reached. Shortly afterwards we met again in Istanbul, but before the deal was confirmed, Paul said, 'We're not signing anything yet. We want to go to Trabzon to look at the facilities.' The following morning we did just that on the president's jet. This was my biggest fear: there wasn't much in Trabzon to attract foreign players (nice houses, and the training ground was good, but little else), and I was sure Kevin would be put off. He also had a young wife, and I remember thinking, *What are they going to do here?* But Kevin liked what he saw and duly signed.

We were delighted. Kevin was a proven goalscorer and the president loved him, but … could we get a tune out of him? Could we hell! If he ran to the near post, the ball went to the far; if he went far, the ball went near. And on it went. You'd almost have thought he was doing it deliberately! I couldn't work him out. We'd ask him why he was making all these (wrong) runs and he said, 'Well, if the lad with the ball mishits it, I'll be in!' He was full of theories, Kevin (he was a striker, after all). But he always gave 100 per cent and improved quickly. In November we played Galatasaray at their Ali Sami Yen Stadium. (Fatih Terim – Mr Angry – was their manager. We didn't get on then. We didn't like each other and were very competitive, although we get on okay now.) We beat Galatasaray 5-3, a massive win for us, and Kevin scored a hat-trick. He was brilliant that day, a true reflection of his potential and quality.

Four months later, Kevin returned to England, signing for Walter Smith's Everton. The Blues were struggling, big time, but Kevin came in and scored nine goals in his first eight matches, almost single-handedly steering Everton away from the threat of relegation. We could have done with a bit of that form but, in the end, we got our money back and a bit more. I always thought Kevin was better than he believed himself to be. He was a good lad, popular, and with plenty of ability. I wasn't sorry that Trabzon missed out. He signed for a big club, so good for him, Walter Smith and Everton. He could have been the new Les Ferdinand, after all! But he didn't do too badly as Kevin Campbell, did he?

Chapter 21

I'D HARDLY been at home a week. As summer turned to autumn, one afternoon, sitting in the garden reading the paper, I overheard Edith on the phone. Trying to work out who was on the other end, as the conversation ran on, it had to be one of her friends or a member of the family. Wrong. After saying, 'It's good to talk to you, I'll put Gordon on,' Edith emerged and whispered, 'It's Bobby.' My good pal Mr Robson had recently been appointed manager of his beloved Newcastle United, his boyhood club. He'd come home. With stories of visiting St James' Park as a youngster with his dad, it was like a fairy tale.

'What are you up to?' was his opening line. Typical Bobby, and so similar to the call (never to be forgotten) he made to me all those years before when I'd just finished at Leicester City.

'Hello to you too, Bobby. I'm just enjoying sitting in the garden, reading the paper.'

'That's no bloody good,' he shot back. 'You'll soon get fed up with that and you'll be on the supermarket run before you know what's hit you – Edith will make sure of that! I'm at the Gosforth Park Hotel in Newcastle, and free for lunch tomorrow. Come up and join me, we can have a good chat.'

He wouldn't be conscious of how far you had to travel, nor even consider you might say no. He was always so positive, and assumed that whomever he spoke to was of the same mindset.

I hit the road early the next morning. Bobby was a stickler for puntuality so I arrived in good time and was in the lounge when he bounded in with a hearty handshake and a beaming smile, greeting me like a long-lost brother, and waking up anyone in the vicinity who may have been having a quiet nap. Everyone knew him, of course. He was back in his native North East, the genuine warmth of the people towards him was infectious and he responded accordingly. Chatting over lunch, it was obvious how proud he was to be Newcastle United's manager, and how much it meant to him to make a success of it. He'd appointed Mick Wadsworth as his first-team coach, who he knew and respected from his FA days, and Charlie Woods, Bobby's long-time ally and chief scout during his Ipswich and England days, was about to join too. Charlie was scouting for Spurs at the time, a bloody good job, but couldn't resist teaming up again with his old pal. Bobby was obviously happy with his backroom staff and, in his view, Newcastle United Football Club was in good hands.

The time flew by, but where was this enjoyable lunch taking us? Bobby had hardly consumed anything, so energetic was his enthusing. 'I'm trying to put together a team I can trust, Gordon, and would like to think there's room for someone like you.' Still on the main course, I suddenly lost my appetite. 'So … what do you think?' he asked.

I paused. 'Well, you've given me nearly 30 seconds to think about it – I suppose that's long enough. I have to say I'm interested,' I replied, my voice no more than a whisper, as if the adjoining diners were trying to eavesdrop. Which they probably were.

Little more was said. When the time came to leave, Bobby waved me off from the hotel steps: 'Drive carefully, and I'll see you at Newcastle United soon, son!' There were plenty of people around. I imagine they all thought he was talking to a player! Bobby didn't care. When discussing his beloved club, he was oblivious to his surroundings. I can't remember the long drive home, other than heeding Bobby's advice to drive carefully as it was getting dark on an otherwise most enlightening day.

Throughout my career, Edith has totally supported and stood by the many decisions, good and bad, that I have made along the way, never getting too involved in the circus, preferring the responsibility of bringing up three sons (enough of a challenge in itself). She was in bed when I got home, but not asleep. 'How did you get on?' she shouted.

'I'll bring you a cup of tea,' I shouted back. Five minutes later, tea in hand, I headed upstairs. 'Bobby has offered me a job,' I said.

'Doing what?' Edith replied, before giving me a kiss and turning over. I couldn't answer. The words 'doing what?' hadn't even been uttered during my conversation with Bobby. I didn't sleep much that night.

The following day, the phone rang. 'Gordon, it's Bobby. I've not had a chance to see the chairman yet but will talk to him tomorrow. Will give you a ring then. Got to dash.' The phone went dead. Everything was going 100 miles an hour, typical in Bobby's world, which, understanding the situation and knowing the man, I fully understood.

Upstairs, Freddie Fletcher, the Scottish chief executive at Newcastle, was a fiery little character for whom I had the greatest respect; a passionate, intelligent man, hard-working, with vision and a great sense of humour. He was the brains behind the huge stadium development and fought numerous battles with supporters, single-handedly too, when they were having to give up treasured season tickets in the main stand, which some families had held for years (all was forgiven when the magnificent new stand was finally completed in 2000, and the stadium and supporters proudly moved into the 21st century). Freddie, a big smile on his face, a big drink in his hand, and a big cigar in his mouth, would dispatch huge clouds of smoke, along with anything else, at regular intervals all over whomever happened to be in his proximity while they listened to his humour and words of wisdom, as I did on so many occasions. It was a privilege. In later years Freddie said to me, 'You should have been Bobby's number two.' But that wasn't for me. Today, coaches have all sorts of people around them and it's taken for granted. It was different back then, but Bobby was ahead of his time. His experience abroad had opened his eyes to different methods, not just of coaching but management structure too.

Freddy Shepherd, the chairman, fully supported Bobby and made me feel most welcome too. Freddy was a man's man. He had a lot of bluster about him and could blow his top quite easily, but by the next day he'd be over it and would move on. He wouldn't mind if you stood up to him and had a go back, either. He could be aggressive when standing his corner, Freddie Fletcher likewise. Together, in the interests of Newcastle United, they formed a formidable and powerful partnership, two totally different characters who didn't always see eye to eye but had a mutual respect, both proud in honouring their responsibilities, both fully committed to the ambitions of a massive club in a hurry.

Bobby's enthusiasm was impossible to resist. I accepted his invitation to join him, but in what capacity? What would I add?

Where was I going in all of this? How could I justify Bobby's support, and what exactly did he expect from me?

It soon became clear: to be there for him at all times; become the link between the academy and the first team; be a sounding board for the top brass if required; operate an open-door policy should any member of staff require assistance; and to oversee the scouting and transfer policy alongside the manager and chief scout. You don't need me to tell you the job title most befitting of such a role: the dreaded director of football. In truth, though, Bobby wasn't interested in any of that, he just wanted me (and Charlie) alongside him.

Having experienced the role twice before, and not getting on with it either time, the obvious question is why accept the position for a third time? The answer is: I don't know. I didn't even ask myself the question. Was it simply due to Bobby's magnetism? Probably. I'm not sure I'd have done it for anyone else. Charlie felt the same. Without becoming too romantic, that lunch with Bobby at the Gosforth Park Hotel echoed his efforts in lining me up with Beşiktaş. He cared about me then, and he still cared now. I was coming to the tail end of my career and perhaps subconsciously I saw it as a last hurrah, one that would play out alongside an old friend. Either way, I felt comfortable, fully understanding why I was at the club. All that mattered was that Bobby was in a good place, which he most definitely was, and he soon got them going. An 8-0 victory over Sheffield Wednesday in his first home match wasn't a bad start! He had a good team, well balanced, with good performances and results, and a brilliant new stadium, always full of fanatical support. Newcastle was a great place to be. Driving to a match, even to training, there was as good a buzz as anywhere. For Bobby it was about pride, and lots of it.

On my first visit to the training ground I was apprehensive. Post-playing, this would be the first time I'd be introduced to a group of players who I wasn't going to coach. In his own endearing way, Bobby made me feel like a new major signing in front of all the lads, finishing with a lovely line: 'How he survived nine years in Turkey, I'll never f***ing know!' For my part I kept it brief: 'I'm pleased to be here, and I hope I can be of some assistance.'

Soon after I joined, sitting in my office in the magnificent new main stand, I received my first-ever memo: 'Mr Milne' – not Gordon – 'Mr Milne, we'd like to inform you that in all matters concerning incoming and outgoing players, full authority and responsibility lies with the board of directors, and no one else.' I thought it odd. Wasn't this a big part of my job? But in the eyes of the hierarchy, clearly not. In other words, 'Gordon, stay out of it.' Lesson one, fully understood. A couple of days later the chairman asked, 'How are you getting on, Gordon? Let me know if you need anything.' The memo wasn't mentioned and, given Freddy's manner, I could only assume it had been intended as clarification, and nothing more. None of this was Bobby's doing, of course. He remained as reassuringly unconcerned as ever. 'Gordon, never mind trying to justify what you're doing. You don't have to do that.' Comforting words expertly conveyed.

The fans' passion, the size of the club and the mood within formed an intoxicating mix. I soon found an apartment in Gosforth, a nice convenient spot, and got my feet under the table. My office was next to Bobby's. His loyal PA Judith, and Gemma who handled Charlie's and my correspondence, were adjoining, and Alan Irvine who ran the academy was adjacent too. Bobby loved this, as most afternoons we were all together and he could bounce in any direction he wished (sometimes two or three at the same time). It felt like the hub of the club and, away from the training ground, was where Bobby came to life.

The demands on Bobby's time were immense, and he wasn't good at saying no. 'How can I let them down?' would regularly ring through the office windows while diaries were being juggled weeks in advance. It was at these times – Charlie, Bobby and myself in the office, long after the staff had gone home – I felt most useful, and the most satisfaction. We'd unwind, talking about anything and everything, with the day's events often the last topic of discussion, with Bobby (apparently) listening patiently. Charlie used to say, 'I've been talking for half an hour, and I don't think he's listened to a f***ing word I've said!' But he did listen. He wanted our input – on certain matters – but what he did with it, we never knew. On many occasions he'd say, 'Hell, it's seven o'clock. Come on, let's have dinner, it's on me.' There was a little Italian restaurant close to the ground where the conversations continued over pasta and a glass.

Our offices were a floor below Freddy's, so we'd all know when the chairman called Bobby for a chat. Sometimes it would only be ten minutes, but the longer he was gone the more uneasy we became. And when he did return, obviously uncomfortable, would he declare himself? No way. 'Judith, thanks for waiting, we'll catch up tomorrow. Gordon, Charlie, let's have a drink before we go.' To have immediate breathing space after any confrontation can only be truly valued when you've experienced it yourself, which I had, many times. Left on your own, you stew. But if you can let off steam to someone you trust, the load is immediately lightened. And that's how it was. A couple of gin and tonics for Charlie and me, soda water for Bobby (although he often looked like he needed something stronger) before he'd say, 'Usual stuff lads, we've heard it all before. Nothing new.' It was about all we'd get out of him, but it was what we were there for, to share that immediate decompression. Three old pals in a deserted football ground; I was so glad we were there for him.

The summer of 2000 saw the club pick Washington DC as a pre-season destination. Bobby wasn't impressed – Europe was his preference – and made his thoughts known upstairs. One day, out of the blue, the chairman summoned me, Bobby and Charlie to his office. For what, we wondered – was this goodbye? Freddy soon put us straight: 'Now, this f***ing trip to America is happening no matter what you [pointing to Bobby], you [Charlie] and f***ing you [me, although I don't know why I got the heavy bit] have to say. Do I make myself clear?' Freddy's face bulged with aggression and perspiration; we didn't feel inclined to challenge him. He turned to me once more: 'By the way, this f***ing academy is costing us three million a year and it hasn't produced a single f***ing player!' This was the first time Charlie and I had experienced Freddy in full flight, and it wasn't much fun. Was this what Bobby had to put up with on his bad days?

I was dispatched to Washington with Carol Beverley (representing our kit manufacturer) to check out the facilities. The university's training ground was more than adequate and totally private, the hotel five-star and palatial. I returned with good news. The trip duly went ahead and the players enjoyed every minute, as did Bobby and the staff, with no problems along the way. We came home and began the season by winning three of our first four matches. We all agreed: good decision by the chairman.

* * *

Bobby did a tremendous job that first season, steadying the ship before gradually instilling some belief into the team. We finished 11th and reached the semi-finals of the FA Cup, unfortunately losing 2-1 to Chelsea. Despite that disappointment it was still some achievement but, more importantly, Bobby had brought hope back to the Magpies. The following season brought consolidation in the shape of another 11th-place finish, and with the squad then boosted by signings such as Craig Bellamy and Laurent Robert, hopes were high for the new millennium. The stadium was now magnificent, a fitting home for those loyal fans who filled it to capacity week in, week out. The place was buzzing.

Those high hopes looked justified when, in late November, we topped the table, albeit only for a few short hours, although that same month brought a minor derailment (remember, it doesn't take much to flip the train off its tracks ...). We were in Spain for some warm-weather training, and one evening were to attend a dinner held in honour of Sir John Hall, the club's president and former chairman. However, four players – Craig Bellamy, Carl Cort, Kieron Dyer and Andy Griffin – failed to turn up. Freddy Shepherd, naturally, went ballistic. The following morning while the players were training, I visited those four players' rooms and placed their passports on their beds. The message was crystal clear: they were being sent home, and quite rightly so. Two of the four objectors surprised me; I didn't see Carl or Andy as that way inclined (time would prove me right) but they, along with the others, had no choice but to face the music for their indiscipline and lack of respect. It was an isolated incident, unusual for the time, but Bobby dealt with it in his usual style. He put it to bed with the minimum of fuss, and we moved forward.

On the pitch, Bellamy had clicked with Alan Shearer, and they were ably supported by the likes of Nobby Solano, Gary Speed and Laurent Robert. Five more wins put us back on top at Christmas. No question, Bobby was working his magic. It was never going to be easy to keep it up though, and so it proved; a slip-up here, a mishap there, and our title challenge gradually petered out. However, Bobby had steered Newcastle to 20 more points than the previous season and, more importantly, a fourth-place finish – Champions League football would return to St James' Park!

The momentum stayed with us the following season, bringing another serious title challenge and a more than respectable Champions League run. There were numerous memorable moments along the way: a 4-0 opening-day home win over West Ham; home and away defeats of local rivals Sunderland; incredible European nights, particularly wins over Juventus, Dinamo Kiev and Feyenoord. Come the spring of 2003 we were still fighting for the Premier League and Champions League. We eventually finished third in the Premier League and succumbed at the end of the second group stage in Europe. On the pitch we were most definitely heading in the right direction; anyone could see as much.

* * *

Bobby had his team around him but remained his own man. He'd reveal little of his conversations with the chairman, which Charlie and I knew were often difficult at best. Freddy didn't mince his words, and we all knew it. Bobby tended to keep what had been said to himself, and although he'd be interested in our opinions, he'd always handle a situation his own way.

One such situation arose in training when I was watching on. I'm not sure what sparked the flame, but the upshot was Craig Bellamy storming off the training ground, effing and blinding about how s**t everything was. It's well known that Bellamy was a fiery lad but in no way did that give him free rein to be so disrespectful. Bobby, being Bobby, just carried on. The session continued in the pouring rain with the rest of the squad respecting the manager's position (and I dare say not too happy themselves with Bellamy's behaviour).

Over lunch in the canteen Charlie and I had plenty of time to analyse events and discuss how we'd handle the situation. The players had finished their meal and as usual the captain, Alan Shearer, asked the manager whether they could leave. 'Yes,' replied Bobby, 'but I'd like to see Craig Bellamy at two o'clock in my office.' Bobby swiftly dismissed the rest of us as well. 'You might as well go too, lads, see you all in the morning.' Within five minutes he'd shut down any potential opinions on, even any references to, that morning's incident (incidentally, both Charlie and I would have dropped Bellamy for the weekend, but we never got the chance to say as much). Bobby wouldn't be side-tracked by anyone. He'd learned to shut out the exterior noise, even from trusted (and forceful) lieutenants. He wouldn't be influenced by others, even if much of what he was hearing made sense to him. At the end of the day, he alone would make the decision.

That's exactly what happened with Bellamy. Only two people knew what was said that day, but the eventual outcome was one person doing what he was good at – scoring goals – and the other, in Bobby's own words, just doing his job. Regardless of what had happened, Bobby was thinking, *How do I give ourselves the best chance of winning this weekend?* And in his mind, it was with Bellamy in the team. He was right, too. He picked him, Bellamy scored twice and Newcastle won.

In football, you practise more than you play, so every day situations come and go, some volatile, some not, but as so much goes unreported, much of a manager's work is never seen, even less credited. Bobby versus Bellamy was a classic example.

* * *

Managing any football, anywhere, has one common denominator: results. We have one match on Saturday, the result of which is of course crucial, but it's only 90 minutes of one day, in one week. What about the rest of the time? Footballers train more than they play, so every day the same faces are working in a confined, competitive environment, 30 players on top of one another, some not playing enough, some not playing at all, different personalities with different strengths, weaknesses, attitudes and opinions. And with the heat on constantly, something has to give. Training sessions can be interesting, to say the least, but they also turn the screw and separate the wheat from the chaff. There's always more going on during the week than on a Saturday. Fortunately, Bobby's squad had a sound foundation in the likes of Alan Shearer, Gary Speed, Shay Given and Warren Barton, senior pros who could stand their corner and did so, men who took pride in their jobs. But not all players are the same.

After a lunchtime kick-off one Saturday afternoon at St James' Park, Bobby received word of an incident involving two Newcastle United footballers in a nightclub in Ipswich. He initially dismissed this as nonsense as it was impossible to get from Newcastle to Ipswich in that time. However, a couple of hours later he received confirmation, and that the two players in question were Kieron Dyer and Titus Bramble (both former Ipswich Town players), who had flown by private plane to Ipswich directly after the match. Bobby couldn't believe what he was hearing, not only that the pair were indeed in Ipswich, but now in trouble too.

What could Bobby have done about it? Nothing. There were no rules preventing players from doing what they did, but it flew in the face of professionalism and, frankly, common sense. Bobby, Charlie and I couldn't understand why they'd do that. But such situations, alongside the behaviour of certain senior figures, began to drive the narrative that Bobby had lost control. It was nonsense but had to be dealt with, more behind-the-scenes management that went unseen.

The senior pros such as Alan and Gary would occasionally join the rest of the lads on a night out but knew how to conduct themselves and steer clear of bother. At the time though, Freddy Shepherd's sons, who were good lads, would be in the clubs at the same time as the players, and being the chairman's sons and big fans, they were accepted into that inner circle. Quite naturally, as young lads rubbing shoulders with their heroes, they lapped it up. But the old adage comes to mind: admire your heroes from afar. You can get too close when a footballer's guard is down and form an opinion that can easily be clouded or influenced by personal bias – but can also be inaccurate. In such environments, gossip festers and requires no assistance to flourish. Talk of Bobby losing the dressing room was a load of crap, but critics don't need much ammunition. Charlie and I saw it for what it was: basic disloyalty to Bobby, pushing him to the limit, taking the p**s. In his defence, Dyer later admitted to letting Bobby down, and in his subsequent coaching career – like Craig Bellamy too, who seemed to become a different person – showed a great deal more maturity. But back then, incidents like crashing his new Ferrari in Newcastle city centre didn't help.

* * *

When things are right at the top of any organisation you have a template that understands the challenges ahead and can adapt to change and pressure. When things are *not* right at the top, everything can unravel, and invariably does.

Sir John Hall and his family were the major shareholders at Newcastle United. His son Douglas was a long-time board member, although by the time I joined, Sir John had taken a back seat due to health issues. Douglas was a completely different character to his father, but influential, nonetheless. Sir John was a difficult act to follow: a very successful businessman, with a natural passion for the club and his own take on how it should be run. Football clubs are different from other businesses though, and with Sir John now somewhat distanced, Douglas would always be fair game to the fans. He was his own man, did his own thing, in his own way, occasionally even giving the chairman concerns. Bobby, who never got too excited about what was happening upstairs, once said of Douglas, 'I don't know much about him, but I think he could be a loose cannon.' It's fair to say Douglas was never going to match his father's contribution to the club. But would Bobby's words ring true?

In 2004 we reached the semi-final of the UEFA Cup in which we faced Marseille. A 0-0 draw at home meant we had work to do in France, but at half-time in the second leg we trailed 1-0. As I headed inside for a cup of tea, Douglas, along with other board members, was heading in my direction. He spotted me, pointed at me, and began shouting and screaming at the top of his voice, 'SHITE! SHITE F***ING SHITE!' before disappearing past the startled spectators. And it was only half-time! Recalling the incident now, the word 'venom' quickly springs to mind.

After European matches it could be two hours before we boarded the coach, as security controls, media responsibilities and all the rest take time. This was bad enough when you'd won but that evening we'd lost. The fans' reaction was negative, big time, which was unusual. I can't recall any other occasions when they showed their own team such hostility. Unfortunately, their displeasure only added fuel to the fire and gave Douglas and the board more ammunition to fire towards Bobby. The hotel, 45 minutes away, was where a dejected group eventually sat down to eat, although some players went straight to their rooms. As usual the staff were on a separate table but with one member missing. To this day I don't know whether Bobby was corralled by the board directly after the match, but they'd got to him, I'm sure, and words had been had. My toxic encounter with Douglas was only the half of it. Typically, when Bobby eventually arrived, not much was said. The mood was low but emotions were running high, particularly at board level. We had a drink and went to bed.

It was the beginning of the end. What was coming was only a matter of time. The powers that be had, in my view, clearly decided they no longer wanted Bobby as manager, although I never thought it would mean the end of his time at the club. I assumed there would always be a place for him somewhere at Newcastle United. I recognised that I was unable to influence the situation in any way, so I left – of my own accord – following the 2003/04 season, a couple of months before Bobby's dismissal. My parting conversation with Freddy was amicable but the pleasure in my role had evaporated and there was a different mood about the club. The warmth was no longer there. I felt it was in everybody's best interests that I left. Bobby, though, was typically more concerned about me than himself: 'If you're not enjoying yourself, Gordon, best to step away.' It was a true measure of the man.

Ultimately, as well as the men in the squad there were also the boys, the young blowhards on too much money, with too much to say, and these kids had the ear of the board. As the negativity slowly festered, Sir John's support began to waver. Bobby was now getting it from both sides: rebellious players (although not all of them) on one side, an unsupportive board on the other. The rot had truly set in. Simultaneously, Douglas had become a thorn in the club's side with his constant criticism and abuse of Bobby, and not helped by his father, quoted in the national press as saying, 'Fourth place is not good enough for this club.' There was no justification for that, especially when considering Bobby's recent track record, never mind his overall career. It usually takes a season or two for any manager to really find his feet, and Bobby, since joining (when morale was extremely low after a poor start that season under Ruud Gullit), had steered Newcastle to league finishes of 11th, 11th, 4th, 3rd and 5th – hardly shabby! There were also European adventures and the odd cup run to consider. What's more, this was hardly a young manager just starting out, this was somebody with a lifetime of experience, who had been around the world and succeeded, and who was now pushing his home-town club into the top tier. This wasn't luck, it was down to the quality of the man. So why would you sack somebody like that? All this made Bobby's dismissal more unbelievable, disrespectful and undeserved even than it first appeared. The two major shareholders were deserting him in their own different ways.

The chairman had the heavy responsibility, which I know he didn't relish, of conveying to Bobby the board's decision. Bobby's reaction – complete shock and devastation – made Freddy even more uncomfortable. Despite all the noise, Bobby had genuinely not seen this coming. He'd lived and worked in hostile environments before, of course – 80,000 Barcelona fans waving the white hankies at him would have dwarfed the pressures at Newcastle – but, in his head, he was just experiencing another. We all knew who was messing about and who wasn't, but Bobby's mindset never wavered: 'I'll sort it out.' He'd handled similar situations all his life and had no doubt he'd handle this one too.

There's no question in my mind: that day had a serious, negative effect on Bobby's health. It was an arrow through the heart of a true and loyal Geordie. When he picked up the phone to talk to me, he could hardly speak. Elsie, Bobby's wife, and the rest of his family felt he'd been guillotined, all in disbelief over what had happened and how it had been handled. In fact, Bobby's dismissal shocked the whole football world.

Would it have been wrong for Freddy to have explained to Bobby the board's desire for change? That could have meant Bobby moving into an ambassadorial role, and I don't believe there would have been a single dissenting Geordie voice. He'd already completed a year at Barcelona occupying a similar position and, in effect, was already doing that job for Newcastle three or four nights a week anyway. 'Part of his duties,' as he'd have said.

I don't know what Bobby may have thought of such a proposition, presented in good faith and with the right intentions. He might have reacted positively; equally, he might well have told them where to stick it. (In fairness, it has been suggested that Bobby was indeed offered such a role, although he and Freddy allegedly clashed over this issue.) But the bottom line was, they wanted Bobby out, and executed their desire accordingly.

Sir John, Douglas, the board, had been responsible for bringing Bobby to Newcastle. Five years later when Bobby was dismissed, Sir John made a statement saying it was the players who got Bobby the sack. So the board signed him but the players sacked him. Really? I often wonder what Alan Shearer, Gary Speed and the other men in the squad thought about that.

Bobby was dismissed after just four matches of the next season. Two or three months later I was in the area, so paid him a visit. As I pulled into the driveway of his beautiful home, Urpeth Hall in County Durham, I saw a guy sitting on a big lawnmower going back and forth cutting the grass, wearing a Newcastle United training top and a woolly hat pulled down over his ears. When he spun round at the end of the lawn, I saw it was Bobby. We began chatting – trying to – over the deafening din of the lawnmower's engine.

'What day is it?' he yelled.

'It's the 30th, Bobby,' I yelled back.

'No, no, no, no, no!' he spluttered, finally turning off the engine. 'Not what date, what *day* is it, Gordon, what *day*?'

'Saturday,' I replied.

'Of course it is! It's f***ing Saturday!' He paused. 'Now, Gordon, if you had said to me just a few months ago that today – a Saturday afternoon – I'd be driving a f***ing lawnmower up and down, I'd have thought you were insane!' He paused again. 'But d'you know what? I'm enjoying every minute of it.'

The look on his face gave me so much pleasure; he genuinely meant it, and I could see as much. Normally, at this time on a Saturday he'd have been on the touchline, midway through the second half with the floodlights on, warm breath and mist drifting through the shadows. But instead, here he was, at home, mowing the lawn – and loving it.

After a while we said our goodbyes. I set off up the drive and saw Bobby heading in the opposite direction. Only later did I realise he was actually heading in a new direction, towards all he'd go on to achieve for the Sir Bobby Robson Foundation. Bobby's cancer, ironically, gave him a new lease of life, and he devoted the rest of his days to raising funds, always out and about, meeting people, generating publicity, and loving every minute of it. Like most of us in the football world, I suppose, I imagine he never thought he could live without the game, but he proved himself, and us, wrong. His illness motivated him, as helping other people was part of his nature, and always had been. Along the way, Bobby helped hundreds – maybe thousands – of people, in many different ways. I was lucky to be just one of them.

* * *

Time was up, I felt. With my spell at Newcastle ending somewhat disappointingly, and not getting any younger, I didn't think there was a great deal left out there for me. But, incredibly, Beşiktaş came calling once more.

Erhan Solu and Ilhan Durusoy were both board members during my first spell at BJK, both speaking fluent English, with sound knowledge of the game and a true affection for the club. They'd provided me with a shoulder to lean on during those early traumatic days in Istanbul, and how I'd needed it. They've remained true friends to this day. It was Ilhan who called me out of the blue. The new president was keen to modernise the youth programme and improve standards, in step with the bigger European clubs – quite a big ask. Ilhan asked if I'd meet the president to discuss his ambitions further. How could I refuse? The president, Yıldırım Demirören, was in Paris on business so I flew to France, where the meeting went well. Mr Demirören was courteous, enthusiastic and positive about his objectives. Over a very pleasant dinner in one of Paris's better restaurants he asked if I was prepared to take on the challenge, bearing in mind this was a completely different role to my previous responsibility at the club. I stressed that this wasn't a five-minute job. He fully understood and immediately offered me a three-year contract. We clinked glasses. I was on my way once more.

My priority on day one was to meet French legend Jean Tigana, now head coach at Beşiktaş, his first role after leaving Fulham. I wanted to make it crystal clear to him that my responsibilities lay with the youth programme and nowhere else. It was vitally important he knew this. As a former head coach, I didn't want to be stepping on his toes. Thankfully, Jean was so easy to get on with, with a calm, laid-back approach, and there was never any conflict. Furthermore, with the youth facility in Istanbul and the senior camp being in Ümraniye, some 15 miles away on the opposite side of the Bosporus, our paths hardly ever crossed (although we did meet socially on occasion). I did my job, he did his.

I soon found out, however, that mine would be more complicated than I ever anticipated. Given the sheer size of the city, travelling from A to B was always a challenge. At rush hour, when kids were trying to reach the training ground for a 6pm start, with or without the help of parents, it became a challenge of monumental proportions. Sessions could start with small numbers of eager smiling faces, and grow gradually as the evening evolved, weary parents eventually delivering their precious cargo, or when little Mustafa and his pal Mehmet turned up on their own, having undergone three bus trips and a long hike, apologising for being late. Those images of hardship and stress, which families endured so their kids had the opportunity to play organised football for a couple of hours at their beloved club, remain with me to this day, as does the enthusiasm and pleasure in their young faces, totally immersed in a different world, escaping reality, and pleading with coaches to play ten more minutes (they never wanted to go home). Those memories will never leave me. I've always wished I could have offered them more.

Because Istanbul is so vast, the kids would train at little satellite clubs scattered across the city, clubs where a board member or even just a fan would be in charge. I was based at one such club (actually the training ground I used with the first team all those years ago) where a board member ran the show – and he was a pain in the arse, a little jumped-up general who didn't want to let go of his empire, so looked upon me as a massive interference. This was just one of the obstacles blocking my path.

Initially, the club did a lot of things right for me (I got a nice house quickly; Edith came over, and we were in good shape) but frustrations began to creep in. It was no one's fault, it was just the structure – amateur, although not negative. There was no one to criticise for this, they were all trying to do the best for the club but, for me, linking it all together was a major challenge, especially without proper funding and facilities. Resources were primarily for the first team, of course; there simply wasn't enough investment available for anyone else. Looking back, I wonder: would a consultancy of six months – me offering my observations and recommendations – have been a better way forward for all parties?

After a year or so I was going nowhere, and without investment that wasn't going to change. It became increasingly difficult to speak to the president, and there were also echoes of my past: my wages – or rather, lack of them – once again became an issue. I was unable to achieve anything worthwhile, and felt I was no longer wanted. I'd experienced such difficulties before and didn't want to go through them again. All this led to the inevitable. I struck a deal with the board: pay me what you owe me and forget the rest. I left Beşiktaş halfway through my three-year contract. My time in football was over. This time, for good.

Epilogue

AS A young man, during my two years' National Service and five as an apprentice joiner (I was still able to play for Preston North End, although obviously not full-time), I occasionally brought my wood shavings to the dressing room – but most definitely not my rifle! Unusual times. I learned so much from the army: discipline, organisation, humility; working as a group; respecting the man standing next to you on parade – you mustn't let him down because he won't let you down. This was in your face 24 hours a day, seven days a week. In an infantry unit such as mine, these were all principles intended to keep you alive. I later learned that those very same principles could help you win football matches – and also survive.

The military had invaded my life for two years, but it was a different situation altogether for Shanks and my father. Overnight, their football careers were decimated and their lives changed forever. Thankfully, Shanks and my dad survived, picked up the pieces and got on with life; two tough Scottish pals from similar backgrounds, football being their lives. Their playing days – cup finals at Wembley in front of 100,000 fans and challenging for league titles – were over. The world had changed, but management beckoned for both; they'd continue the journey. I often wonder how I'd have reacted to a world war during the prime of my career, bearing in mind I have vague memories of running into our air-raid shelter in the garden with my mother, hoping they wouldn't drop bombs on Deepdale.

For me, the army was deadly bloody serious, especially as there was no guarantee I wouldn't be sent abroad to fight, so when I was allowed out to do the odd bit of training, life became that bit more enjoyable – although not for long. Football was a relief – and a release – from the ever-present tension, but in the back of my mind I always knew I'd soon be returning to the barracks. Throughout this period my emotions were well and truly mixed and I didn't realise or appreciate at the time that those two years of my life broadened my thinking and introduced me to the real world and real values. It wasn't by choice that I undertook that journey as an innocent 21-year-old boy. But when that journey came to an end, a wiser, tougher, more mature 23-year-old re-emerged a better person.

After the army there were two things left in my life: family and football. On paper, that might not look much, but it was all I ever wanted. My life has been truly blessed. Any journey through football has twists, turns, good times and bad. I've had my fair share of them all. Disappointments are part and parcel of the game, but without the lows you can't appreciate the highs.

Facing Pelé in the Maracanã; Best, Law and Charlton at their peak; 134,000 in Hampden Park; Wembley, against Yashin, Gento, Puskás, Eusébio and Di Stéfano; lining up alongside Greaves, Moore, Banks, Armfield and Wilson. I still get goosebumps. And the icing on the cake? A Preston-born lad playing alongside his Preston-born hero Sir Tom Finney throughout the great man's final season, and especially in his final match on his own patch at Deepdale. It couldn't – it didn't – get any better than that.

It's been a long journey, but all the more interesting because of that. The list of those I've met along the way reads like a who's who of football and is truly humbling. From Shanks to Sir Bobby, and everyone in between, I've been incredibly fortunate, often in the right place at the right time, and often, thankfully, just when I needed to be. And it feels appropriate to have begun my career as a little kid parking bicycles in my garden, and ending some 60 years later coaching kids of the same age as they set off in pursuit of their own dreams; to call it rewarding doesn't do it justice.

Six decades – a life – in the world's favourite game. First it was Shanks, and my dad. Then me. How lucky am I?

Acknowledgements

I'D LIKE to take this opportunity to thank most sincerely Steve Younger for his patience and understanding, and for pushing me to open the memory box and look back in time. His passion, knowledge and understanding of the game while supporting his beloved Liverpool FC made the many hours spent together – which were so important for me – feel like I was in the company of, and talking to, an old team-mate. A pleasure indeed.

I've known Trevor East for more than 50 years now and without him this book would never have got off the ground. Trevor has been instrumental in helping both Steve and I navigate the world (new to us both) of sports writing and publishing and has been a driving force and constant source of encouragement. Trevor, for all you've done and your unwavering support, I thank you.

I'd also like to thank everyone at Pitch Publishing, especially Jane Camillin for her insight and advice, but most notably for her patience too. This book has taken some time, so Jane, thank you for your tolerance and for sticking by us.

I'm extremely grateful to Mark Lawrenson and Gary Lineker for their kind forewords and would also like to recognise all those who get a mention (as well as many who don't) throughout this book; the career I had is thanks to them, and it's to them I owe a huge debt of gratitude.

Lastly, but most certainly not least: I remember Shanks saying to me one day, 'Never mind interviewing the player, son – make sure you interview the wife first.' Advice still valid to this day. I must have listened, as Edith and I have been married for over 62 years; unquestionably the best signing I ever made. Edith, thank you for putting up with me throughout all this time; I know it can't have been easy, but had it not been for you, in no way could I ever have lived the life I have. I'll never be able to thank you enough – for everything.